OLD
PETERSBURG
and the
BROAD RIVER
VALLEY
of Georgia

Their Rise
and Decline

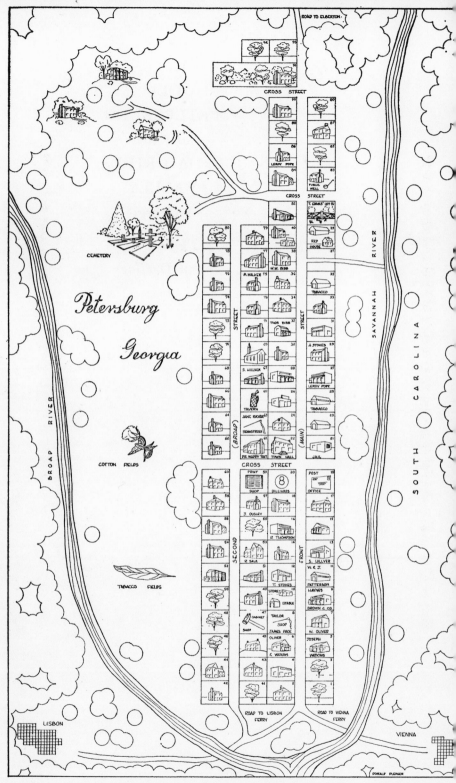

This plan was constructed from the deed records in the Elbert County Courthouse, Elberton,

ELLIS MERTON COULTER

OLD

PETERSBURG

and the

BROAD RIVER

VALLEY

of Georgia

Their Rise and Decline

UNIVERSITY OF GEORGIA PRESS Athens

Contents

~~~~~~

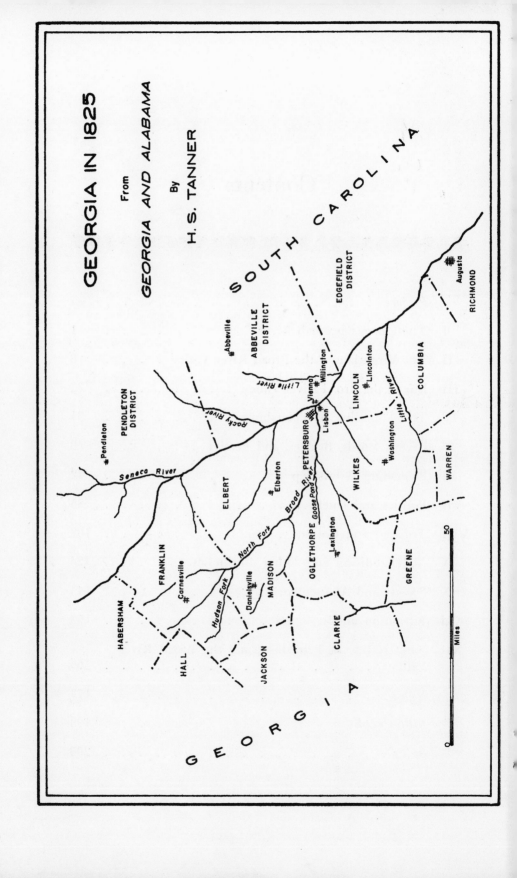

GEORGIA IN 1825

From

GEORGIA AND ALABAMA

By

H. S. TANNER

Preface

IF THE TITLE of this book were given in the style often used in the olden times, it might well read: "Old Petersburg: The Story of the Rise and Fall of a Georgia River Town, Embracing an Account of Some of the Principal Families both in Petersburg and in the Hinterland, Also Giving Attention to the Broad River Country and its Principal Inhabitants, who Made Petersburg an Outlet for their River Trade; Including Efforts at Improving the Navigation of the Savannah and Broad Rivers; Together with Incidents, Such as Duels Which Were Fought in the Vicinity; and Offering Reasons why Petersburg and its Satellites Grew up, Flourished, and then Utterly Disappeared."

But in modern times, a table of contents gives in brief form what was set forth in these old-style titles. Of course, it should be understood without having to be stated either in title or preface, that a title should be short and only indicative of what the book includes. So, indeed, this book is more than the life history of the Broad River Valley and of that "40 acres" called Petersburg, lying between the Savannah and Broad rivers where they ran together about forty miles above Augusta.

Petersburg did not exist in a vacuum. It was the result of economic and social forces in the upper Savannah River country and its tributaries; and to leave out of the picture this background would make the town stand out in space like a mirage. And even the larger picture in which this region was a detail must also be included when it had a part to play.

But this book is primarily about the Georgia segment of the upper Savannah River country, for that river was the dividing line between two states; and Petersburg being on the Georgia side was more a reflection of Georgia than of South Carolina.

These two states had been rivals from Colonial days, and although economic and social forces were not as ready to respect prejudices as were political maneuverings, yet they were important. And largely because of all these rivalries, the South Carolinians set up their own town, Vienna, across from Petersburg, and here sought to reap whatever rewards were to come from upper South Carolina as well as all they could get from Georgia.

Petersburg was much more than a combination of storehouses, warehouses, dwelling houses, streets, and people; it was a symbol of the atmosphere of the times and of the forces that pulled and pushed people around and along—a symbol of land and commercial speculation spreading out as far as Philadelphia, New York, and Boston, of an era of transportation involving the navigation of rivers and of the creaking of wagons across the countryside and the cracking of whips of the drivers of four-horse teams; of the rise and decline of tobacco and the growth and spread westward of the cotton kingdom; of the coming of plantations and slavery; and of the westward movement of population. All of these developments and more helped to make and unmake Petersburg and the Broad River Valley.

E. M. C.

1

The Upper Savannah River Country

PETERSBURG, Lisbon, Vienna, Edinburgh, Alexandria! These names of great cities in the Old World were adopted in the New by ambitious villages sprouting up in the upper Savannah River country. All but one were in Georgia; Vienna was in South Carolina. During the late eighteenth and early nineteenth centuries they grew up, aspired to greatness, and disappeared before any one had become a half-century old.

They were born of economic and social forces and out of the imagination of pioneer settlers and land speculators. They lived, breathed, thrived for a time, and then utterly disappeared, leaving not even the legacy of their names. Only three approached any prominence: Petersburg, Lisbon, and Vienna; and Petersburg alone gave early signs of developing into a great metropolis, for at one time it was the third largest city in the state—only Savannah and Augusta were ahead. But by the mid-twentieth century even its site was no longer visible, for it was covered by the waters of a great lake made by the Clark Hill dam on the Savannah River some miles below.

Before 1763 Georgia was cramped into a small area along the coast from the Savannah River as far south as the Altamaha River and inland and up these rivers as far as the tide went. Her limits as set by England were much greater (the land between these rivers and lines drawn from their headwaters to the "South Seas"), but a treaty with the Indians in 1733 had freed for settlement only the coastal area. Nevertheless, James Edward Oglethorpe, the founder of Georgia, set up an outpost at Augusta, far up the Savannah River beyond where the tide ended. However, not until the end of the French and Indian War in 1763 did Georgia secure this additional territory by treaty with the

Indians, which now gave the white people the right to settle up the Savannah River as far as Little River, about twenty miles above Augusta, and down the coast to the St. Marys River.

South Carolina as far up the Savannah River as a dozen miles above Augusta had long been freed from Indian ownership, and in 1755 the Creeks ceded the upper part of the Colony as far as a point about twenty-five miles beyond the mouth of Broad River, where Petersburg was later to grow up. By 1779 the Indians had given up all of South Carolina except a small slice in the extreme northwestern corner. So, before the end of the American Revolution practically all of upper South Carolina had been opened up for settlement by land-hungry frontiersmen, who were set into motion by the coming of peace.

Georgia was not as fortunate as South Carolina in freeing her lands from the Indians; however, in 1773 the Colony, taking advantage of some big debts owed to Indian traders by the Creeks and Cherokees, made a treaty with the Indians in Augusta, signed on June 1, wherein the Indians gave up more than 2,000,000 acres in payment of these debts. This cession extended northward about sixty miles beyond Little River, almost to the point where the Seneca River emptied into the Savannah from the South Carolina side.[1]

Georgia was now ready to welcome land-hungry people from as far north as Maryland to these lands, generally called the "New Purchase" or the "Ceded Lands." Sir James Wright, the third and last of Georgia's Colonial governors, made the settling of this region one of his principal ambitions. He had made a trip to England in 1772 with the definite purpose of interesting the British government in promoting this cession. Because of the support he had received from the Earl of Dartmouth he renamed the Broad River (in the midst of the New Purchase) the Dart River. He also made plans for a town and a fort on the point of land between the Dart (Broad) and Savannah rivers, to be called respectively Dartmouth and Fort James—the fort in honor of himself.

Wright had argued in London that a new Indian cession would attract immediately 600 families from outside the Colony and that a modest price for the land would bring 125,000 pounds. This would be a second founding of Georgia and an enduring monument to Wright by bringing in more people than had ever lived in that small cession gained in 1733. (Wright's namesake, a town called Wrightsboro, had already begun in a settlement made by Quakers in the upper part of the cession which had been gained by the Treaty of 1763. In the course of the next century the town was to disappear as completely as Petersburg, though, unlike Petersburg, it was never covered with water.)

Sir James (now a proper title for Governor Wright, since he had been granted this honor while in England) lost no time in appointing surveyors to run the boundary line of the New Purchase and to issue a proclamation in the form of a handbill to be circulated and posted on bulletin boards to the northward, inviting settlers to come. The land could be had in tracts of 100 to 1,000 acres—100 acres to the head of a family, 50 acres additional for the wife, each child, slave, and white servant, and 40 acres for every woman servant. Quit rents were not to be levied for ten years. The land was well watered and especially suited for "wheat, indico, Indian corn, tobacco, hemp, flax, &c. &c. &c." To reassure prospective settlers of their safety in these new lands, Sir James added: "That, to the end the said settlers may be safe and secure with respect to their persons and properties and in order to prevent any interruption to them by disorderly hunters, vagrants and wanderers, or by straggling *Indians,* a fort will be forthwith built, and garrisoned by a competent number of Officers and Men to be employed as Rangers for the security and protection of the settlers."[2]

The surveyors graded the land into six classifications. In instructions to commissioners, who should hold sales successively at Augusta, Wrightsborough, and Dartmouth (Fort James), Governor Wright set the general price of from one to five shillings per acre, but certain strategically located areas such as mill sites should bring a higher price, and "All lands situated on Savannah River four miles above and below the Town of Dartmouth be rated at one Shilling Six Pence per acre over and above the valued quality." And the same specifications applied to the lands on the Dart River, with some additional variations of prices of land on both rivers farther up. In the forks of the two rivers the town of Dartmouth was to be laid out on 800 acres reserved for that purpose. Apparently Sir James had visited this site because in his instructions he directed that a fort be erected in the forks "at the place already marked out by his Excellency the Governor."

Sir James did not name the fort, which came to be called Fort James (undoubtedly in his honor), but he did give its dimensions. It should be 120 feet square with bastions (abbreviated blockhouses) on the four corners of the enclosure. Two of these bastions were to be roofed over, while the other two were to be left open to the sky, and all four were to be made of squared logs. To make the enclosure, these bastions were to be joined by walls (curtains) made of split logs and by the outer sides of the officers' houses, the barracks, and the "goalhouse and magazine."[3]

With the building of this fort, there was now no need for another fort which South Carolina had erected in 1765-1766 across the Savannah about a half mile down the river. This was Fort Charlotte, which had been designed to keep the Indians quiet after that Colony had secured the cession of 1755.[4]

According to a description of Fort James given by William Bartram, the famous naturalist, who visited the fort on a trip in the late spring of 1776, it covered "about an acre of ground." If this was the area of the enclosure, the fort was about three times as large as Sir James had specified, but it is probable that the fort was built larger than originally planned. Bartram was purposely exaggerating or was unable to make valid estimates. He had already travelled sufficiently to make him an expert on judging distances. In a more minute description, Bartram said that swivel guns were mounted on the second story of the bastions and that there were loop holes breast high for small arms along the walls between the bastions. The commander's house was a "good building," flanked on each side by officers' quarters and barracks for a garrison of about fifty rangers (including officers), "each having a good horse well equipt, a rifle, two dragoon pistols, and a hanger, besides a powder horn, shot pouch and tomahawk."[5]

The perilous times of 1776 required the fort to be manned, and certainly now the members of the garrison were Georgia revolutionary patriots, for Sir James Wright had already fled the Colony. Fort James was there, but the town of Dartmouth had not yet been able to rise from its paper description and would not do so until the Revolutionary War was over, when the town that was destined to grow up there would be called Petersburg. But when Bartram was there, he could merely write in his journal that the "point of peninsula between the two rivers, for the distance of two miles back from the fort, is laid out for a town, by the name of Dartmouth"; but he made no mention of any lots having been laid off or buildings constructed.

Sir James' proclamation of June, 1773, inviting settlers to come to Georgia did not bring in as many as he had expected. There was little time left before the Revolutionary War, and there were more important matters to engage the attention of prospective settlers. Yet within the next year or two there was a good sprinkling of North Carolinians and some South Carolinians applying for lands in the New Purchase; and, of course, most of them came to the land office operating at Fort James. They selected locations up the Broad River (Dart soon being dropped) and the Little River to the southward, and their tributaries, as well as up and down the Savannah. Broad River and its tributaries were the favorite regions, where warrants for more than 20,000 acres were granted. North and South Carolinians, in almost equal numbers, made up by far the bulk of these settlers. According to incomplete records, there were only fourteen warrants issued to Virginians, eleven to Pennsylvanians, three to Englishmen, two to New Jersyites, and one each to Irish and Scots.[6]

The Scotsman was James Gordon, who secured warrants for 5,000 acres in the Broad River Valley and on Chickasaw Creek, a tributary, on condition that he bring over a certain number of families to be settled on these lands. According to long-standing and persistent tradition, Gordon brought over a considerable number of settlers as indented servants, and when the Revolution broke out he went back to Scotland; however, not before selling them for whatever he could get, after taking most of them over into South Carolina. George R. Gilmer (born in Wilkes County in 1790) said that while attending school in South Carolina he boarded with one of the Scottish families which Gordon had brought over—named Sutherland and originally from the Orkney Islands. Gilmer could have been correct in this assertion, but he was mistaken when he said that the Scotsman who brought the settlers to Georgia was George Gordon, the agitator who later led the anti-Catholic London riots in 1780. Gilmer's mistake came to be accepted and repeated many times thereafter, and in making this statement in 1854 Gilmer was probably repeating what he had heard.[7]

Some of the names which were to appear in the galaxy of Georgia Revolutionary heroes (and heroines) first appear in this migration into the New Purchase. There was Elijah Clarke, who fought throughout the war and thereafter continued against the Indians; the redoubtable Aunt Nancy Hart, cross-eyed, freckle-faced, a terror to Tories, who stood her ground on Broad River and never left the state until years after the war was over; John Dooly, foully murdered by the Tories, whose son John M. Dooly became a judge and a wit unequalled in the annals of the Georgia bar; the Lamars, a family most prolific in men of prominence in American history; and other families who fought for independence and whose names became ornaments in the history of the state thereafter.

The war left a destruction probably unequalled in any other state and a legacy of hatred and social turmoil relieved only somewhat by the confiscation of Tory property and the banishment of some of the best and worst citizens. But in Georgia and out there was released a great urge to move on and upward in a bold new world, now set going by release from the control of Great Britain. This moving might be to secure a better life in areas already somewhat populated, or it most likely meant setting out to a land of even better promise.

In Georgia the New Purchase, interrupted by the war, was now open again for settlers. In the state's first formal constitution, made in 1777, this region had been erected into a county, named for the famous English statesman John Wilkes. The course of empire in Georgia was now into Wilkes County, which would later contribute in whole or parts to six counties and which by 1790 would include almost half the people of the state. The heart of Wilkes County was the Broad River valley with its tributaries; but there were other streams, many of them, for Sir James Wright had not been guilty of mere rhetoric when in his Proclamation of 1773 he had said that the New Purchase was well-watered. As an indication of their number and a tribute to the imagination of the early settlers, there were these creeks: Powderbag, Pistol, Troublesome, Buckhead, Hound, Wildcat, Panther, Beaverdam, Buzzard, Doves, Lightwood Log, Cedar, Bluestone, Millstone, Coldwater, Dry Fork, Deep, Big Shoal, Fishing, Rocky Comfort, Hardship, Long, War, Red Lick, Drunken Camp, Mud Lick, Flat Rock, Camp, and Town. It was a land of pines, but more so of hardwoods and decidious trees—walnut, poplar, white oak, ash, pine, hickory, chestnut, birch, and beech—with carpets of wild grasses, pea vines, shrubs, and reed canes along the streams.

All of this was west of the Savannah River. Nature had made the regions east of the Savannah much the same, but man had come along and named the country South Carolina and given it another government. Thus it was that upper South Carolina was by nature about the same as upper Georgia; however, the Savannah River separated two authorities over the lives of the people in this great kingdom of the upper Savannah, and there was not always co-operation and friendly relations. This rivalry tended to develop two economic units, and the New Purchase was not to be greatly helped by the divisions east of the Savannah, sometimes called districts and sometimes counties. Those lying directly across this upper part of Georgia were Pendleton and Abbeville, with Edgefield immediately below, fronting all the way down to Augusta and farther. South Carolina had at least one advantage over Georgia; for the great stream of people passing southward from as far north as Pennsylvania and New Jersey must first pass through the upper part of that state, and if any of these settlers were attracted by what they saw they might stop there and Georgia would be the loser. But this was not a great hindrance to the growth of Georgia, for upper South Carolina was not large, and many passing into Georgia had first settled in South Carolina.

When peace came after the Revolution the New Purchase, now Wilkes County, had few settlers. Of those who had come in before the war, some had remained faithful to England and being Tories had been killed or driven out; some had been killed in the war as soldiers or had died natural deaths; and some who had left the state for safety during the fighting had not returned.

The state both during and soon after the war had been passing land laws designed to attract settlers. A law passed in February, 1783, was much more liberal than Sir James Wright's terms had been. Any head of a family might have 200 acres by merely paying the "office and surveyor fees," and could obtain additional amounts up to 1,000 acres by paying ascending prices beginning at one shilling an acre. With the opening up of new lands lying northward and westward of Wilkes County, obtained through Indian treaties in 1783, a new scale of prices not so liberal as the former scale was set in a law of February, 1784. The price was now raised to three shillings per acre with a limit of 1,000 acres; however, in the multiplicity of laws, rules, and regulations it was still possible to get land in Georgia for nothing if a person belonged to five different classes relating to service in the war or if he merely had remained in the state without "plundering or distressing the country." In February of the next year the legislature amended the state's land policy by removing all charges for land except office and surveyor fees, but the maximum amount allowed to one person was still 1,000 acres. This was the law until 1803, when the Land Lottery System was set up, under which the remainder of Georgia's public domain passed into private ownership.

2

The Virginians of the
Broad River Valley

GEORGIA LANDS appeared attractive to certain Virginians who
had entered this region as Continental soldiers during the Revolution; and when the fighting was over, a small group of them
headed by George Mathews returned and petitioned the legislature for a grant of 200,000 acres. The petition was granted on
condition that 200 or more families would be brought in. Instead
of settling in the new lands obtained from the Indians in 1783
and established the next year as two new counties, Washington
and Franklin, the Virginians spread out up and down the Broad
River Valley, which until 1790 lay wholly in Wilkes County.
Beginning in 1790 this region was cut up into four counties,
leaving Wilkes county with only a small frontage on the south
bank. First Elbert County was set up, extending from the mouth
of Broad River up the north bank almost to the end of the valley.
In 1793 Oglethorpe County was taken from Wilkes south of the
river and was made to include at least half of the upper valley.
Then three years later the lower part of the valley beginning at
the mouth of Broad River and extending up the south bank to
the Wilkes County line and southward to Little River was
erected into Lincoln County.

Not all of the Broad River settlers were Virginians. The
remnants of those who had come in before the Revolution were
largely North Carolinians or South Carolinians of short dura-
tion in South Carolina before passing on across the Savannah
into Georgia—these latter having come for the most part from
North Carolina. Such were the Doolys, the Harts, the Clarkes,
the Lamars, and others whose names were less well known. These
Wilkes County Carolinians were concentrated largely in the
valley south of Broad River. Before the end of the Revolution they

8

had formed the nucleus of a settlement which became the county seat of Wilkes County. It was named Washington in 1780, being the first town to so honor the great Revolutionary patriot. With the breakup of Wilkes into three additional counties, courthouse towns of necessity were established—Lexington for Oglethorpe, Lincolnton for Lincoln, and Elberton for Elbert. In all of these the Virginia element dominated. In addition to these three towns there was another which in the period of its glory was to become, for that time only, the cultural and economic center of the whole valley. That town was Petersburg, at the mouth of the Broad River Valley.

These Virginians were a remarkable group, constituting an element in the population of the state, whose importance would be hard to overestimate. Concentrated to a large extent in Oglethorpe and Elbert counties, they provided four governors for Georgia and two for Alabama, besides United States Senators, Representatives, judges, and other leaders of lesser standing in politics and public life. For their leaders at least six Georgia counties were named.[1]

George Rockingham Gilmer, one of these Broad River Virginians, writing in 1854 declared that it was "not known that any so small community of planting people, ever created so much wealth, and filled so many offices in so short a time." He praised them for their "extraordinary industry, economy, and honesty, and the honors conferred upon them on account of their patriotism and integrity."[2]

Not all of the Virginians who came to the Broad River Valley were of the elite. There were some who, either before coming or later, slid into that class known as "poor whites," and settled "every poor vacant piece of land in the Broad River neighborhood." According to Gilmer, "Most of them would cheat for six and a quarter cents, and sue each other for a quarter of a dollar"; and only one of them "rose to greatness even in rascality." Some were good at horse swapping; but one less cunning and intelligent gained the name of Coony for having climbed a tree to capture a coon and sawed off the limb between himself and the trunk of the tree, with the result that Coony and the coon fell among the dogs and both were bitten.[3]

Also, Gilmer had no great respect for the North Carolinians, not for any feeling that they lacked intelligence but because they were rivals in politics. In the Old Dominion also the latent feeling of superiority of Virginians over North Carolinians was long prevalent. Gilmer thought that some of the North Carolinians tried to escape that stigma by calling themselves Virginians since before coming to Georgia they had lived near the Virginia line.[4]

Apart from Gilmer's prejudices against those Broad River people who were not Virginians and the "poor white" Virginians, the prominent Virginian families who came to the Broad River Valley made up "the most intimate friendly social union ever known among the same number of persons";[5] but Gilmer in making this statement should have included that kindred but more cosmopolitan group who made up the little Petersburg kingdom down the Valley at the mouth of Broad River. In both cases there was much intermarrying with the consequent formation of tribal interests in kinship and business. The families were generally large; ten and twelve members were not uncommon at this time

Those first family Virginians in the Broad River Valley included, among others, the Gilmers, the Lewises, the Strothers, the Mathews, the Meriwethers, the Johnsons, the Crawfords, the Barnetts, the Harvies, the Taliaferros, the McGehees, the Jordans, the Marks, the Freemans, the Lumpkins, and the Barrows. Their origins before reaching Virginia were English, Irish, Scotch, Welsh, Dutch, French, and Italian. The peak of the influx of these families to Georgia was the period from 1783 to 1790.

Among the first to come was Thomas Meriwether Gilmer. His grandfather George Gilmer had been born near Edinburgh, Scotland, and had migrated to Virginia where he married a second and then a third wife, his first wife having died in London. His second wife was a sister of Dr. Thomas Walker, well-known for leading an exploring party to Kentucky for the Loyal Land Company in 1750, and his third wife was a sister of Dr. James Blair, founder and first president of the College of William and Mary. Thomas Meriwether Gilmer was descended through his grandfather's second marriage. The Meriwether in his name came by means of his father Peachy Ridgway Gilmer's marriage to Mary Meriwether of the well-known Virginia family of Meriwethers.[6]

Thomas Meriwether Gilmer was a fat boy from childhood, weighing 200 pounds by the time he was eighteen, and later almost 300. Living on the Shenandoah River about a mile or two below the school which he attended, he would in the summer months float and swim home down the river. Before he was of age he married Elizabeth Lewis and the next year he set out for Georgia. He settled on the south side of Broad River and built on the hill above the river bottom lands a log house, which later he replaced with a two-story frame dwelling.

Bringing with him to Georgia little except his wife, Thomas Meriwether Gilmer at the time of his death in 1817 left a widow, nine children, a great many grandchildren, and a sizeable fortune. His chattels, including seventy-three slaves, were conservatively appraised by the administrators of his estate at more then $55,000. His cash on hand at his death amounted to $1,485 and notes due stood at $7,956. The value of his real estate was not appraised at the time of the settlement of his estate; but he had already given land to some of his children and he left the residue to his widow, who was to live many years longer. She was still living in 1854, being then 89 years old.[7]

The items found inside Thomas Meriwether Gilmer's house and out in his barnyard and pastures should give some indication of the kind of life a Broad River grandee lived in the late eighteenth century and the first quarter of the nineteenth. Among the pieces of furniture and dining room and kitchen utensils in his house at the time of his death were 10 jugs and 17 butter pots, knives and forks, a cupboard, one caster and 5 dozen plates, a dozen silver table spoons, a dozen tea spoons, a dozen dishes and 4 pitchers, a lot of pots and saucers, a set of China and tea ware, waffle irons, a lot of glasses and candlesticks, 19 table chairs, 4 tea kettles, 2 flour barrels, a spice mortar, 4 tin kettles, 6 pine tables and a pair of birch tables, a walnut desk, a clock (valued at $100, probably a grandfather clock), a pair of field glasses, 2 shotguns, a powder and shot flask, a shot bag, 27 "sitting chairs," 4 pairs of fire dogs, shovels and tongs, sadirons, 8 beds with curtains, a dozen counterpanes and 4 coverlets, a "dressing glass," 10 trunks and a chest, and 320 yards of homespun (valued at $220), and many other items to be found in sitting rooms and kitchens. There were $70 worth of books, items notoriously undervalued by appraisers of estates.

Outside in the stables, barnlots, and pastures were 18 horses and a yoke of oxen, 107 cattle, 75 sheep, and 210 hogs. There were growing crops of cotton valued at $6,720 and of corn, at $3,600. On hand were 450 bushels of wheat, 400 bushels of oats, and fodder worth $200. In their appropriate places were a flax wheel, 9 spinning wheels, a loom and web, 9 pair of cotton cards, 3 bags of feathers and 7 of wool, 59 pairs of shoes (stored away for the slaves), 16 axes, wedges, frows, leather worth $25.00, raw hides,

sythes and reaping cradles, 31 hoes, 26 plows, a dozen pairs of
plow gears, wagons, carts, blacksmith tools, 300 pounds of iron,
dairy furniture, and $228 worth of fat, tallow, and salt. There
were 11 beehives, a cotton gin, and a riding chair.[8]

Thomas Meriwether Gilmer's children intermarried with the
Taliaferros, the Harvies, the Johnsons, the Barnetts, the Marks,
the Mathews, the Bibbs, and the Jordans. Six of them did not find
the Broad River country as inviting as the new lands opening up
to the westward. Five moved to Alabama and the sixth continued
on to Mississippi. Of those who stayed in Georgia, George Rockingham Gilmer was the most prosperous and famous. He had a
short military career, after which he became a member of the
United States House of Representatives and governor of Georgia.
His fame was doubtless kept greener on account of the book which
he wrote in 1854, entitled *Sketches of Some of the First Settlers of
Upper Georgia, of the Cherokees, and the Author.*

A frank but loving reviewer of the book said in 1855: "We
thank Gov. Gilmer for his book. It has been said by some of his
friends that it has injured his fame,—there is too much gossip in
it, too many hearts wounded, too much of the old man's infirmity.
We dissent from these imputations. Of itself, and on its own
pedestal, it is worthy of respect. It differs from all other books;
it is the beginning and end of a peculiar freedom of the press,
which, as an experiment, will scarcely be repeated. The author
was full of images, and overrun with facts. He was beseiged; he
found no rest.

"Writing them down, by way of depletion, afforded some relief;
yet the Broad River community, with their forests, fields, and
cabins, log schoolhouses and rough hospitality,—with their whole
issue of children and grandchildren, intermarriages, and associations thus formed, illustrated by pedigrees from English knight-
hood and Indian princes, including humbler degrees of ancestral
reputation,—all had to be noticed; and nothing less than publication would answer. Gov. Gilmer is no voluntary author: the book
was extorted from him."[9]

Among the other Gilmers and their kindred who moved from
Virginia to Georgia to grace the Broad River Valley was John
Gilmer, an uncle of Thomas Meriwether Gilmer. He had been
an officer under Lafayette in the Revolution. He had none of the
business acumen nor acquisitiveness of his nephew, and it was his
wife (who had been Mildred Meriwether) "whose industry and
economy prevented her husband's generous wastefulness making

his children destitute." Of his nine children, five moved on westward—one each to Illinois, Kentucky, Alabama, Louisiana, and Arkansas.[10]

Another of the Gilmer kin to come to Georgia was Meriwether Lewis with his mother and her family and his step-father. Since her husband William Lewis had died, she married John Marks and together they decided to try their fortune in that promised land of the Broad River Valley. They arrived in 1784 or 1785, at the time when Meriwether would have been either ten or eleven years old. They acquired an estate and prospered. Meriwether was sent back to Virginia for his education, and, therefore, spent only his long vacations in Georgia. Traveling back and forth and communing with the deep forests and open fields of the Broad River country conditioned him to achieve that fame which came to him when he led the Lewis and Clark expedition to the Pacific Ocean in 1804-1806. On one occasion in the early 1790's when there was great alarm among the Broad River settlers over an impending invasion by Cherokee Indians, a group of the settlers fled for protection to a deep forest recess. In the midst of night while they were gathered around the campfire and momentarily expecting an attack, Meriwether had the presence of mind to dash a bucket of water on the fire and thereby restore confidence to the group. Meriwether's mother was again a widow before 1792, and in that year she decided to move back to Virginia. Meriwether, now in the army, came back to Georgia to supervise the return of his mother to the old homestead in Albemarle County, Virginia. Mrs. Marks still owned property in the Broad River country, for in 1797 she made a trip to Georgia to bring back in three wagons the slaves who had been working the plantation lands. In 1806 Mrs. Marks made another visit to the Broad River region, and the following year she was still collecting certain moneys due her; but probably by this time she had disposed of all her Georgia property.[11]

The most colorful of the Virginians to come down to the Broad River Valley was George Mathews, who with a few associates (as previously noted) was largely responsible for the migration of the Virginians to Georgia. He was a son of John Mathews, an Irishman, who migrated to Virginia in 1737. George Mathews took part in Lord Dunmore's War and was in the Battle of Point Pleasant on the Great Kanawha. He fought through the Revolution and was personally known to George Washington, whom he always admired and held to be the only American he would look up to. He was captured by the British and confined on a prison ship. On being exchanged he joined General Nathanael Greene's forces in the Southern Department, and in this way became acquainted with Georgia.

He removed to Broad Rivēr in 1784 and settled in the Goose Pond district, which got its name from the large number of geese and ducks which on their flights back and forth would rest for a time on a small pond made by the flood waters of the river. By 1809 the post office of Goose Pond had been set up to serve the many Virginians who had settled in this region.

Immediately Mathews became a political power not only among the Broad River Virginians but also throughout all of upper Georgia. Before he had satisfied the three years residence requirement for governor, he was in 1786 elected to that office, but since the term did not begin until November, 1787, he was seated. Also he served another term from 1793 to 1796, and became involved in the so-called Yazoo Fraud, by signing the famous bill providing for the sale of much of Georgia's western lands. Being dubbed a Yazooist, he became so unpopular that he threatened to leave the United States and did leave Georgia to return only infrequently. In 1798 President John Adams sent his name to the Senate for confirmation as governor of the Mississippi Territory, but as sharp objection was raised in that body because of Mathews' connection with one of the Yazoo land companies, the President withdrew his name. In 1811-1812 Mathews as an agent of the United States Government became involved in the movement to seize East Florida. He occupied Amelia Island, but his action was disavowed on the grounds that he had misunderstood his instructions. Greatly incensed by this treatment, Mathews set out for Washington to get an explanation from President Madison with the determination that if he did not get satisfaction he would subject the President to personal chastisement. Since he was in this highly excitable state, his health broke when he reached Augusta, and there he died and was buried in St. Paul's Churchyard.

Mathews was a short thick man with a florid complexion, militarily erect with his head thrown back. His speech and pronunciation were picturesque; he spelled coffee *kauphy* and he was saved from these peculiarities in his public papers only by his secretary. On occasion he dressed in a three-cornered cocked hat, high-top boots, ruffled shirt in front and at the wrists; and sometimes he carried a long sword at his side.

George Mathews was married three times. His first wife died;

he got the legislature to divorce him from his second wife; he lived infrequently with his third wife. John and William, his first two sons, remained in Georgia; George, his third son, was appointed by President Jefferson in 1805 as an interim judge in the Mississippi Territory and the following year he was given an appointment as judge in the Orleans Territory; Charles Lewis, his youngest son, married a sister of Governor Peter Early and lived in Goose Pond until her death, after which he moved to Alabama. His daughter Anne married Samuel Blackburn, an Irish schoolteacher, and after a residence in Georgia, they moved to Virginia, where Blackburn became a person of some importance.[12]

No Virginia family which moved to the Broad River Valley was quite the equal of the Meriwethers in their connection through marriage with other important families, in the number of children who constituted this widespreading tribe, and in the part they played throughout the state and nation. According to one of their number, "No one ever looked at or talked with one of them, but he heard or saw something which made him listen, or look again."[13]

Nicholas Meriwether along with his two brothers came to Virginia from Wales in the late seventeenth century and was the progenitor of the Meriwethers—there being no male issues from the families of his brothers. One of his daughters married Robert Lewis, whose descendants were most of the families of that name in Virginia, Georgia, and Kentucky. Descendants of Nicholas Meriwether were part of the great migration to the Broad River Valley, where they became outstanding in the development of that region and in the political life of Georgia. One of the children of Thomas Meriwether (a grandson of Nicholas), was Frank who moved to Georgia and of whom it was said: "He had no pride or vanity. His house was the collecting-place for the poor and ignorant, the rich and learned."[14] Another, a daughter, Lucy, married William Lewis and became the mother of Meriwether Lewis. After William's death she married John Marks and moved to Broad River, as previously noted. Others of these children married into the Gilmer family. David, a brother of Frank's, married Mary Harvie, who was reputed to weigh from 300 to 400 pounds; Elizabeth, a daughter of Frank's, married William Mathews, a son of Governor Mathews; and Tom, a son of Frank's, married Rebekah Mathews, a daughter of the Governor.[15]

Coming down another line of descent from Nicholas Meriwether were General David Meriwether, well known in Georgia politics, a member of the United States House of Representatives

from 1802 to 1807, and often a commissioner to treat with the
Creek Indians; his son James, a graduate of the University of
Georgia, a Superior Court judge, and a member of the United
States House of Representatives; and his grandson James A., a
graduate of the state university, a Superior Court judge, and a
Representative in Congress for several terms. Another son of
David Meriwether's, William, was a graduate of the state univer-
sity. Other sons moved on to Alabama and to Tennessee.[16]

Probably the most prolific and certainly the weightiest of the
Virginians who moved to Broad River were the Harvies. John
Harvie came to Virginia from Sterling, Scotland about forty years
before the Revolution and became the father of nine children.
Since John was dead before the great migration, his widow and
her children joined the exodus to Georgia. A physical characteris-
tic of the family was their great weight. According to those who
were reputed to know, the combined weight of the nine children
was 2,700 pounds. They intermarried with the Taliaferros, the
Moores, the Hulls, the Cosbys, the Harrises, the Wattses, the
Davenports, the Meriwethers, the Jordans (reputed to be descendants of Pocahontas), the Bradleys, the Johnsons, and the Andrews
(John Andrew, the father of James Osgood Andrew, the Methodist
Bishop, whose ownership of slaves broke the Methodist Church
into Northern and Southern divisions in 1845). As daughters of
the Harvie name tended to predominate, the spread of that name
was no indication of how extensive the original Harvies who came
to Broad River had become.[17]

Many of the Broad River Virginians had come from Albemarle
County, but other parts of the Old Dominion provided their contributions. During early Colonial times two brothers from Italy
settled near Williamsburg. They were Taliaferros. Thomas Jefferson referred to the Taliaferro clan which arose from this beginning as respectable and prosperous. George Wythe, signer of
the Declaration of Independence and high judge in Virginia, married into this family. Zachariah Taliaferro, who lived in Amherst
County, was the immediate progenitor of the Georgia Taliaferros.
He did not go to Georgia, but several of his eight children caught
the Georgia fever. The most prominent was Benjamin, who fought
through the Revolution, first under Washington and then in the
Southern Department under Benjamin Lincoln and Light-Horse
Harry Lee, until he was captured at the siege of Charleston. Pa-
roled, he returned to Virginia, married Martha Meriwether, and
in 1784 set out for the Broad River Valley. He settled on the south

side of the river about ten miles above Petersburg. He raised a family of ten children, nine by his first wife, and a tenth "by marrying a dependent young woman of the neighborhood, . . . about whom any romance would have been ridiculous."[18] His tribe did not become very extensive, though they intermarried with the Gilmers, Watkinses, McGehees, Barnetts, Bibbs, and Harvies. The only one to attain any particular fame was Benjamin, himself, who played an important part in state politics, becoming a member of the senate and its president, a delegate to the constitutional convention of 1798, a judge of the Superior Court, and a member of the United States House of Representatives from 1799 to 1802, when he resigned.[19]

Nicholas Johnson was, doubtless, the most flamboyant and eccentric of all the Virginians who came to Broad River. As a young man in Louisa County, Virginia, while acting as a deputy sheriff he committed some deed that made it desirable for him to depart that region. His arrival in Georgia was talked about for years thereafter. He appeared on a blooded charger, accompanied by three servants. He wore a blue coat, red vest, and buff pantaloons; and he often remarked that such a dress would set a man off in good fashion, for bystanders would be led immediately to remark, "Who is that? Who is that?"

He later married Mary Marks, a daughter of James Marks, and raised nine children before his wife died in 1814 or 1815, after which he moved to Alabama. His eccentricities still remained with him. Living alone, he indulged his affections on dogs and cats, keeping about seventy of each breed. His children who remained in Georgia intermarried with the Jordans, Taliaferros (Betty marrying a son of Benjamin Taliaferro), and the Gilmers.

In his Georgia days he had been addicted to strong drink, and one day while in his cups, he very near let his wife drown in Broad River; however, after rescuing her, he never "touched another drop." His plantation adjoined that of Governor Mathews', and in giving advice to the Governor's son Charles on the best method to get elected to office, he specified traveling through the country talking to the women, inquiring the price of chickens and eggs, drinking a glass of cider at crossroads stores, and kissing the children of the neighborhood. Though truthful and honest, he was prone to exaggerate and to emphasize what he was describing, as when he told his wife that he had come upon a partridge nest with a bushel of eggs in it. When his wife expressed her doubts, he reduced the number to a dozen.

Colonel Johnson (a title by courtesy) owned a large plantation and thirty or forty slaves. When an organ-grinder with a monkey happened by, he would call his Negroes out of the fields to be entertained. His dinner table generally groaned under the weight of several hams, a large hunk of beef, dishes of fowls, and vegetables galore. His wife kept seven chicken houses, while the Colonel was reputed to own 500 sheep and uncounted hogs—probably some more of the Colonel's exaggerations. Since his first children were daughters, he was so pleased with the arrival of his first son that he is said to have planted in his fence corners and at other likely spots 100,000 walnuts, expecting that by the time the boy grew into young manhood, the trees would be worth a dollar apiece for timber. This report might well be considered another exaggeration.[20]

The Crawfords were originally from Scotland, but as other Scots had done, some came to Colonial Virginia. Among them were the ancestors of Joel Crawford, who lived in Amherst County, Virginia until in the midst of the Revolution he migrated to South Carolina. At the end of the war he moved across the Savannah into that part of Richmond County, which in 1790 became Columbia County. Here Joel's sons William H. Crawford and Joel, Jr. grew up; but in the course of time both moved northward into the Broad River Valley. Although they were not of the Broad River Virginians, they were cordially received without any condescension. William H. Crawford became a resident of Lexington in Oglethorpe County, while his brother Joel settled farther down the river on the north side in Elbert County. In a short while William H. Crawford was entering a career of national importance which led him to the very verge of the presidency of the United States while Joel, on the other hand, seemed content to be a tobacco inspector in one of the warehouses in Petersburg.

Another family from Amherst County, Virginia, was headed by Nat Barnett, who had intermarried into the neighboring Crawfords before he set out for Georgia. They came about the time of the outbreak of the Revolution, and by-passing the Broad River Valley, they settled down the Savannah in the northern part of what later became Richmond County and which still later was cut off into Columbia County. Two of his young sons, William and Joel, played an important part in the Revolution, and later, like the Crawfords, moved up into the Broad River Valley. Joel became a planter in Oglethorpe County, which he represented several times in the state senate and then, like many other Broad River people, moved on into Alabama where he became an even richer planter.

William Barnett settled in the Elbert County part of the Broad River Valley, where he became sheriff and thereafter was frequently elected to the state senate. He served in the United States House of Representatives from 1812 to 1815. Then, like his brother Joel, he caught the Alabama fever and moved to Montgomery County, where he died in 1834. The Barnetts intermarried with the Broad River Virginians as much as if they had been of that clan—the Meriwethers, Gilmers, Taliaferros, and the Mathews.[21]

Another family of Scottish descent which migrated to the Broad River Valley was that of young Micajah McGehee, who had married into the Scott family to which Winfield Scott belonged. At first looked upon by the Scotts with unfriendly eyes, Micajah and his wife moved to Georgia, where in the course of time they reared a dozen children, said by one chronicler to have numbered fourteen. They intermarried with the Gilmers, Taliaferros, Watkinses, the Olivers, and, of course, with many others in succeeding generations. The Broad River Valley was not broad enough to hold all of the second generation, of whom some moved to Alabama, Mississippi, Louisiana, and to Texas. Micajah built a frame house in a time when log houses were the style. It had four rooms on the first floor and several upstairs. The house was painted red and became a great gathering place for frolics, consisting of dancing by the young people and card-playing by others—principally whist. The older ones enlivened their temperament with a touch of brandy, but not enough to befuddle the brain. Micajah was the first to plant an extensive peach orchard in the Broad River Valley. He turned most of his fruit into brandy which he sold for at least $1,600 a year. Drinking brandy was customary, but not to the extent to which Micajah consumed it. It was said that when he was young he could drink brandy all day without becoming drunk. In his old age he confined himself to a quart a day.[22]

As has already been noted, others besides Virginians[23] mingled into this kingdom of the Broad River Virginians, and some, even Virginians, were hardly a part of the close-knit clan. There was John Lumpkin, who settled on Long Creek, a tributary of Broad River, and who was important in Oglethorpe and Georgia officialdom. His son Wilson became governor of the state, and another son Joseph Henry became the first chief justice of the State Supreme Court. There were also the Barrows, coming down from Virginia but not until later establishing great land-holdings on

Syls Fork across the Broad River watershed, which drains into Little River and thence into the Savannah. The Barrows intermarried with the Lumpkins, the Popes (who had come directly from North Carolina), and various other families forming a kinship of great proliferation.

From far-away Italy came Ferdinand Phinizy, who settled on the upper stretches of Long Creek. Everything he touched seemed to turn to gold. He became a merchant prince, first in Lexington, and after 1800 in Augusta, where he had moved in 1800.[24]

Coming to Georgia as a clerk in Phinizy's store in Lexington was George Paschal, a North Carolinian, who had fought in the Revolution. In 1802 he married Agnes Brewer, who was a member of a little tribe of North Carolinians who had settled on Long Creek. George Paschal later ran a store of his own, became an unsuccessful farmer for a short time; and being an extremely well-read man, he taught school at various times. About 1812 he left Oglethorpe County to engage in a paper-making project at Scull Shoals on the Oconee River, in Greene County; and after failing in this enterprise he returned to Oglethorpe County, where he died in 1832. The admiration he gained for characters in some of the books which he read and for living acquaintances he showed in naming some of his children: Augustus Burrell Julius Nicholas, Isaiah Addison Sanders Goode, Franklin LaFayette Warren Greene, and Lorenzo Columbus George Washington. His wife Agnes became the grand lady wherever the family happened to live, and after her husband's death she moved to the gold diggings in North Georgia and spent the remainder of her ninety-four years in Auraria, as "Grandma" Paschal to a thousand miners who needed her administering kindness. Her sons spread out to the West and became important in Louisiana, Arkansas, and Texas— and one in the nation's capital after the Civil War.[25]

A lone Irishman, a bachelor then and always, Francis Meson, wandered into the Broad River country and settled in Lexington about 1800. He ran a store, became wealthy, and left his fortune to the Oglethorpe academy, which immediately changed its name to Meson Academy, which for the next century was the outstanding educational institution in the Broad River Valley, drawing its students and headmasters from a much wider region. As a New Yorker said of it, "I would rather have the fame of Meson than of Alexander [the Great]."[26]

Coming from Mecklenburg County, North Carolina, about the end of the Revolution and settling in the Broad River Valley was

James Jack. According to tradition, he had carried to the Congress in Philadelphia a copy of the famous though disputed Mecklenburg Declaration of Independence of May 20, 1775. He was probably celebrated in his Georgia home for this exploit, but he seemed not to have capitalized on it politically, for no record indicates that he even reached a position as high as membership in the state legislature, though his son Patrick attained that position.[27]

Although the Virginians dominated the Oglethorpe and Elbert parts of the Broad River Valley, they were not the exclusive inhabitants of these parts; and although they were sprinkled in the Petersburg kingdom in the lower Valley and in the Wilkes County part, they controlled neither one of these regions. As will be seen later, Petersburg was more cosmopolitan than any other part of the Valley, and from Long Creek eastward through Wilkes County the North Carolinians were largely in charge.

3

Life in the Broad River Valley

PEOPLE FLOCKED into the Broad River Valley because land was cheap and they had heard how good it was. By the early 1800's the Valley appeared to be about full when any effort was made to secure land there from the state. At this time if a person wanted land in the valley he would have to buy it from private owners and the price would vary greatly, from less than a dollar an acre for poor gravelly upland to $3.00 to $5.00 for first grade hickory land, being also much higher for the richest bottom lands. Their holdings generally ran from a hundred or fewer acres to three thousand or more.

The Virginians and others came in bringing their livestock, slaves, and wagons loaded down with children and household effects. They immediately set the slaves to work clearing land and preparing for the first crop. Tobacco had been their principal interest back in Virginia, and naturally their first main crop in Georgia would be tobacco. Some of the larger planters raised as much as 11,000 pounds a year and anyone who might modestly call himself a farmer would probably gather at least 1,000 pounds. Tobacco was sent down Broad River to Petersburg by boat or by wagon over the main road, or in large casks pulled by horses or oxen—called "rolling tobacco"—over the long ridge road to Augusta. This marketing of tobacco often resulted in warehouse receipts, called "tobacco notes," which circulated as money in large purchases.[1]

Although tobacco was at first a principal crop, with the invention of an easily workable cotton gin in 1793 and improvements added in subsequent years, cotton soon came into prominence. But at no time was the Broad River economy severely controlled by any one crop. A great deal of corn was raised, along with wheat, flax, sweet potatoes, and the variety of products of kitchen gardens which enriched the lives of the people. Orchards, especially peaches, were soon being planted.

This diversified agricultural economy was closely interlocked with a widespread ownership of livestock and fowls. From the late 1780's on down through the first quarter of the nineteenth century, typical livestock holdings were such as these: John Mc-Elroy in 1796 owned 6 horses, 30 head of cattle, 64 hogs, and 15 sheep; Zachariah Lawrence in 1811 owned besides his oxen and horses, 31 cows, 26 sheep, 54 hogs; at the same time Charles O'Kelley owned in addition to oxen and horses, 43 hogs, 24 sheep, 22 goats; Micajah McGhee also this same year owned in addition to other livestock 41 cows, 18 sheep, and 190 hogs; Jeffery Early in 1812, unlike most Broad River settlers, owned mules (four of them), also 100 hogs and other livestock. As for fowls practically all of the people owned chickens, some owned ducks; however, geese were a specialty. Geese were not only good for food, but their greatest contribution to the economy and comfort of their owners was their feathers. No house was complete without feather beds. The number of geese owned by any one family generally ran from a dozen to as many as 50 and sometimes even more.[2]

Slavery became entrenched in the Broad River Valley from the beginning. Most settlers brought along a few slaves, and as they prospered additions came from purchase and natural increase. The small farmers had from two or three to a dozen or more, while the planter class owned from 20 up to about 100. For instance, Martha Harvie (widow of John Harvie) in 1801 owned two boy slaves along with Letty and her two children, Milinda and Mintilda. John Billups in 1817 owned more than seventy slaves which were valued at almost $35,000.[3] As early as 1800 there were 2,600 slaves in Oglethorpe County.[4]

Slavery was not a condition of living to be chosen by any sensible person, yet the life of a slave in Oglethorpe County was as likely as not to be no worse than that of anyone who had to work for his living—and in some respects better, for the cost of sickness and old age was the concern of the master, not the slave. And as for being held to the land, the common condition of the people of Oglethorpe County was no different, for either by necessity or choice few of them traveled far beyond their own neighborhoods. The patriarchal attitude toward slavery was evident in many families, as is shown in their wills. The widow Harvie left her slave Letty to her son William and at his death Letty might choose which

of William's children she would like to serve. The widow Harvie
further directed that "in token of her mistresses Regard for her,"
she should receive five dollars a year. If Gabriel should like to be
sold, then William was to sell him "to whom he may choose to
serve," and he should receive a present of ten dollars.[5]

Moses Parks had an unusually keen conscience and a humble
attitude to those who were less well off than he was. In 1797 he
willed that his two slaves John and Bet "enjoy that freedom, the
human species have a right to by nature," and he directed that
the legislature "Ratify this clause in my will." He gave $150 "to
school them," and if they should die before it was used "then
it shall go to the poor for ever." If certain other bequests were
not used he willed that these and the remainder of his estate go
"to the help of the poor for ever Viz: the Real poor, the halt &
maim'd lunitic &c &c to be appropriated to their use, according
to the Judgment & good Conscience of my executors, & the glory
of god to whom I give all."[6]

In 1827 James Bradley wrote in his will that it was to be "ex-
pressly understood if any of my Negroes wish to go to the American Colony on the coast of Africa they are to be left out of the
division [of his property] and their expenses paid out of my estate
to the nearest port when a vessel is fiting out for the Colony." He
had about forty slaves, and most of them chose to go.[7] The reference here was to Liberia.

The planter whose disposal of his slaves became a tradition to
be passed around for a hundred years thereafter was Richard
Huff (sometimes Hoff), a bachelor, who in 1850 owned 93 slaves,
all "B" (black)— no "M" (mulattoes), according to the census.
In addition he owned real estate worth $15,000. He lived in
Oglethorpe County on Long Creek, which separated Oglethorpe
and Wilkes counties, with practically all his property being in
Oglethorpe. According to tradition he sent two ship loads of his
slaves to Liberia, 100 on each ship. As the United States Census
of 1850 reported that he owned only 93 slaves, it is evident that
the tradition is greatly in exaggeration. Since in 1860 he owned
33 slaves it might well be assumed that he sent 60 of them to
Liberia—he would hardly have sold any in the light of his offer to
let those who so desired go to Liberia. Thus, he must have sent
most of his slaves to Africa and they might well have been trans-
ported on two ships. As late as 1908 an old Negro working on the
plantation of Colonel James Monroe Smith in Oglethrope County
was receiving a letter now and then from his father, who was one

of the last to go to Liberia where he had greatly prospered and was reputed to be worth $100,000.[8]

Slaves were used especially in the heavy farm work, but there were also lighter tasks for them to perform, such as looking after livestock and aiding in the distilling operations, which were carried out on almost every plantation and farm. Brandy was a favorite drink, used on almost every occasion, from the celebration of births and weddings to the last rites for the dead. In the first quarter of the nineteenth century, drinking was not frowned upon, even by the preachers, some of whom were referred to as "brandy Baptists." No sale could be held without the cryer putting in a charge for brandy or whiskey, and it extended even to the executors and appraisers of estates. For a sale in settling the estate of Benjamin Knox in 1805, these items of expenses were listed: "for crying sale $15" and "for brandy at sale $11.62½." The size of the brandy charge evidently indicated that the crowd attending the sale had been treated. The price of brandy was generally a dollar a gallon.[9] In the case of appraisers the charge for brandy was much less, since only three or four people were necessary for this work. "Spirits on the day of appraisement," 75 cents, would indicate that the appraisers had consumed about three-fourths of a gallon.

The household industries included especially spinning and weaving, both of cotton and wool. Necessary for these operations were cotton cards, spinning wheels, and looms. Mrs. Micajah McGehee bore the reputation of being one of the most clever weavers throughout the Broad River Valley. George R. Gilmer, who apparently knew all the people on Broad River and all the characteristics and foibles that they had, wrote of her, "She spun, wove, cut out, and made up a petticoat in one day, and wore it the next."[10] Making butter and curing hams and bacon filled up many a larder and smokehouse and provided articles for exportation to Petersburg and Augusta. In the early days beavers were common on Broad River and its tributaries; hence there was trapping; but this activity soon played out.[11] Grist mills run by water power were common on the streams, and at least one cotton factory was built on Broad River. It was located at the Anthony Shoals and consisted of a four-story brick building, containing 1,500 spindles, 20 looms, "an extra number of Cards," and all things necessary for making yarn, osnaburg, sheeting, and shirting.[12]

Many of these proud Virginians never got out of their log

houses; and when they needed more room they would add another
log house connected by a "breeze way" or "dog trot." Sometimes
they would build other log cabins in the yard nearby. Frame
houses, which were one-and-a-half or two stories, were unusual,
and the white-columned houses, long associated with ante-bellum
planter aristocracy, never found lodgment in the Broad River
Valley during its first half century of settlement. Moving from a
log house into a frame one called for a frolic of dancing lasting
late into the night, as was the case when the Thomas Meriwether
Gilmers moved into theirs.[13] A few settlers built frame houses in
the beginning, as did Benjamin Taliaferro, Micajah McGehee,
and Abraham Hill.[14]

Life, indeed, had its lighter moments. There were amusements
of all sorts, eating and drinking (but generally neither to excess),
dancing, card-playing, horse-racing, cock-fighting, hunting, gander-
pulling, foot-racing, rifle-shooting, wrestling, quoit-pitching and
"pitching into one another,"[15] and on rare occasions, bull-baiting.
Militia musters, though by law considered to be serious business,
soon became so detested that they were made into horse-play. The
person most likely to be elected captain was the one who promised
that he would not hold another muster.[16]

In addition to what has already been said about what was
owned by the Thomas Meriwether Gilmer family, a look into the
houses of these Broad River people and out into their yards shows
much of how they lived. Besides kitchen and dining room utensils
there were many other items less well known a hundred years
later, such as candle moulds, piggins and churns, brass skillets,
pot racks, funnels, jugs, pewter and earthenware, steelyards,
smoothing irons (sadirons), coffee mills, and mouse traps. In the
sitting room and bed rooms, besides such expected furnishing as
window curtains, carpets, and feather beds, there were trundle
beds, candle snuffers, folding tables, at least one of a variety of
clocks (wooden for $30, brass for $80, and in a few homes, musical
clocks rated at $125), and some of four styles of chairs classified
as "sitting chairs," "easy chairs," "common chairs," and "windsor
chairs."

Among personal adornments and accessories were "gold re-
peater" watches, silk handkerchiefs, gloves, "umbrillas," "black
velvet breeches," great coats, and knee and stock buckles.

On the outside premises there might be found in the great
house besides the ordinary accouterments for riding and driving,
such items as saddle bags, side saddles, "hunting saddles," compass

and rifle guns, curry combs, and bells probably to use on sheep and cattle. Then at their proper places could be found "riding chairs," sulkys, bee gums, Dutch ovens, sun dials, hogsheads and barrels, flax hackles and wheels, spinning wheels and looms, grindstones, grubbing and weeding hoes, clevises, swingletrees (singletrees, whippletrees) and doubletrees, foot-adzes, files, chisels, drawer-knives, hatchets, steel-traps, log-chains, axes, shovels, crowbar, crosscut and whip saws, augurs, wedges, frows, pinchers and nippers, and broad axes.

More so in the Broad River Valley than perhaps in any other part of the Georgia frontier, books had their place in the homes. Histories, biographies, and religious works predominated—Martha Harvie's collection ran from "Clarendon's History 6 vols., $8" through "Foster's Sermons" and "the life of God in the Soul of Man" appraised at 25 cents each. Appraisers had little sense of the value of books and generally listed them at almost nothing, as: "1 writing disk [desk] & a parcel of old books, $4"; "lot of books, $6"; 1 bible, hymn book & other old books, $5"; but some times a surprisingly large value was put upon a lot of books or, most probably, the price was still small but the collection was large, as $43.50 for "1 Lot Books," owned by Josiah Jordan. Very frequently books were thrown in as a make-weight in placing a value on various items, which added a ludicrous incongruity to intellectuality, as: "1 flat Iron, knife & book, 75 cents"; "2 pr Sizors 7 books 1 looking Glass, $2.62½"; "1 lot of old tools & books, $3.37½"; "chist hinges & old books, $1.50"; "chairs, books, gimblets, $4.50"; "Books flax & cotton wheel, $7"; "1 Lot old Books & 1 small Bell, 87½¢"; "1 pail 1 churn 1 box of 3 books & brush, $2.50"; and "Books, looking glass, cloth Brush, sizors, etc., $2.50."[17]

There was no state organization of schools beyond the fact that a state university was chartered in 1785 and set going in 1801. It was the head of a system which included an academy in each county, endowed with land and later aided by the income from a secondary school fund. Parents too poor to pay tuition charges for elementary education might send their children to neighborhood schools and the state would take care of the charges from a "poor school fund." For the Broad River people there were two well-known academies, the Meson Academy (previously mentioned) and the Academy of Wilkes County. The other counties in the Valley had academies, but they were not so well conducted. The elementary schools, over which the state exercised no con-

trol, were often called "poor schools" because the schoolmaster
was aided by the poor school fund. They grew up haphazardly.[18]

Anyone who had the inspiration to teach a school set about
collecting enough pupils to make it worthwhile, although he
might have little learning himself. Pedagogues wandered over the
country seeking schools. When one ingratiated himself in a neighborhood sufficiently to secure as many as twenty pupils he started
his school in some empty building near the edge of an old field
(a one-room structure, probably built for a school, but also possibly built for some other purpose and then abandoned). He
lodged with any family which would have him in return for educating their children. In the neighborhood of the Thomas Meriwether Gilmers in the Goose Pond district the school was taught
at one time by a deserter from the British navy, who established
navy discipline and whipped accordingly. In cold weather when
the schoolhouse might not be heated he would line his pupils up
in a circle and make them dance around the room to keep warm,
applying the switch now and then. Sometimes he set the boys to
wrestling to speed up the circulation of their blood.

Another teacher who appeared in this neighborhood was a respectable man from North Carolina; however, he found someone
he loved more than teaching schools so he married her and quit.
He was followed by a "wandering, drunken Irishman" who
"knocked, kicked, cuffed, and whipped at a great rate." Some of
the boys he whipped as many as ten times a day. This Irishman
gave way to a Virginia gentleman, whose love for brandy was so
great that on some days he would slip away to a brandy still, and
then school would be out for those days. The next Goose Pond
schoolmaster on week-ends incapacitated himself with drink whenever he could afford it; and after his tenure the Broad River people were done with these ne'er-do-wells and began hiring their
home-grown schoolmasters.[19]

These Broad River people were ambitious, industrious, and
intellectual within bounds, but they were rather indifferent to
religion. Lorenzo Dow, "the crazy preacher," wandered up the
Valley in the early years of the nineteenth century and set the
people to wondering what their future life might be like; but the
most persistent seeker to save the souls of the people was Francis
Asbury. He was the first to introduce Methodism into the Broad
River Valley. One of the early Methodist preachers in this region
was John Andrew, up from the Puritans of Liberty County. He
preached a little, ran a store, and did some school-teaching. He

was no success in any of them; but in another respect he was a success in that he was the father of James Andrew, who became a great preacher of Methodism and was elected a bishop in the 1840's. Because he owned slaves a controversy arose which split the Methodist Church into a Northern and a Southern division. He grew up in the Broad River Valley where he "worked hard in the field during the day, collected light-wood knots on his return home, and toiled by their light after knowledge during the night."[20] A great Methodist revival which hit Broad River in 1809 produced lasting effects for the good of the church.[21]

The Baptists had already made their entry into Georgia before the Methodists came. These Baptists appeared first in the Kiokee River valley to the southward, and from there their contagion spread into the Broad River country. The Presbyterians made their first permanent lodgment in this region when John Newton brought the message to the people in 1785. He settled where Lexington would later flourish and died near that town in 1797, leaving an estate of $1,717.38, of which $41.50 was the estimated worth of his books. There was a note due him "on the members of new hope Church $198.77" and an amount of $15.50 owed him by "Bethsalem church for the year 1796."[22]

Broad River played a conspicuous part in the beginnings of the two state political parties which were later to bear the names of Troup and Clark. The Yazoo sales was the principal issue that started the process, and also at stake was the reputation of George Mathews, the governor who signed the bill. Logic played little part in the way the coalescing of different groups worked itself out. The Yazooists were associated nationally with the Federalists, despite the fact that they were the democratic frontiersmen; while the pretentious aristocratic Virginians were the supporters of the Democrats (Democrat-Republicans or Jeffersonian Republicans). The North Carolinian Clarke family (Elijah who spelled it *Clarke* and his son John—later governor—who spelled it *Clark*) were Yazooists, while Virginian William H. Crawford was a Democrat (the later Troup Party in Georgia) and Virginian Mathews was a Yazooist and a Federalist. Broad River Virginians, in general, were Troupites, while the North Carolinans were Clarkites. So excited were the Broad River people in the national election of 1800 that a first-class scramble took place among the younger people when someone brought up the subject of politics at the housewarming of Thomas Meriwether Gilmer's. According to one who was present, dancing and whist games were stopped, and "every one present became agitated, and most talked as fast as they would have fought."[23]

In addition to Broad River being infested with politicians, there were doctors, midwives, merchants, and pedlars. Diseases and births called for both doctors and midwives. Families were too prolific for the few doctors who were called in to attend to those who might be suffering with "bilious fever and other diseases created by extensive clearings, a warm climate, Broad River, and its low grounds."[24] Therefore, skilled midwifery became a lucrative frontier profession.

No society was ever perfect enough not to sprout a few crimes. Broad River was no exception, though the crimes found here were neither numerous nor heinous. The whipping post and stocks were still used in the early eighteen hundreds as the method for punishing petty crimes. In 1800 Rowley Lunsford was found guilty of "malicious mischief," and the judge read the sentence that he was to be taken "forthwith from this Bar to the Public whipping Post in the Town of Elberton and there receive thirty nine lashes on your bare Back with a Cow Skin & be discharged."[25] The next year in the same town, "John Albriton being brought into court for disorderly Behaviour in the court yard, and he continuing refactory, Ordered that the Said Albriton be confined in Stocks for the Space of Thirty Minutes."[26] On any frontier a crime considered equal to murder was horse-stealing. In Oglethorpe County during the late 1790's three criminals convicted of this crime were hanged.[27]

The Broad River, itself, was kind to its settlers. Its waters provided fish for their tables and sport in catching them. Since much of its watershed was never denuded of its timber and vegetation, the rains seldom ran off in such quantities as to produce devastating floods—only one impressed itself sufficiently on the memories of those who saw it and of succeeding generations who heard about it, to be used as a point from which to reckon time. That was the great flood of 1796, known as the Yazoo Freshet because it came the year the Yazoo Act was passed. Broad River's bottom lands were as fertile as any to be found anywhere, and much of its uplands were almost as good for tobacco and cotton as the bottoms were for corn. In fact, the Broad River Valley was a good place for those who chose to come and to stay.

4

The Founding of Petersburg

BEFORE THE REVOLUTION, when the New Purchase had been secured from the Indians, the most strategic region in upper Georgia was the lower Broad River Valley. Governor Wright thought so when he ordered a fort to be built at the juncture of the Broad and Savannah rivers. South Carolina Governor William Bull thought likewise when earlier he had had Fort Charlotte constructed nearby. Now with the great influx of settlers after the Revolution, this location took on even more significance. Fort James had been an outpost to protect the settlers, but now a fort was little needed. Commerce, not protection against Indians, called for a city instead of a fort.

Not only had the Colonial governors of Georgia and South Carolina sensed the strategic importance of this region around the mouth of Broad River, but there were others who saw great possibilities there. Among them was Dionysius Oliver, a Virginian who came to Georgia about the time of the outbreak of the Revolution. He is reputed to have been captain of a privateer (so stated on his tombstone, which, however, is of twentieth century origin), to have been with General Benjamin Lincoln's army at the seige of Savannah in 1778, and subsequently to have fought at Kettle Creek and Kings Mountain.[1] It seems highly unlikely that he was at Kings Mountain, for the year before (1779) he was appointed a magistrate of Wilkes County and shortly thereafter was serving on a jury.[2] This service would not have precluded his having fought at Kings Mountain, but it seems that his war career was already over. Certainly he soon began to capitalize on his war services and take advantage of the loose administration of the Georgia land laws. In July of 1784 he received these grants, 650 acres, 200, 300, 500, 400, 600, 650, 1,000, and in September another grant of 950. All of this land lay in Wilkes County and amounted to 5,250 acres.[3]

A part of this land included the old Fort James and the town of Dartmouth site between the Broad and Savannah rivers, an area which came into the possession of the state on account of its previous ownership as public domain by the Colonial government or by confiscation from the Loyalists. At the same time Oliver was wisely locating his lands, another Virginian, Zachariah Lamar, who had come down before Oliver and had received from Sir James Wright in 1773 a grant of 400 acres on Broad River, was becoming a leader of importance.[4] This grant could not, of course, have included the Fort James area, but it is possible that it was located just across Broad River southward at its mouth. If not so, another grant of 700 acres which Lamar received in 1784 undoubtedly did lie in this area,[5] for in February, 1786 the legislature authorized him "to lay out a town on his own land, situate on the south side of the mouth of Broad river," to divide it into half-acre lots, and to offer them for sale. The town should be named Lincoln. Also he was authorized "to erect a public warehouse for the reception and inspection of tobacco."[6]

The legislature thought all of this was called for, because it was necessary and would "be greatly conducive to the general convenience of the citizens in the upper part of this State, that a town should be laid out, and a tobacco inspection established at the mouth of Broad river in the county of Wilkes." In the same law there was the germ of the town of Petersburg, for the legislature recited that Dionysius Oliver had petitioned the body for authority to erect a warehouse "on his own land, in the aforesaid county of Wilkes, in the fork of the aforesaid Broad river, and the Savannah, for the reception and inspection of tobacco," and that they were now giving him that authority. There was no mention of a town to be laid out, but, of course, there was no prohibition against Oliver doing so.

It could be easily seen that Oliver had the strategic location, and seeing so himself he speedily drew up a map or plan[7] of a town he would erect there, which he called Petersburg—a name in honor of Petersburgh, Virginia, in or near which he was born in 1735. The next year Oliver bought 100 acres nearby, probably with the idea of hemming in the new prospective town of Lincoln, or at least to profit from its expansion.[8]

Lamar soon realized that Oliver had the superior location for a town and he lost interest in promoting the town of Lincoln, for before the end of the year he bought three lots in Oliver's town of Petersburg.[9] It seems that he never took advantage of the permission given him to erect a tobacco inspection warehouse or if he did, then another warehouse was authorized by the legislature in 1797 at the mouth of Broad River on the south side, on the lands of Thomas Walton, Jr.[10] This location would indicate the same spot where the town of Lincoln had been authorized, and suggests that Lamar might have sold his lands there to Walton. In 1796 this region had been cut off from Wilkes County and erected into a new county called Lincoln. The selection of this name for the county may have made it seem desirable to change the name of what was then or what was supposed to be the town of Lincoln to Lisbon. Certainly it was called Lisbon as early as 1805 when it was reported that a mercantile firm there was being dissolved.[11]

Lisbon never reached proportions sufficient for it to be considered an honor to the Portuguese town for which it was named. If it ever erected a warehouse for the inspection of tobacco, it was overshadowed by those in the growing town of Petersburg directly across Broad River. There was little incentive for people to settle in Lisbon and as a service to the few people who did move in and to the planters in the hinterland south of Broad River, a merchant or two set up shop and caught the trade of those who did not want to go to the trouble and expense of being ferried across to Petersburg. In 1827 it was reported that Lisbon had only three or four houses and that it had "dwindled almost to nothing"[12]—an expression which indicates that earlier it might have taken on some life. But there was a germ of life that still lingered in an old store building and a gigantic oak until they were snuffed out by the waters of Savannah and Broad rivers which were backed over them in the mid-twentieth century by a gigantic dam some miles below.

Lisbon, as well as Petersburg, had a rival across the Savannah in South Carolina, which sought all the trade it could get. This town was called Vienna, to honor the gay and cultured city of Austria-Hungary. It was set going about 1795 when the South Carolina legislature appointed public packers of beef and pork to be located at this point on the Savannah River. And a few years later it was predicted that "this village bids fair to participate in much of the upper country trade."[13] Although there was a long-standing rivalry between Georgia and South Carolina, this fact had little to do with the prosperity or lack of it that accompanied

Vienna's struggle for supremacy. The compelling force of money
and economic trends cannot be turned aside by mental attitudes—
even in time of war it is difficult to keep enemies from trading
with each other. It was, therefore, no dislike that might have been
between the governments of Georgia and South Carolina that
hindered the progress of Vienna. Its growth was stunted by its
location as compared with that of Petersburg. It probably got a
good share of the hinterland trade of the Carolinians but little of
the Georgians. The ferries plying across the Savannah likely carried more trade to Petersburg than Petersburg and the Georgians lost to Vienna. This little river town having been laid out
"in expectation of becoming a place of considerable commerce,"
had by 1829 been almost deserted. In its heydey of great expectations it had promoted a little satelite town on the hills above,
which was called South Hampton.[14] It showed so little life that it
soon faded away and its very name was soon forgotten.

The promotion of Petersburg became the marvel of the times.
Its location between its two rivers made it appear to all who had
its position described to them or its location viewed on a map,
as the commercial center of all the upper Savannah River country.
Here was a bonanza for investors that should not be ignored. All
those Virginians who had settled up the Broad River Valley would
be tributary to Petersburg as would the people living up the
Savannah, on both sides of the river. The down river towns of
Augusta and Savannah would court the trade of this upcountry
metropolis. Its fame would not stop short of Philadelphia, New
York, and Boston. This was the era of the Yazoo Speculation,
when Georgia lands and lots were being hawked and bought as
far away even as Europe.

Dividing his town into eighty-six lots of one-half acre each
(later increased to 93 with some irregularity in sizes) Oliver was
almost beseiged with buyers. From 1786 to his death in 1808, he
had disposed of all of his lots and his adjacent lands. To some
purchasers he sold several lots, but to his favorite son, John, he
sold all out-lying lands he had between the two rivers. First in
1793 he sold him 300 acres, a tract which surrounded the town
but which, of course, did not include the town lots which John
did not already own. In 1805 Dionysius sold to John the remainder of his land between the two rivers for $1,000. John
bought and sold lots extensively in Petersburg, where he became
one of the biggest merchants. Also he ran a large plantation on
which at the time of his death, in 1816, he had sixty-four slaves.[15]

Although there were eleven children in the family of Dionysius Oliver, John seems to have profited most from the Oliver estate. Martha, one of the daughters of Dionysius, married Thomas Hancock of Edgefield District, South Carolina, and their daughter Sophia Ann married Benjamin Ryan Tillman, who became the father of Benjamin R. Tillman, the famous governor of South Carolina.[16]

Not only did the residents of Petersburg speculate in Petersburg lots, but men with money in Augusta, Savannah, and in other parts of the state became interested. For instance, in 1802 Eleazar Early, a merchant of Augusta, sold to Thomas Hills, a merchant of Savannah, Lot 36, for $1,200.[17] One of the outstanding speculators in Petersburg lots was Daniel Dennison Rogers of Boston, Massachusetts. In 1790 he bought from Edward White, a merchant from Burke County, Georgia (a speculator, himself) fifteen lots for 400 pounds, which would be about $1,700 in American money of that time.[18]

The greatest resident speculator in Petersburg lots was LeRoy Pope, an important merchant, postmaster for a half dozen years, and one of the principal men of the town until he moved to Alabama to found the town of Huntsville and become a banker and power in that new state. He was allied through marriage relations with the Watkinses and the Walkers, other prominent residents of Petersburg. He was already buying and selling lots when in 1797 he bought all fifteen lots which Rogers of Boston owned. With this supply, he carried on an active real estate business for some years thereafter.[19] In 1793 Pope became involved in a Franklin County land speculation through which he received a fradulent grant of 104,000 acres out of a total of more than 2,600,000 acres which went to the other participants.[20]

Since there was no bank in the town, Northern merchants, money-lenders, and speculators played an important part in the economic life of Petersburg. Indeed, there were no banks in all of Georgia until 1807 when one was set up in Savannah, followed by another one three years later in Augusta. These Northern dealers loaned money to Petersburg merchants, acted as their factors, and through accepting Petersburg lots and plantation lands as collateral they sometimes came into possession of much real estate. In such instances they engaged in real estate transactions, but in general they did not primarily deal in Petersburg lots. It is not known when Harry Caldwell and his wife Katharine of Newburg, Orange County, New York, came into possession of Lot 12, but they sold it in 1798 to Jeremiah Walker, II for $150.[21] The previous year they had sold Lot 14 to James Manning for $150, according to "plan laid [off] by Dionysius Oliver ... and exhibited to the first purchaser."[22] This couple may have been engaged in a mild case of speculation.

John E. Caldwell Company (John E. or C. and Josiah), who were suppliers and money-lenders, were merchants of the city of New York. In 1808 they became creditors of Joseph Watkins and wife Delia for $3,500 and as security they received Lot 40, on which there must have been a substantial house, as it was described as "improved." Ferdinand Phinizy, the Lexington merchant who had moved to Augusta, as previously noted, acted as agent for this New York merchant house.[23] In 1811 in supplying credit of $1,500 to Archibald Stokes they accepted as part collateral a mortgage of $750 on Lot 50.[24] Memorable Walker in 1802 secured a loan of $1,500 from Samuel Corp of New York by mortgaging Petersburg real estate.[25] The mercantile firm of Memorable and James S. Walker were heavy debtors to New York supply merchants. In 1802 to secure notes amounting to $1,806.51 given to William Minturn & Robert H. Bowne and Thomas Service, merchants of New York, they offered a plantation on Broad River;[26] and the next year they gave a promissory note to Joseph Strong, a New York merchant, secured by their homeplace on Broad River.[27] Other loans made by New York merchants were $2,000 in 1809 to LeRoy Pope by George Newbold,[28] and another the same year by the same merchant to Thomas Stokes for $3,377.30.[29] The next year Newbold extended another credit to a Petersburg customer, Nathaniel Allen, Jr., for $1,800.[30] All of these credits or loans were secured by Petersburg real estate. Another New York merchant who did business with Petersburg residents was Henry Kneeland.[31]

These transactions with Northern firms seem to have been mutually advantageous; but occassionally misunderstandings arose. In 1825 Archibald Stokes was in dispute with a New York firm which insisted that he had guaranteed certain notes. Stokes denied that he had done so, and in a letter to a kinsman, William S. Stokes of Madison, Georgia, he remarked that they could "prove what ever they wish to in New York"—an expression that might have meant that a New York jury would accept any charge against a Southerner, or that Stokes would not pay, whatever the verdict might be.[32]

It is quite evident that merchants and other businessmen in Petersburg, and in other parts of the South for that matter, were much dependent on Northern firms for credit. And apparently prices of merchandise bought on such terms were accordingly high. As one Petersburg merchant reported in 1821 on a visit to New York: "Money is a great article here; for cash you may buy goods at your own price."[33]

Not all of Petersburg's financial transactions in real estate and mercantile supplies were with Northern firms; many were transacted with Augusta and Savannah houses, and quite a number with South Carolina businesses. Some of these Georgia and South Carolina firms may first, however, have secured their supplies from Northern markets. It would seem that better prices might be secured from the North direct, rather than through Southern middlemen firms. Some of those firms and individuals in South Carolina dealing with Petersburg were George Whitfield & Joseph Bunkley of Abbeville, James Hamilton of Columbia, James Russell of Vienna, and Jonathan Care and David W. Credie of Charleston.

The time of Petersburg's greatest prosperity and prospects for future growth was around the turn of the nineteenth century and the first decade following. These are some of the prices for lots from 1798 to 1809, depending, of course, on how far they had been developed: $2,000; $1,800; $1,500; $1,250; $1,000; $650.

As an indication of Petersburg economic instability and the fluctuation of real estate values, the life history of Lot 34 for twenty years should prove of interest. In 1787 Dionysius Oliver sold it to Robert Watkins for an unstated price. For the next ten years it passed through unknown ownerships until it reached Mary Easter, who in 1797 sold it to L. O. Whitfield for $100. It then reached the ownership of George Whitfield & Joseph Bunkley of Abbeville, South Carolina, who included it as part collateral for $1,300 owed to J. Holliday & Company. In 1801 J. Holliday & Company in a transaction involving $1,800 passed the ownership to Eleazar Early, the Augusta merchant, who the next year mortgaged it to James Hamilton of Columbia, South Carolina, which was involved in a debt of $1,470.47. After changing ownership a few more times it was back under mortgage to James Hamilton again, who in 1817 foreclosed on it—the highest bid was $15.[34]

Unlike that closely-knit group of Virginians who were going

into the Broad River Valley and giving tone to it, those who boomed and settled Petersburg a little later were a conglomeration with origins as far north as the New England states. As has been seen, Dionysius Oliver, the promoter of Petersburg, was a Virginian and also were many of the others who were to play prominent parts in the growth and decline of Petersburg; however, speculation and business ventures drew people from farther north after Petersburg began to announce itself to the world.

One of the most prominent families to settle in Petersburg and its environs was that Virginia family of Watkinses out of Prince Edward County. They must not, however, be confused with the Thomas Watkins of Chickahominy, whose branch settled around Augusta and produced Robert and George Watkins, compilers of the famous Watkins *Digest of the Laws of the State of Georgia,* published in 1800. The Petersburg Watkinses were not only prominent in the business life of the town but they were also notable in their many marriage connections and in their migrations westward, principally to Alabama.

James, I, a son of William Watkins, in his old age moved to Petersburg in 1796 and died there two years later. He lived with some of his children who had previously come to Petersburg and its vicinity. He had married Martha Thompson of another prominent Virginia family, which was also to become outstanding in Petersburg, and to this union came nine children. His eldest son William became a merchant, tobacco warehouseman, and a dealer in real estate, before moving on to Tennessee and from there to Alabama in 1808. A daughter Sarah Herndon married her first cousin Captain Robert Thompson, a Petersburg merchant familiarly known as "Old Blue,"—so-named because he kept his money in blue denim bags. They later moved to Huntsville, Alabama. One of their daughters, Pamelia, married Thomas Bibb, the second governor of the State of Alabama, his brother William Wyatt Bibb having been the first.

Samuel, a son of James Watkins, I, married Eleanor Thompson, a sister of "Old Blue." He became a Petersburg merchant in partnership with "Old Blue," and also ran an extensive cotton plantation, which lay up the Savannah River, above Petersburg. His wife, quite an aristocratic lady, took great pleasure in her home and flowers, and when riding about in her coach she was always attended by her black maid. Most of their children moved to Alabama, but Samuel and Eleanor did not follow until 1825.

Another son of James Watkins, I, was Robert Herndon Watkins, who married Jane Thompson, a niece of Dionysius Oliver's, being the daughter of Eleanor Oliver, who married Drury Thompson.

John was the sixth of James Watkins', I, children. He married Susan Daniel, a lady from North Carolina (or Virginia, as is sometimes stated), and lived a few miles out from Petersburg on his plantation, which he named "Thornville," sometimes called "Thorn Hill." After her death he married Mary Moseley, a daughter of Joseph Moseley, from Virginia. His son John Daniel Watkins married a daughter of Joseph Christopher Yates, governor of New York from 1822 to 1824. John remained on his plantation until his death in 1841.

The seventh child among the nine children of James Watkins, I, was Thompson Watkins. Thompson married a sister of old Benjamin Taliaferro, the Revolutionary hero who had settled some miles up Broad River from Petersburg, in the south side. Like so many other Broad River people, Thompson caught the western fever and moved to Alabama.

James Watkins', I, eighth child was Joseph, who married Mary Sayre, and after her death, her sister Delia. There were no children by either marriage. The Sayres were of a New York and New Jersey family. A persistent tradition grew up that Joseph Watkins invented the cotton gin, for which Eli Whitney received a patent and the credit—though not much cash. "Robert Watkins of Petersburg," who must have been his brother, was advertising a gin in 1796; but the story of Petersburg's part in the cotton gin invention must be reserved for its proper place in this narrative.

Isham was the youngest of James Watkins' nine children. He married Emily Taliaferro, a daughter of Benjamin's and had ten children, who spread out over Alabama, Mississippi, and Tennessee.

The second son of pioneer James Watkins', I, in his family of nine children was named James, II, also. He married another Jane Thompson, also a niece of Dionysius Oliver by Isham Thompson (a brother of Drury Thompson) having married Dionysius' sister Mary Ann. All of this means that two Oliver sisters had married two Thompson brothers, and that each couple had a daughter which they named Jane—this would mean that the two Janes were "double first cousins." James, II, son of pioneer James, I and his wife Jane lived on a plantation on the

Savannah River above Petersburg and raised a family of eleven children. Most of them made significant marriages and some of them and their children moved on to Alabama. They follow:

Robert H. Watkins (named for his father's brother), became a planter and a merchant in Petersburg, and in 1812-1813 he was a member of the Georgia Senate. He married Prudence a daughter of John Oliver (Dionysius' favorite son) and later moved to Alabama.

Mary Watkins married Dr. Asa Thompson and lived in Petersburg, where he practiced medicine and engaged in cotton-planting. Later he moved to Alabama.

Sarah Watkins married Stephen Willis Harris, who later became a Superior Court judge and lived in Eatonton. After his death his widow moved to Athens. Judge Harris was a graduate of the University of Georgia in the Class of 1805; he became a Trustee of the University in 1820 and continued until his death in 1828.

Martha Watkins brought in another tie with the Taliaferros; she married Benjamin, a son of old Revolutionary Benjamin Taliaferro.

Jane Watkins married James Minor Tait, a brother of Charles Tait (eminent in Georgia and Alabama history). After his wife's death he moved with his children to Mississippi.

Susan Watkins became the second wife of John Oliver, her brother Robert H. (as previously mentioned) having married Prudence, Oliver's daughter by his first wife Frances Thompson. After Oliver's death, which occurred in 1816, Susan (also called Susanna) married Dr. William N. Richardson, an outstanding Petersburg physician, and they later moved to Alabama. Mary, one of the children by her second marriage, became the wife of Gabriel Toombs, a brother of the famous Robert Toombs.

Eliza Watkins married William McGehee, a son of Micajah, as his second wife. After some mercantile experience, not very successful, he moved to Mississippi.

Sophia Watkins married Eli S. Shorter, who became an eminent jurist. After a residence in Eatonton, they moved to Columbus, where he died in 1836.

Garland Watkins, the oldest son, served in the War of 1812, returned home and studied law, and died early unmarried; Theophilus died when only fifteen; and James (III), married Jane, a daughter of John Urquart of Augusta.

An indication of some of the plantation possessions of a Peters-

sufficient importance to publish a part of it. In referring to the "Matrons and Daughters of Columbia," he declared that the fate of the nation rested with them. Their responsibility was great, for "mankind receives more knowledge previous to the age of seven years, than in the whole subsequent part of life." Addressing himself to the young ladies, he said, "Remember that he who neither loves liberty nor his country, is incapable of loving you; and grant him that punishment which every virtuous American views with more horror than death itself—let him be banished from your engaging society."[37]

On February 19, 1803 this news item appeared in the *Augusta Chronicle:* "MARRIED, on Thursday the 10th instant, Doctor William Wyatt Bibb, of Petersburg, to the amiable Miss Mary Ann Freeman, of Wilkes County." Mary Ann ("Polly") was a sister of Fleming Freeman, who had married Bibb's sister Martha. The Bibbs and the Freemans had been close neighbors across Broad River in Wilkes County, and the children of both families must have attended the same school. This fact lends some credibility to a little sentimental tradition which seems never to have been denied: One day at school Mary Ann came up not knowing her lesson, whereupon the teacher (in keeping with those stern times) threatened to whip her. Young William arrested the uplifted switch and said, "Don't strike her. Whip me. I'll take it for her." The teacher seeing the nobility in William's action relented and said, "William, you are a noble boy, and, for your sake, I will excuse Mary." This was the Mary Ann he married ten years later.[38]

John Williams Walker, three years younger than Bibb and to graduate three years later from Princeton College—and destined for an eminent career in Alabama—now living in Petersburg, wrote to his friend Larkin Newby, who had moved away to Fayetteville, North Carolina, that Dr. Bibb had "taken to his embraces the 'amiable' Miss Polly Freeman a few days since; and they have just arrived in town this evening, to fix their permanent residence here.—He's a clever fellow, I wish him well."[39]

In 1805 Bibb bought from John Williams Walker for $1,000 the house on Lot 38, which his father Jeremiah Walker, a Baptist preacher and a merchant, had occupied before his death.[40] The practice of medicine was not sufficient to satisfy Bibb's worldly ambitions nor to fill his pockets with needed money—especially so the latter—for in 1805 he was notifying through the press that he wanted people owing him to pay up. He said that he expected his patients to pay "immediately after his services are rendered."[41]

So, the very year of his marriage, he decided to enter politics by running for the Georgia House of Representatives. He was successful and continued to be elected, serving from 1803 to 1806.

Now with politics uppermost in his mind he allowed his medical practice to gradually play out for he entered the race for the United States House of Representatives in 1806 while still a member of the legislature. He was successful, taking his seat in 1807, and continuing through successive elections until 1813. Bibb's election in 1810 was hotly contested by John Clark (son of Elijah Clarke), in which he received the highest number of votes in the state. A poem, sung to the tune of Yankee Doodle contained this stanza:

> "With one accord BIBB shall be sent
> To represent the state, Sir,
> While Clark in sorrow shall lament
> The just decree of fate, Sir."[42]

Bibb resigned in 1813 to accept election to the United States Senate in order to fill the vacancy made by the resignation of his friend William H. Crawford. He served in this position until 1816, when he resigned to accept the appointment of governor of the Territory of Alabama. He now moved to Alabama, and when the territory was admitted as a state in 1819 he was elected its first governor. The next year while Bibb was riding horseback his steed became frightened in a sudden thunderstorm and threw him. This accident resulted in his death. William Wyatt Bibb was succeeded in the governorship by his brother Thomas; and so Petersburg provided Alabama with its first two governors.[43]

It would be a singular occurence in the history of Georgia or of any other state in the Union, that both United States Senators should come from a small town or its vicinity. But this was the fact in Georgia from 1813 to 1816, when Bibb's colleague was Charles Tait. Both Bibb and Tait lived near Petersburg, Bibb having moved out of Petersburg to a plantation a few years previously.

Charles Tait, born in 1768, was the oldest child in a family of ten children born to James and Rebecca Tait, in Hanover County, Virginia. The family moved to the Broad River Valley in 1783 and settled near the site of the future town of Petersburg. Charles attended the Wilkes County Academy, and probably through the influence of Bishop Francis Asbury, he continued his education at Cokesbury College, in Maryland, remaining there from 1788 to 1794—the last several years there he instructed classes in French. He studied law while at Cokesbury and was admitted to the bar when he returned to Georgia; but instead of practicing, he accepted election to the headship of Richmond Academy in Augusta. He remained there two years, during the last of which, William H. Crawford was one of the teachers. In 1797 he resigned and entered the practice of law and politics, living on his plantation "Retreat," not far from Petersburg. In 1803 Tait made a bitter fight against John Griffin for election by the legislature to the judgeship of the Western Circuit. Tait and Crawford were leaders in the faction against John Clark, Griffin being allied with Clark, especially since both had married sisters, daughters of Micajah Williamson. Tait was elected and remained as judge until 1809 when he was elected to the United States Senate. At the end of his term in 1819 he retired and moved to Alabama the same year. In 1820 through his old friend and associate in politics, William H. Crawford, now Secretary of the Treasury, Tait was appointed by President Monroe to be United States District Judge for Alabama. This was another Petersburg casualty for the up-building of Alabama.

Tait had married Mrs. Anne (Lucas) Simpson of Baltimore in 1790, while at Cokesbury College. The year before Tait moved to Alabama she had died, and in an obituary the *Augusta Chronicle* referred to her as "a lady of great piety and benevolence." The Taits were strong Methodists, with whom Bishop Asbury often stopped on his trips to Georgia. Tait named one of his sons for the Bishop—James Asbury Tait, who preceded by one year his father to Alabama. By the time Judge Tait had been in Alabama three years, his longings for his old Georgia surroundings of former days drew him back on a visit; and he returned to Alabama with a new wife, the widow of his old political enemy Judge John Griffin. In 1826 he resigned his judgeship and spent the next eighteen months traveling throughout the eastern United States during which time he attended a Yale commencement and visited many prominent people, including former president James Madison. He died in 1835.[44]

Another Virginia family which was planted in Petersburg was the Walkers. They were brought there to preside at the very birth of the town by Jeremiah, a Baptist preacher, whose name in the vernacular of the day was spelled like it was pronounced "Jaramah." He bought town lots, an island in the Savannah River, plantation lands, and slaves—thereby accumulating a small fortune. Yet he had time to preach sermons and funerals and to inculcate Baptist principles into some of his Petersburg listeners. He died in 1792, leaving land, city lots, slaves and books to all his seven children.[45]

Following the custom of giving to children such names as these, Moaning, Lamentation, Prudence, and Charity, he named one of his sons Memorable, who later became an outstanding merchant in Petersburg. As an indication of how a successful merchant lived and what he accumulated, the appraisers of Memorable's property at his death in 1803 listed 23 slaves (valued at $1,000), 7 horses ("Post Boy," "Paddy," "Kiddy Caddy," and so on), 2 yoke of oxen, 17 head of cattle, 75 hogs, 25 geese, 2 stills with 18 hogsheads for "stilling," a variety of plantation tools and equipment, a mahogany side board and other furniture (including 11 Windsor chairs), silver cutlery, 3 pictures (probably paintings of ancestors), 40 books and pamphlets, 9 trunks, a half dozen saddles (2 for women), and a great many other items which would go into a well-furnished residence. In addition were his mercantile supplies and plantation lands. Certain items were offered at a sale, at which Dr. W. W. Bibb, John Oliver, and other prominent residents of Petersburg bought many items; Charles Tait bought a *History of Modern Europe* for $17.50, and another attendant bought William Gordon's *History . . . of America. . . .*[46]

Memorable Walker was only 26 years old when he died. The *Augusta Chronicle* in announcing his death said, "We would wish to pay his character the eulogy it merits. But his virtues were so eminent that perishable materials could add nothing to their indelibility."[47]

The most famous of Jeremiah Walker's children was John Williams Walker, who after receiving his preparatory education under the tutelage of the well-known schoolmaster, Moses Waddel, was graduated at Princeton in 1806. He married Matilda, a daughter of LeRoy Pope, and moved in 1810 to Alabama, where he took a prominent part in organizing the Territory and State government of Alabama and became the first of its two senators to take his seat in Washington.[48]

Another progenitor of a Virginia family which moved to Georgia was Holman Freeman; however, unlike most Virginians who came to Georgia he arrived before the Revolution. Attracted by Sir James Wright's proclamation inviting settlers to the New Purchase, Freeman came in 1773 and took up 400 acres of land on Chickasaw Creek, a tributary of Broad River flowing in from the south, not far from old Fort James, the future site of Petersburg. There were five sons and four daughters in Holman's family.[49]

Being too old and unwell to enter the war, he could give personally only his loyalty to the cause of Liberty and Independence, but his sons took an active part in the Revolution. In this internecine civil war ("The War of Extermination") which accompanied the Revolution in Georgia, a party of Tories came to the home of old Holman Freeman and after nearly beating him to death, took him to Augusta (then in the hands of the British). There after catching the smallpox he was allowed to return home in a dying condition. His son John, bent on avenging his father's death, learned the identity of the two leaders of the Tory party. He went to the home of one of the Tories and found him in the field plowing with his little daughter riding on the plow. John asked the Tory "if he had not plowed enough." The Tory replied that he wanted to finish the field. John said "it was not worth while to finish it, and shot him on the spot." Never relenting his quest for vengeance, John traced the other Tory leader to Augusta and found him lying on a blanket in the shade of a tree. When John called his name, the Tory covered his face with the blanket, realizing that his end had come. John shot him dead, and putting spurs to his horse galloped away.[50]

There was only one child in John Freeman's family, Rebecca. She married Shaler Hillyer, a native of Connecticut, who had recently come to Petersburg to engage in the mercantile business. (An extended account of Hillyer's career will appear under a discussion of the merchants of Petersburg.)

Another son of Holman Freeman was named for his father Holman. After the war Holman Freeman, II, secured grants of land amounting to 3,300 acres up and down Broad River and elsewhere.[51] Of his three children (Fleming, John, and Mary), Fleming married a sister of William Wyatt Bibb and about 1816 moved to Alabama, and, as previously noted, Bibb married Mary ("Polly").

Of the many other families who were residents of Petersburg, there were the Remberts, the Welles, the Raglands (in John R. Ragland's family there were seventeen), the Easters (in Richard's family there were fifteen), the Patons (from New Jersey), and the Stokes. Another family name was Pope. The Popes had scattered over Delaware, Maryland, Virginia, and North Carolina. LeRoy Pope's branch, it is thought, came from North Carolina, and William and Alexander (Pope brothers), from Delaware.

Another family who helped old Dionysius Oliver found Petersburg was the Cades. Unlike so many other Petersburgers, they stayed there to the bitter end. They lived in the last house in the deserted village before the waters of Broad and Savannah rivers empounded by the Clark Hill Dam mingled their floods fifty feet deep over the site—the Cades being the lares and penates of departed Petersburg.

Many families were tributary to Petersburg, who never lived in the town. The Goose Pond Virginians, up Broad River in Oglethorpe County, were too far away to visit much in Petersburg; but some of their heavy products such as tobacco, cotton, corn, and bacon were floated down Broad River or hauled on the highway to increase the commercial importance of that town. Old Elijah Clarke, living up the Broad River, came to Petersburg now and then when he was not fighting the Indians, or engaging in filibustering on the Florida border, or devising land speculation schemes. After his death in 1799 some of his children found Petersburg a good trading center—his son John, when not governor of the state or too deep in politics, and Elijah's daughter Elizabeth, who married Benajah Smith and lived up Broad River at Millford, dying there in 1813.[52] And there was John M. Dooly, famous as a Superior Court judge and a wit who lived across Broad River up in Lincoln County. His business in Petersburg was more concerned with practicing law than with trading.[53] Down the Broad at its mouth, the Lisbonites found Petersburg, just across the river, a much more satisfactory place in which to visit and trade than their own little village. And over the Savannah in South Carolina, the Viennese were likewise attracted to Petersburg. Across the Savannah and inland a few miles was Moses Waddel's Willington school, and although his pupils were not allowed to visit Petersburg, he himself did most of his trading there. Likewise from the Calhoun Settlement not far away, Patrick (brother of the great John C. Calhoun) and other Calhouns were often to be seen in Petersburg.

Thus, Petersburg was not simply made up of buildings; it was throbbing with people, some of famous families and some unknown to fame. There was a great deal of intermarrying among these families, which set up power units in trade and politics not only in Petersburg and Georgia but also in Alabama whither so many Petersburgers went to run that Territory and to set it up as a State.

5

Rivers, Roads, Bridges, and Ferries

The Upper Savannah

PETERSBURG was situated in the fork of the Savannah and Broad rivers for the purpose of taking advantage of the navigation these rivers afforded; they were the life lines of Petersburg until land transportation was developed. From Petersburg southward the Savannah was free of major obstructions to Augusta, where there were difficult rapids on the Fall Line which separated the Piedmont Region from the Coastal Plain. Below Augusta the river was easily navigable (as river navigation went in those days) to Savannah and on to the Atlantic Ocean.

Above Petersburg the Savannah could be used by flat-bottomed boats carrying as much as ten tons, up as far as the confluence of the Tugaloo and Seneca-Keowee, which formed the Savannah. The enthusiastic Georgians considered the Tugaloo navigable as far up as Toccoa Creek.[1] However, only a few miles above Petersburg a series of rapids began and were repeated many times on up the river. It took skillful handling of boats to prevent disaster. From Petersburg up the Broad River boats could ply thirty or forty miles as far as the Goose Pond region and even farther except in time of low water. Navigation on Georgia rivers was never impeded by ice except in the most unusually cold winters, as for instance in 1780, when the Savannah above Augusta froze over thick enough to hold up the weight of a man.[2]

Unimpeded navigation could not be taken for granted; these streams required frequent attention, and the State of Georgia from the very early times carried out a program of improvement on its principal rivers by removing snags, driftwood, and sandbars. The Savannah afforded a troublesome problem beyond river improvements. Because it was the boundary with South Carolina there was contention about which state owned the river. Though the Charter setting up the Colony of Georgia was not clear on this point, the State early laid claim to the whole river. The Treaty of Beaufort between the two states in 1787 seemed to imply that the river belonged to Georgia. With the confusion of its ownership never to be settled throughout the whole of the nineteenth century, the co-operation of South Carolina was never successfully obtained. In 1922 by edict of the United States Supreme Court the boundary was made the middle of the river.

The first move Georgia made to improve the upper Savannah was in 1786, when the legislature passed a bill to promote navigation on the river from Rae's Creek, just above Augusta, to the mouth of Tugaloo River and up that river to Tugaloo Old Town, a point near where Toccoa Creek flowed into the Tugaloo. In the introductory part of the law it was recited that "nothing contributes more to the Advantage of the Citizens, or to the opulence of the State, than making easy, and extending the Navigation of Rivers" and that as "Policy and Justice" dictated that the expense should "be paid by such persons as will immediately be most advantaged thereby," a system was, therefore, being enacted to provide for the expenses. This whole stretch of the river was divided into five districts: First, from Rae's Creek to Little River; second, from Little River to Soap Creek; third, from Soap Creek to the "Mouth of Broad River [Petersburg]"; fourth, from Broad River to Lightwood Log Creek [about 40 miles farther up]; and fifth, from Lightwood Log Creek to Tugaloo Old Town. People owning land along the river were required to pay five shillings for every hundred acres of land "of the first quality," and two and a half shillings for other lands, all of which lay within five miles of the river in the First District, ten miles in the Second District, and within fifteen miles for the rest of the distance up the river. As Broad River was the only navigable tributary in this stretch of the Savannah, the improvements were to extend up that river for fifteen miles. Since enthusiasm for this work had already led both Georgians and South Carolinians to subscribe "large donations," this money was to be added to the assessments on the lands adjoining the river. Five commissioners were named, one of whom was Holman Freeman (II), to supervise the work, and to hire "Artificers, or Persons skilled in clearing Rivers," who should be in direct charge. The plan was to clear the river, place a lock at the lower rapids at Augusta, and charge a toll of five shillings per hogshead against all South Carolinans who had not subscribed to the expenses of clearing the river.[3]

This law was unwise and oppressive because it levied a tax on many people who made no use of the river and it did not touch many others who lived away from the river and did use it. The next year the legislature repealed that part of the law levying the tax, but made no other provision for raising money, which was, of course, equivalent to repealing the whole law.[4] But people up the river were anxious to have the navigation improved, and one of the presentments of the Wilkes County grand jury in the summer of 1790 (no doubt actuated by the Petersburgers, who were still in Wilkes County, since Elbert County had not yet been cut off) was a complaint against not having better navigation between Petersburg and Augusta.[5] South Carolinans were also dissatisfied and led their legislature in 1791 to pass a law, which came to nothing, to improve the navigation on the Savannah,[6] and in 1795 the legislature passed another law establishing a lottery to raise money to be used to "clear out and remove the obstructions" from Vienna down to Augusta.[7]

A lottery! Here was an idea for raising money which the Georgians must have got from South Carolina. Impelled, no doubt, by the Petersburgers and Broad River Valley settlers up the river, the legislature declared the next year (1796) that the improvement of navigation would greatly increase the value of land lying along the Savannah and Broad rivers and provided for a lottery to raise $4,000 to be used on the Savannah from Augusta to Lightwood Log Creek and from Petersburg up the Broad to its South Fork (about fifty miles). The managers of the lottery were made up of five citizens, three from Petersburg and two from up Broad Valley—Benjamin Taliaferro, William Barnett, Oliver Whyte, Robert Watkins, and Memorable Walker. The commissioners to superintend "opening and clearing" the rivers were from the same region as were the lottery managers—six of them among whom were Robert Thompson from Petersburg and Thomas Gilmer up Broad River and father of the future governor George R. Gilmer.[8] Like all previous attempts of both Georgia and South Carolina to improve navigation on the Savannah, nothing came of this legislation.

In 1799 Georgia tacked her sails in another direction. Taxing land along rivers had failed; a lottery had failed; now the state would try incorporating a company to carry on the work. Since "the improvement of the inland navigation of every country is of primary importance to its inhabitants, and few countries enjoying greater natural advantages than this state for the extension of commerce, and it being conceived that the clearing out and removing the obstructions in that part of Savannah River, between the town of Petersburg and the city of Augusta, would greatly conduce to the convenience and interest of the inhabitants settled in the north and northwestern part of this state," therefore, the legislature hereby established a company to be known as the Savannah Navigation Company with a capital of $40,000, which was to be divided into 400 shares at $100 each and offered to the public at Petersburg. This was almost entirely a Petersburg undertaking, with those in charge consisting of the following Petersburgers: LeRoy Pope, Robert Thompson, Memorable Walker, Robert Watkins, and John Oliver. Three others closely associated with Petersburg were Robert Ware, Newell Walton, Jr., and James Hugh.

Whenever the company should have improved the river sufficiently for boats to be able to carry fifteen hogsheads of tobacco, it might charge the following tolls: 37½ cents per hogshead of tobacco, 10 cents per 1,000 feet of lumber, 4 cents per barrel of flour, and 2 cents per 100 pounds for all other articles of commerce.[9] The company never developed beyond the paper setting it up. Besides the failure of this company, there soon arose problems other than snags, sandbars, and rapids which were provided by nature. There were also dams and fish traps, which interfered with navigation as well as with the free passage of fish up stream. Now the question was, which was more important fish or boats. Devising a plan to deal with the situation, the legislature held an even hand over both as expressed in the preamble of a law passed in 1802: "Whereas the keeping open of the River Savannah, is of the greatest importance to the citizens of the back country, as well in consequence of navigation, as the advantages resulting to the citizens generally, by having an annual supply of fish therefrom, *And whereas,* many persons on the said river, have so obstructed the passage of boats by dams, as to render it highly injurious to commerce, and almost totally prevented the fish from getting up the same. . . ." Petersburgers were more interested in commerce up and down the Savannah than in fishing, and were, undoubtedly, largely responsible for the legislation here enacted. Applying to the upper stretches of the Savannah from Augusta and far on up the Tugaloo, the law forbade anyone to stop up or obstruct the water for more than two thirds of the distance across, and the third left open must include "the main sluice."[10] Experience during the next seven years indicated that some changes should be made. Leaving open just a third of the Savannah River was not considered sufficient for the passage of boats, and so in a law passed in 1809 it was forbidden to anyone "to obstruct, or cause to be obstructed, more than one third part of Savannah river, by dams, fish traps, or other obstructions, and the main current shall at all times be kept open for the free passage of fish and boats." The uppermost stretches of the Savannah, called the Tugaloo above the point where it was joined by the Keowee, was considered so precarious for navigation that the old law allowing two thirds of the stream to be obstructed was continued.[11]

Some of the fishermen along the upper Savannah above Augusta paid little attention to this legislation; and complaints came in from both boatmen and those fishermen who lived above some of the most effectual obstructions which prevented the passage of fish up to their part of the river. As the commissioners who had been appointed to enforce the 1809 law failed to carry out their inspection of the river, the legislature in 1812 passed further legislation designating a new set of commissioners to view the river and if they found any obstructions forbidden by law they were required to notify the owners of such traps or dams to remove them within two days. If they refused, then the commissioners were empowered to call out the militia, and if the militiamen refused to respond, then the commissioners were required to remove the obstructions and to enter prosecutions against the offenders, who were subject to a fine of $100 a day for every day they had allowed the obstruction to remain.[12]

Still the Savannah did not flow to the sea unvexed by dams and fish traps; as a remedy, the legislature in 1816 appointed a new group of commissioners, who no longer had authority to call out the militia, but on the refusal of the owners of fish traps and dams to remove them, the commissioners were then required to do so and charge the cost to the offenders. But now the legislature retreated from forbidding the obstruction of two thirds of the river, to its original position of one third for all obstructions set up after February 15, 1817. For violating this section of the law, offenders were subject to a fine of $30 a day, one half to go to the informer and the other half to the commissioners to be used in the performance of their duties.[13]

The battle between the boatmen and the fishermen now sim-
mered down on the Savannah as the day of navigation by steamboats dawned. In 1788 Georgia had granted a patent to William Longstreet on a steam engine, which two years later he
attached to a boat at Augusta and forced it up the river at the
rate of five miles an hour; but it remained for Robert Fulton to
gain fame as the inventor of the steamboat when in 1808 he ran
the *Clermont* by steam up the Hudson River in New York. Soon
Fulton joined a company which got a monopoly of running
steamboats on all the rivers of New York. In Georgia the legislature in 1814 gave Samuel Howard such a monopoly on all the
rivers of Georgia, reciting that Howard proposed "to adopt a
new and improved mode of transporting merchandise upon the
waters of the state of Georgia, by towing and warping the ships,
vessels, boats and rafts, in and upon which the same may be
laden, by means of other boats or vessels impelled by the aid of
steam."[14] Two years later the *Enterprise* steamed up the Savannah
from Savannah to Augusta, towing a boat laden with 3,000 bushels
of salt.[15] A new era in navigation now began on the lower Savannah, but Petersburg was only indirectly affected, for no steamboat could ascend the rapids at Augusta and continue on to
Petersburg. However, Petersburg and all upper Georgia and
South Carolina profited in having quicker transportation to the
sea for their commerce.

To provide needed capital Howard got a charter three years
later for the Steam Boat Company of Georgia[16] but after a few
years the company went bankrupt. In 1824 the United States
Supreme Court freed all navigable waters throughout the country
from steamboat monopolies.

Up until 1815 Georgia had assumed no costs of improving
navigation on her rivers; she merely empowered private individuals through lotteries and stock companies to act. As was
painfully evident, the results had been nothing. But "many years
past" South Carolina had appropriated $10,000 for improving
navigation on the Savannah when Georgia should provide a like
amount; but Georgia had never acted. Now the legislature in
December, 1815 appropriated rather tardily its $10,000, making
its use contingent on whether the South Carolina appropriation
still held. The law named five commissioners to act with any whom
South Carolina might appoint to supervise the work. They were
empowered "to employ a general superintendent or undertaker
of said work." The money was to be expended beginning at

Augusta and to continue up the river as far as the appropriation would permit. The state still hoping for private donations, the commissioners were authorized to receive subscriptions at such places as they thought expedient.[17]

The commissioners met in Augusta in June of the following year and arranged to hire laborers to work on the river, two thirds between Augusta and Petersburg and the other third north of Petersburg. The commissioners divided themselves into two committees, one group to meet in Augusta the next month, and the others to hold a conference in Petersburg in October.[18]

Over the years of futility and failure Georgia, always impressed with the importance of river navigation for the prosperity of the state, evolved in 1817 a general state policy calling for state appropriations for improving the navigation on all of its navigable rivers, and setting up an internal improvement fund of $250,000 to be invested in bank stocks "or other profitable stock." The governor was authorized "to appoint some person of known talents and practical knowledge" to examine the rivers of the state and to report on "the practicability of improving the navigation on said rivers, . . . the expense thereof, and the best mode by which the object can be effected." In addition to appropriating various sums for the principal rivers, the act provided $20,000 (the largest amount for any river) to be used on the Savannah from Augusta on up to the Tugaloo and up that stream to Panther Creek, a few miles above Toccoa Creek. But the troublesome point of the Savannah and Tugaloo being the boundary with South Carolina was ever present, and it was provided in this act that the appropriation was contingent on South Carolina making a like appropriation.[19]

In the meantime the commissioners, who had been designated in the act of 1815 appropriating $10,000, continued their activities, even though South Carolina had not matched the amount. But a Major Wilson, who was the chief engineer of South Carolina, promised to make an exploration of the river a part of the way up to Petersburg immediately, and as time permitted to continue it. The commissioners, meeting in Augusta, in May, 1818, now designated a part of them to accompany Major Wilson up to Petersburg, and another part to continue with him on beyond Petersburg. The commissioners decided to meet the following month in Petersburg.[20]

But as so often happened in Georgia's efforts to improve her rivers, nothing came of all this activity, and on December 18,

1818 the state, abandoning all hope in securing the co-operation
of South Carolina, repealed the part of the law requiring it and
confirmed the appropriation of the $20,000.[21] The next day the
legislature removed the condition attached to the appropriation
of the $10,000 in 1815 requiring South Carolina's co-operation,
and combined the $10,000 with the $20,000, making a fund of
$30,000 to be used on the upper Savannah. Half of this amount
was to be spent on the river from Petersburg down to Augusta,
with the other half applied on the river up to Panther Creek. And
still expecting some private contributions to be made, such monies
were to be added to the $30,000 and spent proportionally. In
the meantime South Carolina had appointed some commissioners
relative to the navigation of the Savannah, but no money had
been appropriated. The Georgia commissioners who were designated in this act were instructed to associate themselves with
the South Carolinians if it could be arranged.[22]

During the year 1819 work on the Georgia rivers was pushed
forward, but with varying results. At the end of the year the
Joint Committee on Internal Improvements of the legislature
after examining the reports of the several commissioners was
much discouraged with what it had learned. It was "compelled
to remark, that the want of science and experience has been
severely felt in almost every attempt which has been made to improve the navigation of water-courses." It recommended that some
attempt be made "to call in to our aid the talents and experience
of the most enlightened persons on this subject." Some of the
river commissioners had done better than others. From Petersburg
up the river "Skill and industry" appeared "to have been used in
the work"; but from Petersburg down the river to Augusta little
appeared to have been done, though some partial surveys had
been made as well as "several ineffectual attempts to procure the
counsel and aid of the state of South Carolina."[23]

During the next several years Georgia got some co-operation
from South Carolina in planning though not in financing the improvement of the river from Petersburg to Augusta; and in 1822
the commissioners for this part of the river, reporting that there
was no necessity for the further expenditure of money here, turned
back to the state $4,556.46 of the $15,000 which had been appropriated.[24] In fact, in 1823 South Carolina had so changed her
attitude toward the improvement of the Savannah that the governor proposed to the Georgia governor that a treaty or convention be drawn up by which both states would fully co-operate with

each other in the whole Savannah River navigation. Before the end of the year an elaborate treaty, providing for appropriations, supervision, and tolls was worked out, which Georgia ratified in December of that year. Two years later South Carolina ratified it; however, as the Federal Constitution forbade any state without the consent of Congress to "enter into any Agreement or Compact with another State," it was necessary for this treaty to be submitted to that body. As the two state delegations in Congress could never agree on acting in the matter, the agreement was never put into effect.[25] And within a few years South Carolina lost complete interest in improving the navigation on the Savannah River below Augusta, for in 1833 the Charleston and Hamburg Railroad had been completed, and was now intended to divert all the river commerce possible over the road to Charleston—rather than let it continue down the river to enrich Savannah. Any attention she would now give to Savannah River navigation would be above Augusta—this attitude was not objected to by the Petersburg traders, for this was the part of the river with which they were most concerned. In 1824 the commissioners for that part of the Savannah River from Petersburg up to Andersonville (a South Carolina river port at the confluence of the Keowee-Senaca and the Tugaloo) reported that they had improved the river sufficiently for boats carrying eighty bales of cotton (about nine tons as measured in the weight of cotton bales at that time) to navigate the river.[26]

By 1821 Georgia's internal improvement fund had been increased to $500,000, yielding a substantial annual income, and plans began to mount for a more scientific expenditure of it.[27] In 1825 a Board of Public Works was set up which should be guided in its work by an experienced engineer. This bright prospect of progress lasted only a year, when the board was abolished and the engineer dismissed. Soon Georgia was to follow South Carolina in her interest in railroads, and the rivers were again to revert to private initiative.

However, the rivermen were determined never to give up, for no promise was held out that there would ever be a railroad to serve the commerce of the upper Savannah. After Georgia had quit making appropriations for improving river navigation, the legislature in 1845, yielding to Petersburgers and others, appointed commissioners for the Savannah above Augusta and gave them authority to use any unexpended appropriations for improving navigation from Petersburg to Augusta.[28] Throughout ante-bel-

lum times the Petersburgers and other upper Savannah River inhabitants never lost interest in their river. In December, 1859,
only a year before the secession movement began, they secured a
charter from the Georgia legislature for a company to be known
under the cumbersome title of the Augusta, Petersburg and Savannah River Steam and Pole Boat Navigation Company of
North-Eastern Georgia, to be capitalized at $100,000 with the
privilege of increasing the amount to $1,000,000. Its purpose was
to open a channel in the Savannah and Tugaloo rivers above
Augusta to accommodate pole and steam boats of fifty tons
burthen.[29] The Civil War soon put a stop to any activities in
which this company had hoped to engage.

THE BROAD RIVER

The other water life-line on which Petersburg's commerce
depended was the Broad River. The history of the improvement
of navigation on this river paralleled that on the Savannah, but
with more and greater emphasis on preserving fishing rights as
opposed to boats and mill dams. Noting that it was "just and
reasonable that all citizens residing within the vicinity of Little
river and Broad river should enjoy the natural and equal privilege of taking the fish of said rivers," the legislature in 1796
forbade the construction of mill dams across these streams without providing a sluice a tenth as wide as the river to be kept
open from the twentieth of February to the first of April to allow
fish to go upstream; and anyone building a fish dam was required
to leave a fourth of the stream open.[30] Some citizens who were
about to set up flour mills and sawmills were much discouraged
by this legislation, and their complaints led the legislature two
years later to make certain exceptions, observing that it was of
much more "consequence to the community at large, to encourage
the manufactory of flour, than the inconsiderable advantage resulting to a few individuals, from the egress of the fish."[31]

This legislation was not taken seriously by the fish trap and dam
men, and by 1808 enough protesting by the citizens of five counties who depended on getting to market down the Broad and
who also fished that stream for the delectable shad, led the legislature to agree that many citizens of those counties were "improperly and unjustly restrained from partaking of the advantages and benefits which nature has ordained and granted them, by
a number of persons whose interest it has become to obstruct and

hinder the passage of fish up Broad River, by stopping the current and stream, in divers places, by fish dams and traps, so as to really become a monopoly to individuals, and detrimental to the inhabitants bordering on said river." The legislature recited further that some of these citizens had made personal contributions and others were expected to do so to keep Broad River open whereby they might "convey their produce to market with more ease and convenience." It reiterated former legislation that at least one fourth of the river, including the main channel, must be kept open to provide "a free passage for boats, rafts or fish." Anyone so bold as to disregard this law should be subject to a fine of $50 a day as long as he allowed his obstruction to remain in the river.[32]

It was soon found that the terms of this law did not make it self operative; so the next year the legislature came back with an amendment requiring a third instead of a fourth of the stream to be kept open and set up machinery for its enforcement. The fine of $50 a day was reaffirmed, the procedure for prosecution was provided, and anyone who reported a forbidden obstruction should receive one half of the penalty incurred. Thirteen commissioners were named whose right and duty it was to view the river and report any illegal dams, first, however, giving the owner five days notice to remove the obstruction; and if the notice were not complied with, then the commissioners should themselves with any aid of other citizens needed destroy the obstruction.[33]

As more people filled up the Broad River Valley and began providing articles of commerce for the market in Petersburg and a reverse trade up the river, the promotion of navigation on the river became of primary importance, but not neglecting the fish men and mill men, for they also provided articles of commerce. If the laws were obeyed, then planters, millers of flour and meal, lumber manufacturers, and fish men all would be properly served by the river. Following the practice for the upper Savannah, commissioners were given permission by the legislature in 1800 to set up a lottery to raise $1,000 to be used in improving Broad River; but like the Savannah River lottery nothing came of this effort.[34]

And now belatedly in 1810 taking a leaf out of the Savannah River book, a group of Broad River Valley citizens got themselves incorporated by the legislature as the Broad River Navigation Company, asserting that few countries enjoyed "greater natural advantages than this State, for the extension of commerce," and that removing obstructions in Broad River "would

greatly conduce to the convenience and interest of the inhabitants
settled on the north and north western parts of this State." The
company was capitalized at $10,000, divided into 1,000 shares,
and was to continue for twenty years. By implication, this law gave
the company permission to obliterate the fish men and the mill
men (though it would certainly not be to their interest to do so)
in granting it the power "to proceed to improve the navigation
of the said river from the confluence of the same with the Savannah river to the mouth of Hudson's fork [about seventy miles or
more upstream], in such manner as the company shall deem best
calculated to promote the object of their association, and for this
purpose shall be, and they are hereby authorized to remove all
and every obstruction in the said river, which may tend to obstruct the navigation thereof." And any one felling trees into
the river or otherwise obstructing navigation should on conviction
be fined not more than twenty dollars. When the company should
have cleared the river, then it might charge tolls on all articles
carried up or down the river, of not more than 25 cents per 100
pounds, except that for lumber the toll could not be more than
50 cents per 1,000 feet (on the face of the law pounds would be
inferred but in a subsequent law, feet was stated). It might also
levy an unstated toll based on the river mileage "for the keeping
the navigation in repair." Although this law seemed almost to have
deeded the river to the company, it was not quite so, for people
living along the river might carry on seining operations, keep
ferries for crossing the river, and travel on the river in canoes carrying anything which they could put into them, provided they
did not come "under the denomination of boats of burthen."[35]

In none of the legislation relating to navigation on either the
Broad or the Savannah was there any mention of passenger service
or rates. The law incorporating this company required it to sell
all of its shares before it could become a legal body. As the sale
of its 1,000 shares proceeded slowly, the legislature the next year
allowed it to reduce the number needed to be sold for this purpose, to 250; but it repealed the provision giving it a life of twenty
years and allowed the state to extinguish its charter on paying for
the original stock with a few accretions and deductions.[36]

The incorporators not having met with success in organizing
their company, after five years of inactivity, they induced the
legislature in 1815 to grant them a reorganization. Now additional
men were brought into the corporation and the toll rates were
reduced; but the charter could be annulled as formerly and the

capitalization remained the same—$10,000. Their powers to improve the navigation were described in more detail—now being authorized "to build dams, cut canals, open sluices, and to do and perform all and every act which may appear necessary to promote the object of their association"; but in building dams they must not obstruct the passage of fish. Now their tolls must not be more than 12½ cents for "every hundred pounds of tobacco, cotton, flour, iron, steel, and all heavy articles"; nor more than 6¼ cents "for every cubic foot contained in all bales, trunks, and boxes of dry goods"; and not more than 25 cents per 1,000 feet of lumber.[37]

Shaler Hillyer, who was one of the incorporators and the leading spirit in the Broad River Navigation Company, secured a bit of special legislation for himself a few days before the reorganization of the company. In providing power for his mill at Muckle's Ferry Shoals he was given permission to build across Broad River a dam not more than four feet high, however, over the main current he must construct a section of the dam twenty feet wide in such a way that it could be lowered "to admit shad to ascend and descend without difficulty" during the time when they were running, which was from the first of February to the first of May. And as a further protection to the fish, in that area of two hundred feet above and below the dam no one should be allowed to fish "with nets, gigs, or any other instrument or machine whatever, (other than the hook and line)," during the season when the fish were running. Any free person convicted of violating this provision was subject to a fine of $50.00, and any slave so offending was subject to ten lashes along with the owner of the slave paying a fine of $20.00. The punishment for a free person of color was thirty-nine lashes.

Boats should be accommodated by a canal or mill race which would run from the dam down to the mill at the Shoals. This canal must be of sufficient width and depth to accommodate "boats of the size of those usually navigating between Petersburg and Augusta." Locks at the mill permitted boats to enter and leave the canal. The enforcement of all these provisions guarding both fish and boats was provided for in elaborate sections of the law relating to the commissioners for keeping open the navigation of the river.[38]

The general state-wide policy of improving river navigation adopted by Georgia in 1817 led to the river appropriation act of that year, previously noted. It allotted $5,000 to Broad River but only on condition that no tolls should be charged on the river commerce.[39] Apparently the company refused to give up this valuable privilege, for without the right to levy tolls it could not spend money on the river. The state had the right to vacate the charter by indemnifying the company, but it must have felt that the promise of $5,000 to improve the Broad was recompense enough. In 1824 the committee of the legislature charged with making recommendations for any further appropriations for the Broad and Savannah rivers recommended that none be voted until a survey should have been made "by a competent engineer" and the "practicability" of further expenses be established. It observed further that the Broad River Navigation Company operated "as a serious injury" to the citizens of Broad River Valley because of its failure to use its privileges and a neglect of its duties provided in the act of incorporation. It recommended that the governor induce the company to surrender its charter.[40]

In the absence of official records long since lost, it is logical to assume that the state refused to recompense the company and that the company, therefore, refused to give up its charter. But finally, in 1828, the patience of the state (and also of the Broad River Valley people) gave out and the legislature proceeded to repeal the company's charter, "any law to the contrary nothwithstanding."[41] There is no implication in the repeal law or evidence otherwise that the company was recompensed.

In the meantime with the company resting on its privileges but performing none of its duties, the Broad River people got a law passed in 1824, striking out on a new principle. Reaffirming all the old regulations as to width of the stream to be left open, dams, fish traps, and the like, the law named a new set of commissioners whose duty it was to establish the main current of the river and to call on citizens of the adjoining counties to remove any obstructions to the main channel. They could not be required to work more than three consecutive days and not more than six days during any one year. They received no wages, but anyone refusing to work should be subject to a fine of $5.00 a day as long as he refused to work.[42]

From this time to the middle of the century, law after law was passed, each generally repeating the previous one but specifying more particularly how the law was to be enforced. Most of these laws were more concerned with the passage of fish than of boats, and most of them linked Broad River with the upper Savannah in their application.[43] Also it was a continuing problem to provide commissioners to look after river obstructions. Some when appointed refused to act and proceeded to resign; others remained inactive when they accepted appointment, being influenced by local interests; and most of these commissioners were not in any way qualified in the science of river engineering.

BOATS AND BOAT HANDS

The navigation of rivers, of course, presupposes boats, and their size and structure would naturally depend on the depth and difficulties of the channels they plied. Petersburg was primarily interested in boats that could be successfully used on the Broad and on the Savannah above the town and below to Augusta; but indirectly Petersburg's egress to world markets would depend on how well her commerce fared on the lower Savannah. As tobacco was the principal item of trade in Petersburg's first years, the transportation of this article on the river below Augusta was in what were called "tobacco flats."[44] They were generally of the size to carry from fifty to seventy-five hogsheads of tobacco, though one advertised for sale in Augusta in 1801 was described as able to carry upwards of one hundred hogshead and drawing only three feet of water.[45] Three years earlier there was offered for sale another which would hold from sixty to sixty-two hogsheads and it was asserted that none was "equal to her for running fast."[46]

On account of more difficult channels to navigate, the boats used above Augusta were smaller and of special construction. They were known as "Petersburg boats." The smaller boats plying the upper Savannah and high up the Broad could carry nine or ten tons, depending on the stage of the water; and those on the lower Broad and down the Savannah to Augusta were much larger. A typical Petersburg boat was seventy or seventy-five feet long and five or six feet wide, and when loaded it drew only fifteen or twenty inches of water. It was laden with ten to fifteen hogsheads of tobacco and later, with the coming of cotton, it could carry as many as sixty bales, generally placed two layers deep. It was poled by five or six deck hands, with a captain or patroon at the prow.[47] It could make the trip to Augusta and back within a week. In 1817 one of these boats laden with forty bales of cotton was reported to have caught fire with a complete loss of the cotton.[48]

Petersburg was, of course, the center of the river traffic above

Augusta, and boat owners were ready at all times to engage cargoes. Shaler Hillyer did a considerable cotton trade down the river to Augusta, sometimes engaging the whole boat or only a part, as in 1813 when he wrote that he had "left eight Bales of Cotton to go in first Boat."[49] In one instance he loaded a boat with nineteen bales, but when they were weighed in Augusta, only eighteen bales were reported. He was never able to find out whether the boatmen had lost one on the river, or whether he had been robbed of a bale on the docks.[50] Sometimes this river traffic was provoking in other respects. One Tuesday in 1806 at daybreak a boat laden with his cotton set out for Augusta. It was a beautiful morning and a good river, yet the boat did not arrive until Saturday. In the meantime Shaler had gone to Augusta to provide for its trans-shipment on a boat scheduled for Savannah. The Petersburg boat arrived too late, much to his discomfort.[51]

The deckhands of the boats were almost uniformly slaves, either owned or hired by the patroon. Some of the captains of the boats and their pole-wielders were not above stopping at some convenient place along the river to do a little pilfering of corn, cotton, and other produce. In 1815 the legislature passed a law requiring all owners or agents of boats to carry a bill of lading of their cargoes and papers showing the name of the patroon and the consignee. Furthermore, the next year the legislature brought to an end the evil of allowing Negro or any other boat hands to carry to market any produce described as their own or to trade such items among themselves. The owners of boats were held "liable and compelled to pay for all pillages and thefts committed by their respective crews."[52]

Along the Broad River there was a more friendly attitude and greater honesty of boat owners and crews toward the inhabitants. Boats on their way to Petersburg were always willing to execute little commissions for trading articles in the Petersburg stores, extending these courtesies even to some slaves. These boats were provided with what were called "Petersburg boat bugles," to be used to announce the approach of the boat. They were about five and a half feet long and five inches in diameter at the farther end and were made of smoothly-dressed wooden staves, highly polished, all held together by iron bands. The bugles were as thin and light as if they had been made of tin. The mouthpiece was made of cow horn. The whole construction was such as to add a melody to the sound, which was music to the ears of the Broad River people. With favorable wind conditions the bugle could be heard for miles.[53]

ROADS

Petersburg's location on the point of land where two rivers met was, of course, a great advantage in water transportation; but for traffic on land it was almost equally as great an inconvenience. In the early days the only highway out of the town which did not cross one of the rivers was one leading up the peninsula to Elberton. Of course, there were various secondary roads to plantations and homesteads up the Broad and Savannah rivers and the intervening interior. Yet Petersburg needed land transportation for bringing in the products of plantations (tobacco and cotton especially) to be shipped by river to Augusta, and also for travel. It should be noted in this latter respect, that the improvement of river navigation was designed for commerce and not for passengers. Apart from passenger traffic on the lower Savannah with the coming of the steamboat era, there was little anywhere else on the Georgia rivers. Therefore, since most travel out of and into Petersburg was by land, the development and maintainance of roads was of special importance to the town.

Despite Petersburg's location between the two rivers, it was at that point on the Savannah where land travel from the north and east crossed into upper Georgia. United States mail routes were directed through Petersburg. In 1794 the route from Washington, Wilkes County, ran through Petersburg and on through Elberton to Franklin Courthouse, a distance of about sixty miles, requiring two days for the trip which was made every two weeks.[54] There was also a mail route from Augusta through Lincoln Courthouse to Petersburg and on by Elberton to Carnesville (formerly called Franklin Courthouse), to be served weekly.[55]

A mail route did not necessarily mean a highway which might accommodate wheeled vehicles, for in the earlier days mail was generally carried on horseback; however, Petersburg was accessible from the beginning by wheeled conveyances, and in 1804 a monopoly in stagecoach traffic from Petersburg to Augusta was granted to John Beal. He was allowed to use any road he pleased "for the conveyance of passengers and their baggage." He was required to run a stage at least once a week, and his franchise was to last for ten years.[56] Later an integrated stage line from Milledgeville to Washington, D.C., ran through Petersburg.[57]

Whether mail route or stagecoach route, the Georgia roads were generally in a miserable condition. There was no state system either designated or aided, and private initiative asked for few toll road franchises. Roads were, therefore, considered only of local interest. The road law of 1792 vested in the county inferior courts the right and duty of laying out new roads and appointing road overseers, whose duty it was to keep the roads in good repair. All roads should "at all times be kept well cleared from logs, trees, bushes and other obstructions" for a width of thirty feet and all roots should be grubbed up for a space of at least sixteen feet across. If within sixty feet any trees deadened for making new grounds should fall across a road, the person responsible should suffer a fine if he did not remove the obstruction within two days. To keep the roads in good repair, "all male laboring persons" between the ages of sixteen and fifty were required to bring "proper tools" and work not more than twelve days a year. Wherever two highways met, sign posts either of stone or wood must be set up with inscriptions "in large letters" indicating the "most noted place" to which each of the roads led and the distance thereto.[58] The next year the road law was amended and elaborated. Now, "all male white inhabitants, . . . free negroes and mulattoes, and all negroes and other male slaves from the age of sixteen to fifty years" were required to work on the roads, which should now be from twenty-four to thirty-six feet wide. Besides being required to bring proper tools, every white worker must "carry with him one good and sufficient gun or pair of pistols."[59] It is difficult to explain this requirement unless it was called for to repel Indians, who were at this time on the war path. It could hardly be supposed to prevent the Negro workmen from running away. A more detailed description of how road work was to be carried out may be had from a road overseer's commission: The road must be put "in good travelling order" by "widening said road to Thirty feet removing all loose rocks, raising the middle above the sides, opening all side ditches, trimming the limbs high up the trees & cutting all necessary turnouts."[60]

With all the laws and regulations, the roads continued in almost a state of nature. Too often an overseer would have a pile of brush thrown into a ditch which had been washed across a road and, sprinkling a little dirt on it, remark that "it will do for the present." And then the next rain would wash it all away.[61] A good roads advocate in 1823 argued that it took more than a few axes and hoes to work a road. Plows, scrapes, and other implements were needed. With less than these, "You might almost as well clear up the Okafanoka swamp with a penknife." People should realize, he said, that on "the market roads, corn and fodder, if nothing else, always commands the highest price."[62]

Yet, over rudimentary roads, trails, and horse paths Georgia's overland travel and trade went on from Colonial times far into the nineteenth century. Apart from the few stagecoaches, people traveled in wagons and buggies, in sulkies, and on carts and horseback. A few people in Petersburg made short trips around in their "elegant" carriages. Some hardy people traveled long distances on foot, as did the "crazy preacher" Lorenzo Dow. Bishop Francis Asbury traveled thousands of miles over Georgia's roads and trails and elsewhere on horseback or in his chaise. Eli Whitney in visiting some of his interests in Georgia and South Carolina, in 1802, traveled about 2,800 miles "in a Sulkey & the same horse performed the whole journey."[63]

People migrating to Georgia generally came in wagons and carts, into which they could pack their belongings, with some in these parties riding horses. The Few family, of which William was a member, in their journey from Maryland to North Carolina and proceeding later to Georgia, set out with their movable effects in a four-horse wagon and a cart drawn by two horses.[64] Another party coming from Virginia in 1775, consisting of two men, a woman and her child and a Negro boy, made their way with two horses and a cart drawn by one horse.[65]

Before the coming of railroads, wagonage became a business participated in by many people. Some owned only a wagon or two with the necessary horses, while others made large investments and became wagon magnates, ready to go near or far in this land transportation. Every town of much size had its "Waggon yard," the one in Augusta being an enclosed area with accommodations for both man and beast.[66] The owner of a wagon line in Greensboro advertised in 1815 that he had "four excellent Waggons and Teams, with honest and careful drivers, which he will run to any part of the United States, as he designs to keep them constantly on the road."[67]

Francois Michaux, the French traveler, in 1802 saw large wagons drawn by four or six horses going from upper Georgia and the Carolinas to Charleston, carrying such articles as cotton, tobacco, smoked hams, and deer and bear skins.[68] Bishop Asbury in his Georgia travels during the late eighteenth and early nineteenth centuries saw the roads gorged with wagons going to

Augusta. And one person in a little Georgia town received this
notice in a dispatch sent to a Milledgeville newspaper: "There is
in this village a very *curious little man,* whose occupation being
of a man very sedentary kind, makes it his business to collect facts
concerning matters for which no body else cares a farthing.
Among other things, either for his amusement or information, he
thought proper to count daily the number of waggons which
passed his house," and he found that the average for the whole
year was six coming and going daily.[69]

During the period of the War of 1812, when the coastal traffic
was cut off, land transportation by wagons reached its height.
Cotton was sent as far as Baltimore to be exchanged for merchandise.[70] Shaler Hillyer wrote a merchant firm in New York to send
him salt and sugar by the first wagon possible.[71] A Petersburger
wrote to his friend in North Carolina in 1813 that there were
30,000 bales of cotton piled up in Augusta and equal amounts
each in Savannah and Charleston, and that it would require
10,000 wagons to haul it to Northern markets.[72]

The impetus given to land transportation during this period
put the rivermen in serious competition with the wagon men,
with whom they had to wrestle for years thereafter. In December,
1817, it was reported in Augusta that during the previous eleven
days, 10,000 bales of cotton had been brought to that town by
wagons.[73] Sometimes wagons would either by design or by chance
line up in cavalcades of from fifteen to twenty, and their characteristic narrow-rimmed wheels would make the roads almost im-
passable by the time they had gone by.[74] Ordinarily wagons
traveled from ten to twelve miles a day, but sometimes as far as
twenty four—all depending on the condition of the roads.

A resident of the Petersburg region during the wagon era observed that these wagon drivers were "an institution, a profession,
a community—expert and skilled, with rules, regulations, and cus-
toms governing themselves and the vast number of farmers residing along the different roads leading to Augusta, with whom these
wagons had transactions of various sorts."[75] These wagoners were
white men of the better class, for only such could be trusted with
the kind of business in which they were engaged.[76] A sort of
boisterous camaraderie among them set them apart.

John Lambert, a widely-traveled Englishman, wrote in 1814:
"These waggoners are familiarly called *crackers,* (from the smack-
ing of their whips, I suppose). They are said to be often very rude
and insolent to strangers, and people of the towns, whom they

meet on the road, particularly if they happen to be genteel persons. I have heard of several ludicrous, and some shameful tricks, which these gentry of the *whip* have been guilty of. There are instances of their having robbed people; but in general they confine themselves to a few mad pranks, which they call *jokes*. In almost every part of the United States, there seems to be an invincible antipathy betweens the towns' people and these waggoners, who take every opportunity they can to give each other a thrashing. The waggoner constantly rides on one of the shaft horses, and with a long whip guides the leaders. Their long legs, lank figures, and meagre countenances, have sometimes a curious appearance when thus mounted; especially if a string of them happen to pass along the road."[77]

Bridges and Ferries

Though Petersburg, on the point of its peninsula, was cut off by water from land roads leading in every direction except to the northwestward; it was not in a state of isolation from them, for from the very earliest times it was supplied with ferry service. In fact even in Colonial days when Fort James was there, a ferry must have been maintained across the Broad River at this point. Certainly a Thomas Carter was maintaining a ferry there by the end of the Revolution, for in 1784 Dionysius Oliver received the right to run the ferry which Carter had formerly owned. In this same year Barksdale Ferry was authorized by the South Carolina legislature across the Savannah River "below Fort Charlotte," which, however, could not serve the point of land where Petersburg was to grow up; but this place was taken care of at the same time by the South Carolina legislature authorizing another ferry "above Fort Charlotte" at John Sharp's plantation.[78]

John Oliver, son of Dionysius, soon entered the picture as a ferry master among his many other interests. His father transferred to him ferry rights across the Broad in 1787 (the year after Petersburg was started);[79] and in 1792, when Petersburg began to flourish, the South Carolina legislature granted to him the ferry rights across the Savannah where the John Sharp ferry had run. These were the authorized ferry tolls there: for wagons and four-wheeled carriages, three shillings each; for a one-horse chaise, chair or cart, one shilling and six pence; for a man on horseback, four pence; for foot passengers, two pence; for cattle, sheep, goats, and presumably other animals "ferried or swam over," one penny;

and for a "rolled" hogshead of tobacco with horse and driver, seven pence.[80]

There was constant ferry service across the Savannah from Petersburg to Vienna, which had grown up contemporaneously with Petersburg. By 1817 there were at least two ferries running, for this year South Carolina authorized John Watkins to run a ferry across to the foot of Commerce Street in Petersburg, and at the same time it gave ferry rights from Vienna to Petersburg to James Russell, the unfortunate preacher who had turned commercial. The established ferry tolls were now: wagon or four-wheeled carriage, driver, and horses, 75 cents; riding chair, cart or other two-wheeled vehicle, driver and horse, 25 cents; man and horse, 12½ cents; foot passenger, 6¼ cents; hogshead of tobacco, 25 cents; horses, cows, hogs, sheep, and goats, 2 cents each.[81]

There was, of course, continuous ferry service across the Broad River between Petersburg and Lisbon, and in 1808 the Georgia legislature gave Joshua Grinage the ferry rights across Little River on this road to Augusta for those who did not care to risk the ford there. The following tolls were established: for an empty or loaded wagon with four hourses, 37½ cents; for ox-cart, 25 cents; for four-wheel pleasure carriage, 50 cents; for two-wheel pleasure carriage, 25 cents; for man on horseback, for every "led or drove horse," and for every foot passenger, 6¼ cents; for most "neat cattle," 6⅛ cents; and for goats, sheep or hogs, 2 cents each.[82]

Ferries were, of course, authorized and used across streams too dangerous to ford or too wide for bridges; however, as the state was not spending money on roads it left the building of bridges to local authorities and to private individuals, who were to charge tolls. By the road legislation of 1792 the overseer and his workmen were required to build bridges wherever needed and make them not less than fifteen feet wide; but if the bridge across the swamp or stream could not be built within three days, then it was the duty of the county concerned to have the bridge built and paid for out of a tax levy.[83] Apparently this system was ineffective, for four years later the legislature authorized certain persons named to erect bridges on five streams and to charge certain specified tolls, except that citizens passing "on public occasions, or going to or from divine service," should not be required to pay a toll.[84]

Still the legislature's worries over bridges were not ended, for the next year it repealed this law except for two of the bridges, announcing that it had been "found from experience that toll bridges are prejudicial, and not of that benefit to the inhabitants contemplated"; however the owners were to be recompensed by money raised by a special tax.[85] Then, in 1808 a law provided that the owners of all "toll bridges, ferries and turnpike roads" should erect at a conspicuous place a board painted black with white lettering giving the tolls required, and if anyone failed to do this, no toll could be charged.[86]

Roads, bridges, and ferries served Petersburg about as well as they did any other town in the state, and rivers were Petersburg's special benefactors. Any decline in its prosperity could, therefore, be little attributed to the lack of these forms of transportation. However, with the coming of the next era of transportation, that of the railroads, Petersburg's fate was largely sealed, lying as it did on the eastern edge of the state, almost surrounded by water hazards incident to railroads. The new lines of commerce passed by Petersburg, leaving it far to the side.

6

Petersburg Grows Up

PETERSBURG'S location was a beautiful one, and the mere fact of this attraction, apart from economic considerations, must have played some part in its selection. It was situated on an alluvial plain, broadening out from the point of land where the two rivers met, in a sort of amphitheatre formed by a ridge on the South Carolina side and one on the Georgia side cutting down to the westward, separating the hinterland between the two rivers.

The danger in this location came from any excessively high flood waters coming down the two rivers and mingling here. The famous "Yazoo Freshet" of 1796, which washed away the Aunt Nancy Hart cabin on the Broad and created havoc in Augusta, must have greatly imperilled Petersburg. Descriptions of what happened in Augusta should give some indication of what Petersburg must have suffered. The river rose from thirty-five to forty feet, putting the town under two feet of water and washing away the Wade Hampton bridge.[1] Bishop Asbury happened along soon after the water had receded and wrote in his journal on March 10, "I saw how the flood had ploughed up the street[s] of Augusta: I walked over the ruins for nearly two miles, viewing the deep gulfs in the main street."[2] The *Augusta Chronicle* noted that "the river rose to an alarming height—within a few hours the site of the town was generally under water, and excepting a few houses which stand on the highest situations, the rest were completely surrounded with the water which found its way over the lowest parts of the bank of the river and spread itself thro' the whole town and common."[3]

In the course of time Petersburg spread far beyond the ninety-three lots which had formerly been laid out by Dionysius Oliver. It eased off into one-acre homesteads and on farther into plantation homes. Some of the most well-to-do chose the ridge for home sites. It became a tradition that one of these ridge lots sold for $15,000.[4] As was customary in those days, these estates were given names by their owners, as "Thornville," the home of John Watkins; "Spring Hill," where John Daniel Watkins lived; "Normandy," the D. B. Cade home; "Hebron," where John Williams Walker lived; and "Poplar Grove," where Shaler Hillyer lived.[5]

Bishop Asbury on one of his many journeys through Georgia and elsewhere visited Petersburg in 1801 and was much impressed with the town. "Petersburg is beautifully situated," he said, "has about eighty houses, well-constructed for stores, and about one hundred buildings in all; they are generally one story in height, well painted, with convenient shed attached."[6] George Sibbald, who lived down the river in Augusta, in a work published this same year declared that Petersburg was "in point of situation and commercial consequence . . . second only to Augusta." Continuing he said it "is a handsome well built Town and presents to the view of the astonished traveller, a Town which has risen out of the Woods in a few years, as if by enchantment: It has two Warehouses for the Inspection of Tobacco."[7]

It is difficult to determine whether the Bishop intended to say that there were eighty stores and business houses and only twenty residences, but that seems to be the implication. Certainly Petersburg was more of a commercial than a residential center; and as has just now been noted, many of the people who had their businesses in Petersburg lived outside of the formal city limits.

Tradition has greatly exaggerated the size and the number of people living there. One person has asserted that the city consisted of 700 lots and that there were more than 2,000 permanent inhabitants.[8] Another has written that in the early 1800's there were about 700 or 800 people living there.[9] This latter estimate is, undoubtedly, near the correct number. The United States census for 1810 gave the number as 332, which included the slaves.[10] The Broad River Valley at this time, much of it tributary to Petersburg, had a population of nearly 45,000.[11] By this census Petersburg was the eighth town in size in Georgia, being outdistanced by Savannah (5,215), Augusta (2,476), Milledgeville (1,256), Washington (596), St. Marys (585), Louisville (524), and Greensboro (411). But as Petersburg was a boom town, based largely on speculation, it might well have been third in size around 1800.

For the first sixteen years of its existence the town was governed by the Inferior Court of Elbert County. During this "swaddling-

clothes" period Petersburg was small enough and law-abiding
enough to need no closer supervision than what the Court could
give it. In 1794 the Court appointed William Runnolds as constable for the "district of Petersburg,"[12] and three years later it
ordered a road to be opened from Front Street in a direct line to
the Savannah River. It appointed William Goode and John R.
Ragland to be overseers "to lay out and keep the same in repair."[13] Petersburg, like all the rest of Elbert County, came under
the jurisdiction of the Grand Jury, which regularly made its
presentments to the Superior Court. In 1799 it presented as a
grievance that the streets of Petersburg were "not kept in good
Repair."[14]

As the town grew larger it needed a local government, so in
1802 the legislature passed an act "for the better regulation and
government of the town of Petersburg." Named in the act to be
commissioners were Robert Thompson, LeRoy Pope, Richard
Easter, Samuel Watkins, and John R. Ragland. Their first duty
was to convene immediately and to proceed to organize further
the town government by appointing "a clerk, and such other officers as they deem necessary." They were to hold office until the
first Monday in January, two years hence, when the citizens should
elect five commissioners, and every year thereafter at the same
date new elections should be held. The commissioners were vested
"with full power and authority, to make such bye-laws and regulations, and to inflict or impose such pains, penalties and forfeitures,
as in their judgment shall be conducive to the good order and
government" of the town—but to do nothing repugnant to the
laws and the constitution of the state, "and that the pains, penalties
and forfeitures, aforesaid, shall not extend to life or member."[15]

The commissioners proceeded to organize the town government
by appointing Joseph P. Watkins "city sheriff" with Nicholas
Pope to be his deputy. John Watkins became treasurer and Shaler
Hillyer, clerk. Having thus acted the commissioners turned their
attention to passing city ordinances. No one should ride through
the streets "faster than a common canter" and any one heard
swearing should be fined. Rules were set up to keep the streets
clean, and a tax was placed on billiard tables.[16] Hillyer, in addition to being the "C. B. C." (Clerk of Board of Commissioners—
alphabetical designations were already in style), had the duty of
receiving the tax returns for all taxable property in the town.[17]

Now being a town by legislative enactment, Petersburg developed the ambition of becoming the seat of justice for a new coun-

ty that should include parts of Elbert, Lincoln, Wilkes, and Oglethorpe—a designation that would have had to include most of the
Broad River Valley on both sides of the river. Even before Petersburg had been incorporated there had been rumblings among
its citizens that the town was important enough to be a new
county capital, and Memorable Walker with an assistant had been
sent to Louisville, then the state capital, to lobby for the new
county. This new county movement got nowhere, but it was supposed to have played a part in getting the legislature to incorpo-
rate the town.[18]

Shaler Hillyer's duty as tax receiver for Petersburg (both for
city and, presumably, for state taxes) added nothing to his pop-
ularity, since no one liked to pay taxes and often visited this dislike on innocent officials. The records of what constituted city
taxes have long since disappeared, but state taxes were in more
permanent keeping. Tax acts were passed annually with few
changes from the preceding act. The tax on land depended on its
location, whether near navigable streams or swamps; whether
swamps, high river swamps or low grounds. High grounds were
evaluated by the kind of timber growing on it, "pine lands" or
"oak and hickory lands," divided into first, second, and third
grades. The rates for the year 1803 which Hillyer applied in receiving tax returns are here given. The kinds of land around
Petersburg and in its dependencies were high river swamps and
oak and hickory. Pine lands were only incidental, but where they
were found in sufficient areas to be set apart the rate of tax was
at three quarters of a mill per acre. The only high river swamp
land with which Petersburgers might have been concerned lay
down the Savannah River from the mouth of Broad to Rae's
Creek, and was taxed one cent and five mills per acre for first
quality, eight and a half mills for second quality, and two and a
half mills for third quality. And in this same area, all oak and
hickory lands (cultivated and uncultivated) within a mile of the
river, including all islands, bore the rate of six mills per acre for
first quality; two and a half mills for second quality; and one and
a half mills for third quality. All the land up the Savannah and
Tugaloo and up Broad River from Petersburg, and within a mile
of the rivers, was considered oak and hickory land (with the possibility of some pine land), and whether cultivated or not, was
taxed at these rates: first quality, at four and a quarter mills per
acre; second quality, two and a half mills; and third quality, one
mill. All other oak and hickory land (that is, more than a mile

from the rivers) was taxed for first quality, four and a quarter mills per acre; second quality, two and a quarter mills; and third quality, one and a quarter mills. Since many Petersburgers were large landowners, they had these taxes to pay if their lands lay within the areas described here; however if their lands were in other parts of the state the taxes on them were slightly different.

In addition to land taxes Petersburgers, as well as other Georgians, had other taxes to pay. A poll tax of 31¼ cents was levied on all free male white persons, and on all free Negroes, mulattoes and mestizoes twenty-one years old or above—the same poll tax applied to all slaves who were under sixty years of age.

In addition to taxes which towns might levy, the state placed a tax of 31¼ cents on the $100 valuation "of every lot, wharf, or other lands not herein already enumerated, and all other buildings, within the limits of any town, village, or burrough." The same tax computed in the same manner was levied on all merchandise. There was a tax of one dollar on "all four wheeled carriages (waggons exempted)," and fifty cents on all two wheeled carriages, but carts and drays were exempted. Lawyers and doctors of medicine were taxed four dollars, and there was a tax of fifty dollars on billiard tables. The tax on gambling devices was designed to outlaw them. The sum of $1,000 was levied "on E, O, tables, or other instruments of like construction, for the purpose of gambling."

As Georgia was desirous of bringing in settlers land taxes were purposely kept low; and in "all cases of extreme indigence or infirmity" the poll tax might be remitted.[19]

In receiving tax returns, Hillyer undoubtedly received some complaints with them; and he, himself, may have been confused and perturbed in certain matters. Just what were the boundaries of the town, and how extensive were the town commons? Apparently Dionysius Oliver in laying out his lots had not intended them to be the exact limits of the town, and no one else had thought much about the matter until the question of town taxes came up. Perhaps the question of pasturing cattle on the town commons and of other uses being made of this area may well have been of longer standing.

So, to remedy these matters and to give the commissioners further powers of governing the town, the legislature came to the rescue in a law which it passed in 1804. They were now directed to have a survey made of the town and to "ascertain and lay out the commons thereunto belonging, agreeable to the proposals, upon which said town was settled." A correct plat should be made and deposited as an official document in the office of the Clerk of the Court in Elberton. As some questions had arisen about the powers of the commissioners to purchase land and other items needed in governing the town, the right to do so was now specifically granted. Furthermore, they should have the right to make rules and regulations "respecting the streets, public buildings and taverns, carriages, waggons, carts, drays, pumps, buckets, fire-engines, the care of the poor, the regulation of disorderly people, negroes, and in general all regulations which they may deem necessary for the welfare and convenience of said town, and for preserving good order therein." Undoubtedly there had been some question as to the commissioners' right to assess property and levy taxes on it; they were now given that power and also the power "to inflict pains and penalties and forfeitures" for violations of the town ordinances. As the original act incorporating Petersburg had mentioned by name only the clerk which the commissioners had the right to appoint and since there must have been some opposition to their having appointed other officials, the present law made more specific their power of appointment. They were now given the right "to appoint a clerk, treasurer, sheriff, constable, and all other officers (affixing their salaries, that may appear to them necessary)."[20]

A new set of commissioners had been elected in 1804, the previous ones having been named by the legislature in the original act of 1802. LeRoy Pope and Robert Thompson were returned; but the other three were replaced by John Oliver, John Watkins, and Dr. W. W. Bibb. Now with the additional powers granted to them in this act of 1804, the next year they bought from John Williams Walker for $1,000 Lot 39, "commonly called the Red House lot." Here for the first time the commissioners would have a permanent seat of government in a town hall.[21] They proceeded to have a town well dug[22] and to provide other services for the public—to keep the streets clean, to preserve peace and good order, to appoint other officials, and to perform all other acts necessary and proper for the government of the town.

Under the rule and dispensation of its five commissioners, for the next quarter century Petersburg thrived and grew great and began its decline. The town had been going down hill for some years before 1828, when a new law was passed reducing the number of commissioners from five to three. This reflected the fears of the Petersburgers who were left that the government though

now simplified into three commissioners might fail to function by
their refusal to accept election, or in case no election were held.[23]

The United States postal authorities were slow in establishing
a post office in Petersburg, and there must have been great inconvenience in receiving mail there. Not until 1795 did Petersburg receive this service. William J. Hobby, down from Connecticut, and later one of the editors of the *Augusta Herald,* was the
first postmaster, followed by another New England Yankee from
Massachusetts, Oliver Whyte; then James S. Walker, a brother of
John Williams Walker; and from 1804 to 1810 that Petersburg
nabob, LeRoy Pope held the position, relinquishing it only because of his move to Alabama. Thereafter came in succession
Alexander Pope, John Watkins, Henry M. Watkins, James M.
Hester, Archibald N. Sayer, Felix G. Edwards, Archibald Stokes,
and Mark S. Anthony. The post office was discontinued in 1855.[24]
When a town was able to afford a newspaper it was considered
grown-up and on the road to becoming a city. In June, 1805
Michael Burke and Alexander M'Donnell set up a newspaper in
Petersburg, which they named the *Georgia & Carolina Gazette.* It
was a weekly and cost $3.00 a year. They continued their partner-
ship until December, when M'Donnell became the sole editor and
proprietor, and Burke moved to Louisville.[25] The paper's life was
precarious from the beginning. In its second issue, the editors
had this to say: "In this happy land, where the means of information is within the reach of every individual, it must excite the
most painful reflections, keenest anxiety, for a continuance of her
hitherto unexampled prosperity, when we find men of decent
respectable appearance, whose venerable aspect would have graced
the sage members of the Roman Forum, reply, on being asked to
subscribe for our paper, that their circumstances would not
permit!"[26]

Although subscribers seemed hard to get, even many of those
who did subscribe were "slow pay," and had to be frequently re-
minded of their back dues with threats to stop their paper and
even to cease publication. When the paper was a half year old, the
editors sent out a distress call for subscriptions owed them and
announced that they intended to suspend publication of the paper
for a time "to discover the estimation in which it is held, by
people coming forward to advance for the ensuing six-months—
unless this zeal manifest itself pretty generally, so as to enable us
to get out of our present embarrassment, no longer will the
GEORGIA & CAROLINA GAZETTE issue from the Press of

BURKE & M'DONNELL."[27] They put their threat into operation and suspended the paper for almost a month.

Now and then a public-minded subscriber would come to the
rescue of the paper by sending a communication of praise and
thanksgiving for having such a prosperous town, which had been
much aided by the editors—some expressing the hope that all good
Petersburgers would come forward and subscribe and not let the
paper die. One such person, signing himself "A. B. C.," in a little
philosophical essay praising the value of printing and learning,
observed that since "you have established a press in the Town of
Petersburg, I cannot . . . [keep from] expressing the satisfaction
which my mind has derived from a knowledge of that circumstance." He continued: "Fellow-citizens of Petersburg and its
vicinity! When we reflect that many of us can remember the time
when the spot on which that town now stands was an uncultivated
wild, and the prosperous and happy alteration which civilization
and the hand of industry have already made, we have reason to
felicitate ourselves on the progress and pleasing aspect of our
country. In addition to our other privileges and proofs of progress
in the arts of refinement and humanity, a press has been established, which, we trust will be conducted with such prudence as
to be beneficial to many—injurious to none."[28]

As everywhere else there were in Petersburg wind and weather,
good health and bad, physicians, sickness and death. There was
hot weather and cold, though mildness was generally in the air.
Petersburg being on low river bottom land was protected by the
hills on both sides from the cold winter winds, and its altitude
was sufficiently high to relieve it from the humid heat of places
nearer the coast. But as a health hint the town paper told of a
young man, who being very hot drank too much cold water "and
in less than five minutes afterwards dropped never to rise again."[29]
Dry spells sometimes came and lasted a long time. In 1807 there
was an unusually drawn-out drought. During the late summer and
fall there was no rain for three months; the Savannah River was
no longer navigable even by flat boats, and many of the branches
and creeks had nearly run dry. According to the *Augusta Chronicle,* "the oldest inhabitant in Georgia, it is said, does not recollect
that there has been such a long spell of dry weather as at the
present season."[30]

And as has already been mentioned several times, the very opposite of dry weather could on rare occasions make its appearance
—an unforgettable instance being that time when the heavens

opened their flood gates and spilled out the "Yazoo Freshet" of
1796. Snows were rare in Petersburg, and when they came they
were only skiffs; but in February of 1803 a snow came in quantities long to be remembered. John Williams Walker writing to
his friend Larkin Newby in North Carolina described the land-
scape as very beautiful with the "trees, houses, shrubs, &c. all
clad in the whitest vestments of creation." The boys and girls were
soon outdoors snowballing one another. Walker's eye for beauty
both of women and of nature led him here to make a comparison
and to suggest that the women were envious of the snow: "Yet,
I think beautiful women, those who are possessed of a white skin
and lily white hands can not but regard the snow with an eye of
of envy, as it so clearly and evidently eclipses the clearest and
whitest complexion of their skin."[31]

Just as the Petersburg hills protected the town from the cold
winter winds but added some displeasure by deflecting the gentle
summer winds, they could not keep out cyclones when nature became boisterous. Shaler Hillyer, writing to a friend in Boston, in
early December, 1808 told how "we had a Violent Whirlwind in
Petersburg on last Tuesday week. By which I am considerable
looser [*sic*]. My kitchen, well house, Stable, Smoke-House, Corn-
House & *Little House* were litterally shivvered to pieces so that
I have stored the fragments without any chance of ever rebuilding
them with the same material. And every chimney on the lot were
blown down."[32]

Petersburg's location could hardly have made it a health resort,
although a resident who loved the place wrote in 1818 that "the
health of this place I have always considered quite as good as any
situation near a creek or in flat Lands,"[33] which may not have
been a very convincing comment. At least, a person who knew the
region asserted that it was "subject to billious fevers and chills."[34]
And consumption or tuberculosis, that scourge which respected no
person and few places, claimed its victims in Petersburg—Memorable Walker died of that disease in 1803, and death from the same
cause having claimed his brother John Williams Walker after he
had gone to Alabama. Long before his own time had come, but
soon after his brother had died, John Williams Walker had written to his North Carolina friend, "The messenger death hath
made rapid strides over this part of our country the present year,
His stern mandates have been issued and thousands have obeyed
the summons."[35]

The Petersburg commissioners realized as early as 1807 that

standing water, which soon became stagnant, was a breeder of disease, though medical science had not yet developed far enough to tell them why. This year they passed an ordinance making it an offense to let water stand in a cellar for more than three days, punishable by a fine of $10.00 for every day thereafter. As cellars were not generally open for passersby to look in and as complaint had to be made to the commissioners to put the law into force in specific cases, it seemed to be most honored by neglect. But as the summer approached in 1812 the commissioners published a notice stating that the rule would "be most rigidly enforced."[36]

Some of the wealthier families left town during the summer and fall months and made long journeys in their carriages to the mountain resorts. In July, 1807, Hillyer wrote his merchant supplier in the North, "Owing to . . . the low state of health of Mrs. Hillyer I shall not see you this season. By advice of our Doctor I am to take my family to the mountains to spend the fall months, and early in the spring I shall be in New York."[37] In his efforts to keep from having a break-down over the rough roads which he would have to travel, he said that he was giving his carriage a complete overhauling.[38]

Petersburg, of course, had its physicians, whose services were available in the nearby villages of Lisbon and Vienna, and also in the surrounding country. Among those earliest there was Dr. Benjamin Gantt, a native of Maryland, who died March 18, 1803. He had "for a number of years practiced medicine in the towns of Petersburg and Vienna" and the regions thereabout. "Few men, perhaps," wrote the author of his obituary, "were more remarkable for their equanimity, affable manners, and obliging disposition and behaviour." He knew for sometime of his approaching end and he passed on with fortitude and resignation. He was buried in Vienna, where many citizens from both towns attended his funeral.[39] Indeed, the most famous Petersburg physician, if not so for his medical skill at least for his later career in politics, was William Wyatt Bibb. While in the state legislature and in Congress, when available, his services were sought after and willingly given in and out of town. He had returned from the Medical College of the University of Pennsylvania in 1801 and announced that he was offering "his Medical Services to the Citizens of Petersburg and its vicinity," and that he was expecting to receive soon "a general supply of Fresh Drugs and Medicines . . . [and hoped] by his attention to gain a part of the public confidence."[40] Then, there was a Dr. Casey, who had moved from

Maryland this same year, and who announced that he would "practice Physic and Surgery, in Petersburg and its vicinity," and that he could be found "at his shop opposite Mr. Bruce's store."[41] Sometime later he informed the public that he had "just received a supply of fresh drugs, &c, and an assortment of Patent Medicines, which he will dispose of on the most moderate terms."[42] Another physician was Dr. Newby, before his removal to North Carolina about the end of the century.

And still another in these early years was Dr. Waddy Tate (other families spelled the name Tait). He announced in 1805 that he had received a supply of assorted medicines and had commenced "the practice of Physic." "Those who may have sufficient confidence in HIM," he continued, "to commit themselves to his care, may rely on the strictest attention being paid to facilitate their recovery." His office was at the home of Caleb Tate.[43] Dr. Asa Thompson was another well-known Petersburg physician before he moved to Alabama.

Some of the physicians who came later in Petersburg's history were Dr. William L. Revier and the well-known Dr. William N. Richardson. The latter was one of a group of physicians in Petersburg and Augusta who tried to bring some order into their professional charges by issuing a "Rate Bill" in 1818, and to improve their professional standards by insisting that those who practiced medicine should have diplomas or proper accreditation otherwise.[44]

In announcing their arrival or their continued service, physicians often seemed to place as much or more emphasis on the fact that they had new drugs and patent medicines to sell rather than on any medical skill otherwise; probably it was to be understood that their skill lay in diagnosing the disease and prescribing what drug would produce a cure.

Physician's errors based on their lack of knowledge and the workings of inevitable fate always accompanied their works. The town cemetery with its great flat marble slabs, tall monuments, and modest gravestones bore mute but eloquent evidence of Death's harvest in Petersburg. On a beautiful knoll in an otherwise flat surrounding of Petersburg the cemetery was begun, becomingly decorated with evergreen shrubs and cedar trees, and individual graves with prostrate ivy vines. One of the earliest graves was that of Joseph Denison from Connecticut, "late a Tutor in Yale College." He died in the home of Harry Caldwell in 1789. The old Reverend Jeremiah Walker preached a funeral sermon, "well adapted to the melancholy occasion." The news account added, "The death of this truly pious and learned young man, cannot be sufficiently lamented."[45]

The mortality of children and young adults, so common everywhere in these times, did not pass Petersburg by; but there were some of its inhabitants who lived to that "ripe old age," which was considered the crowning glory of those who were so fortunate as to reach it. One of the earliest graves whose marker resisted the ravages of a century and more was that of James Watkins, who had followed his children from Virginia to Petersburg, and had died there in 1798, age seventy. His wife Martha died at the age of sixty-nine. Another of that long-lived Watkins family, John Watkins, found his place in this "city of the dead" when in 1841 he had reached the age of seventy-five. His wife Susan had preceded him a dozen years, dying at the age of almost fifty-eight. Mary Watkins, the wife of Joseph, a principal merchant of Petersburg, died in 1805 at an age not revealed in her obituary: "Possessed of numerous amiable virtues, and elegant accomplishments —she lived highly respected and died deeply regretted by an extensive circle of respectable connexions and friends to whom she was endeared." That handy preacher and schoolteacher, the Reverend Moses Waddel delivered "a funeral discourse." Her "remains were attended by a large number of mourning friends to the burial ground, adjacent to this Town and there interred."[46]

Veterans of the Revolution were numerous in the early days of Petersburg, and although their fight for liberty was occasionally mentioned no special distinction was given them. Florence (Florance?) Driscol was an Irishman who had come to America in time to take part in the Revolution. He joined the patriots "and behaved with the intrepidity for the cause of liberty, which is peculiar to his country."[47] He died in 1806 at the age of sixty and joined some of his comrades in the Petersburg Graveyard. This hallowed spot became as cosmopolitan in its silent sleepers as was the town in its bustling citizens. Witness this inscription concerning one of them: "Sacred to the Memory of WILLIAM POPE, JUNIOR, a native of the State of Delaware. Obit 4th Dec. 1808— Etat 35 years, who in attempting to visit his friends in this state, after an absence of four years on the wilds of Louisanna, was overtaken by sickness on the way, which terminated in death two days after he had reached the home of his brother, Alexander Pope in Petersburg."[48]

Others who came from the northward to Petersburg to live and there to die were the Patons (Pattons) from Woodbridge, New

Jersey, George and Thomas—and Catherine, who became the first
of three wives in succession of Archibald Stokes. The Stokes
family also was from Woodbridge, with connections in the State
of New York. All were buried in the Petersburg Graveyard.

Providing pathetic representatives of those dying when children
or in early adulthood was the Captain Daniel Bird family. The
Captain married Sarah, a daughter of John Oliver (son of Dionysius), in 1807. Six years later she died at the age of twenty-one,
to be followed less than a year later by her two young daughters,
dying on succesive days. "They were both intered [*sic*] in the
Petersburg burial ground," as related in their obituary, "whither
the mortal part of their amiable mother was followed by her
weeping husband and other friends on the 4th of December last."[49]

Not all Petersburgers who remained steadfast to their town
were buried in the graveyard on the knoll. The instinct of people
to sleep the long sleep near the spot where they had slept in life,
so prevalent among those who lived on plantations, led some town
dwellers not to depart therefrom in death. Captain John R. Ragland, who was one of the first five commissioners designated by
the legislature in 1802 to rule Petersburg, died on the tenth of
July, 1803, at the age of thirty-four, "after a long and painful
illness." He was buried in his garden, where two of his children
had preceded him.[50]

7

Politics and Duels

POLITICS in Petersburg and the Broad River Valley played an important part in the development of the state's political parties. In Georgia's convention in 1788 to adopt the Federal Constitution the decision was unanimous; however this action did not mean that Georgia belonged to the Federalist Party, which came into power in the national government. Soon Federalist centralizing forces created much discontent in Georgia, with the result that the Federalist Party in the state never developed much strength.

Thomas Jefferson's philosophy of government appealed to Georgians, and his party was dominant in Georgia for many years. The state never cast its electoral vote for a Federalist. Hezekiah Niles, the Baltimore editor, said that Georgia politics was like the handle on a pitcher—all on one side, but this did not mean that there was an era of good feeling in state politics, for there soon grew bitter factionalism which Niles again commented on, saying that he did not understand what the parties in Georgia were fighting about but that they did bitterly fight.[1]

It was only an expression of human nature to be contentious, especially in any group of people as large as a state, where there must be a contest for the offices based on personalities if not on principles. In Georgia one of the earliest issues which was at the roots of a factionalism leading to the development of two parties was the sale of the state's western lands in 1795—known in history as the Yazoo Fraud. Land was the most evident thing to get possession of and trade on, therefore, land speculation became the order of the day. But when Georgia sold her birthright of western lands for a mess of pottage, there arose a great uproar throughout the state. All who had had a part in this sale along with their supporters were tarred with the brush of "Yazooists."

The opponents of this sale dubbed the Yazooists also as Federalists, a charge which had little relationship to any Federalist
principles.

Here was the chance to build up a party based on this strong
emotionalism which had spread over the state. James Jackson of
Revolutionary fame, now a Senator in Congress, resigned his
position and returned to Georgia to fight the Yazoo Fraud sale,
and having got elected to the legislature, he was in the forefront
in repealing the law selling this land. From now on to his death
in 1806 he capitalized on the Yazoo Fraud and built a strong
political party on that issue. Being from Savannah, he needed a
leader to bring the upstate area into his political setup, and there
was no more likely person for this position than William H.
Crawford, who lived near Lexington in the Upper Broad River
Valley. Soon there fell into this Jackson-Crawford party such
Petersburgers as William W. Bibb and Charles Tait. Bibb, though
a physician, was in politics as early as 1803, when he was one of six
Petersburgers running for the Georgia House of Representatives.
His election brought forth this comment from John W. Walker,
who would, himself, later be in the midst of politics, "He will
perhaps do as much honor to the County as any member we have
sent for many years."[2]

This combination of the coast and the upcountry made a hard-
and-fast political party, whose coastal branch after Jackson's death
was led by George M. Troup, another Savannahian, who had
been a protege of Jackson's. Crawford, soon gravitating to Washington to become a national leader, did not fail to keep a strong
hand on Georgia political leaders. Jackson had been born in England; Troup was born in that part of Georgia's western country
which later became the state of Alabama. However, the leadership
of the upcountry element in the party was almost entirely Virginians among the Broad River Valley settlers.

The Jackson-Crawford Party, which later became known as
the Troup Party, of course, had to have an opposition party. Here
came the group which had been called the Yazooists and Federalists—the land speculators. The head of this group was the Clarke
family, old Elijah and his son John, and Elijah, Jr., to some extent. Clarke, being a North Carolinian, carried with him most of
that group, many of whom had come to Georgia before the Revolution and also had settled in the Broad River Valley and had become dominant in Lincoln and Wilkes counties in the southern
part of the Valley. Leaders in this group were such Broad River

Valley men, in addition to the Clarkes, as John M. Dooly of Lincoln County and Peter Lawrence Van Allen of Wilkes, formerly of the State of New York. Also known for his Federalism was Shaler Hillyer of Petersburg, formerly of Connecticut, who was a merchant and a planter rather than a politician, of whom it was said that he was "notoriously known to be a bigoted Federalist, and one who is in no way friendly to the principles or conduct of the [Jefferson] Administration."³ Hillyer was, indeed, a true Federalist, but in little or no way related to the Clark Party, as it came to be called. (Elijah spelled his family name Clarke; his son John, for whom the party was named, dropped the e.)

The Clarkites were strongest in the upcountry and especially on the frontiers.⁴ The sharp cleavage between the Virginians and the North Carolinians in politics, and even in other walks of life, was well expressed by the ardent Virginian George R. Gilmer in commenting on Dooly: "Though identified with Wilkes county [really a resident of Lincoln County] as Judge Dooly was, my friends had little or no intercourse with him. The habits and opinions of the old Georgia settlers from North Carolina were so different from those of the Virginians who followed them, to whom I belonged, that there was scarcely any intercourse between them."⁵

Petersburg, its environs, and the rest of the Broad River Valley were long outstanding in providing leadership in both state and national politics and in both political factions. But especially prominent was this little kingdom in its representation in the Naitonal Capital. From 1800 on for the next quarter century with Benjamin Taliaferro leading off in the House of Representatives there followed David Meriwether, William W. Bibb, William Barnett, Wilson Lumpkin, Joel Abbott, Thomas W. Cobb, George R. Gilmer, and Wiley Thompson—all in the House of Representatives. This list is especially impressive when it is noted that at this time in Georgia Representatives were elected on a general state-wide ticket, with no candidates allotted to any part of the state. Beginning in 1807 in the Senate, there was William H. Crawford until 1813, when he resigned to go to France as the United States minister and later to become Secretary of War for a short time before his appointment as Secretary of the Treasury. Finally he was an unsuccessful candidate for the Presidency in 1824.

While in the Senate, Crawford had as his colleague Charles Tait of the Petersburg neighborhood, who had entered in 1809 and remained until 1819. It was unusual in any state for the two Senators to come from such a restricted region as the Broad River Valley, but in 1813 Bibb resigned from the House of Representatives to become a United States Senator and a colleague of Tait's until he resigned this position in 1816—thus here for three years there was the unheard of situation when both Senators came from the same neighborhood—Petersburg. Never before or afterwards was there such a converging of political leadership into such a small area, in Georgia or elsewhere. The combination of Crawford, Bibb, and Tait was yet to make itself felt as a dominant force in the rise of the State of Alabama.

Scientists know something about how weather conditions bring on hurricanes and cyclones, but probably less is known of conditions in the realm of the mind which create hurricanes of mental aberrations resulting in duels. Certainly having a high sense of what was considered honor and a quick response in the protection of it, and by taking undue umbrage at words and acts which could be construed into insults, led men to fight duels. The only good that it might seem could come from this custom was to make men more careful of their language toward their fellows; but political contests created heat spirals in the mind just as air-currents did in nature which led to hurricanes in both realms and to the destruction of life alike.

The year 1802 produced a rash of duels and challenges, though some of the challenges did not result in duels. David Brydie Mitchell, later governor of Georgia, fought and killed William Hunter in Savannah. Although the exact cause of the duel is obscure, it is easy to surmise that it was one of those birth pains in the rise of the two Georgia parties, for Mitchell was an ardent Jeffersonian and Hunter was a Federalist. Another duel which was fought in Burke County, about twenty-four miles from Louisville, then the state capital, grew directly out of the Yazoo sales. Robert Watkins, one of the compilers of the *Digest of the Laws of Georgia, 1755-1799,* in which the Yazoo law was included, and James Jackson, the fervid opponent of the law and the author of the Rescinding Law, fought it out, with Jackson wounded but not badly.[6]

But the hotbed of political turmoil was in the Broad River Valley, with Petersburg and its vicinity providing the fields of honor and some of the Petersburgers using their influence to ward off duels in the making. In all the personal quarrels leading to challenges and to duels themselves, political factionalism was the main cause. A minor affair led to a chain reaction in which four challenges passed resulting in one duel and a death.

The beginnings developed in a trial in the Wilkes County Superior Court on May 11, 1802. George Cook was being tried on the charges of some petty misappropriation of funds, with Charles Tait prosecuting him, and Peter Lawrence Van Allen (also spelled Van Alen, Van Alan, and Vanallen), then the Solicitor General of the Western Circuit, defending Cook. Tait and Van Allen were neighbors in the vicinity of Petersburg. While Tait had been Rector of Richmond Academy, in Augusta, Cook had been one of his students; later when Tait had been moody and despondent he had written little notes of a personal nature to Cook, who had kept them. Now in preparation for the trial, Cook had shown them to Van Allen, who with devastating sarcasm and wit read them before the court.[7]

Tait became so mortified over this impropriety and show of disrespect that he challenged Van Allen to a duel. The political undertone of all this was well shown when Tait selected William H. Crawford to deliver the challenge and in effect act as his second. Crawford first made the affair public by writing to the *Augusta Chronicle* two days after the insult (May 13) which was not published until the 29th, giving the news of the challenge. Crawford charged Van Allen with making "improper expressions" in the Cook trial and that Tait had called on Van Allen "for that satisfaction on which is due to the injured feelings of a man of honor." When Crawford delivered the challenge, Van Allen said that he would answer it in his own time as he thought proper. But that very evening Van Allen went to a friend in town (Washington, Wilkes County) to borrow a case of pistols and ammunition, remarking that he had received a challenge. The next morning Crawford met Van Allen in the company of John M. Dooly and asked for a definite answer. Dooly then handed Crawford an unsealed letter directed to Tait, which he refused to receive since it was addressed to Tait. When Dooly informed him that the letter was unsealed, Crawford read it and found that Van Allen "absolutely refused to make reparation for the injury he had done." A little later in the day Crawford asked Dooly if he was Van Allen's second. Dooly denied that he was. Crawford added that he was giving all of this information to the public that they might judge of the motives which restrained Van Allen "from making that reparation, which, if a Gentleman, he was bound to render."[8]

This letter gave only a bare outline of the developments. In a

letter to the *Augusta Chronicle,* dated June 2, Van Allen gave his
side of the argument. Van Allen said that after he had received
Tait's challenge, he "applied to John M. Dooly, Esq. to be my
second, to which he readily assented," and he asked Dooly for
his opinion whether "I ought to meet him [Tait]," and the next
morning Dooly "gave it as his decided opinion, that from Mr.
Tait's standing I ought not to meet him as a gentleman." Van
Allen said that he then wrote his reply to Tait's challenge, dated
May 12, and unsealed, which Dooly had handed to Crawford. In
this letter Van Allen said, "I think it a duty I owe the community
and my own feelings, to tell you that I consider you not in any-
wise on a footing with a gentleman. But I will assure you whenever you shall have wiped off that infamy, I shall give you a different answer. . . . I know the value of character and honor; but
in the meantime, I should deem it at present improper, in addition to the above reasons, to notice you, because the person whom
you have so basely injured intends to chastise you for your perfidy
towards him [Cook?], of which circumstance I am apprised, and
perhaps attending to your call might deprive him of that justice
which he so justly claims."

Van Allen having thus published his answer to Tait's challenge,
devoted the rest of his communication in the *Augusta Chronicle*
to an attack on Crawford and to direct attention to Tait, calling
him "an *apostate preacher* and *politician*" and charging him with
cowardice; for after that first day in court Tait had not been back
nor had he been seen on the streets of Washington. With bitter
sarcasm Van Allen said, "I was informed that he had taken a room
in col. Willis's loft during his stay in town [Willis being the
keeper of the town hotel]." And as for Crawford, if there was
anything in this communication which he disliked, "I am ready
and willing to give him any satisfaction he may require."[9]

Crawford had started this newspaper publicity, Van Allen had
kept the ball rolling, and now Dooly gave it a kick. In a letter
written the day before Van Allen's but published at the same time,
Dooly gave his version of the affair. He said that Van Allen had
asked him to associate himself with other gentlemen and give
their opinion of whether or not Van Allen was accountable to
Tait. Some of the gentlemen refused to give an opinion, but
without Dooly saying so here he must have told Van Allen as Van
Allen said that he did not consider Tait a gentleman. When this
same unsealed letter was seen by Tait, he read it and refused to
accept it since it should have been directed to Tait's second (an

extreme puncitilio that seemed to indicate that Tait was trying to squirm out of fighting the duel which his challenge had brought up). It began to look ludicrous because Crawford had at first objected to reading the letter because it was addressed to Tait, and now Tait was refusing to accept it because it was not addressed to Crawford. Later in the day, Crawford saw Van Allen and asked for his answer. Van Allen replied that he had no further answer to make. Later the same day Crawford met Dooly on the streets and seemed determined to involve Dooly in the quarrel by asking him if he considered himself Van Allen's friend and "from the great stress laid upon the word friend, and the manner in which it was expressed," seemed to want to know if Dooly approved Van Allen's conduct. Dooly said, "I replied I did not feel responsible for any of capt. Van Allen's conduct. . . . But from the language adopted by Mr. Crawford on this occasion, it would seem that he wished me to be in a situation that would attach accountability from me to him. If so, I can assure the gentleman, that the answer I made him was not produced from any desire to avoid his resentment, and that if he wishes to attach responsibility to my situation, or to make a personal difference of the affair between him and myself, he is at liberty to consider me the friend or second of Mr. Van Alen."[10]

It was now Tait's turn to fire a salvo; but he waited a little more than three weeks to do so. On June 24 he wrote Van Allen, beginning, "I shall not attempt to vie with you in the low arts of scurrility and abuse. I have too much respect for propriety, for the delicacy of the public ear, and for my own dignity, to call you an insidious rascal, a corrupt villian, or a dastardly calumniator, but perhaps I may, with all imaginable ease, prove you such. I shall not tell you how much you are condemned by all honest men, nor in what a delicate point of view you stand with the community in general, but perhaps of this you may be soon sensible, unless a sense of shame, that last hope of expiring virtue, may be entirely extinguished."

Tait denied the charge that he had ever been a preacher, "much less an *apostate* Preacher, in any religious society whatever," and he had never changed his politics or political principles. "My opinions of men may have changed," he cryptically added, "but my political principles remain unchanged." He insisted that his conduct toward Cook was correct: "I never doubted one moment of the fairness and propriety of my conduct toward this man." And the reason Tait did not appear in court on the last day was that

Van Allen had let out the news of the challenge, and "for that reason, and that alone, by the advice of my friends, I did not go out on that day; nor did I change my room, as you have meanly suggested." "Having thus attended to your base attempt to injure me," continued Tait, "and your mean subterfuge to hid your cowardice, I now inform you, that it was not on account of your private character, or general conduct, that I thought you entitled to my notice, for any insult you could give me. It was because you have, by accident, become the Solicitor-General (the *office* you have disgraced) and because, from a combination of circumstances, I though it proper to teach others, through you, that I was not to be injured with impunity." He then accused Van Allen of "corruption in office," citing two affidavits, and now "perhaps take my leave of you forever." And with this parting shot he closed his letter: "You have made your retreat into the Temple of Cowardice; it shall be to you an inviolable sanctuary."[11]

Van Allen was not to retreat into that "Temple of Cowardice." Finding the peace-loving Dooly as good as his word in not wanting to get mixed up in this fury of words or on the Field of Honor, Van Allen was forced to look for another friend or second. He found William B. Tankersly, and in a letter to Tait on July 9, Van Allen disproved Tait's charges of corruption in office. On the same day he gave instructions to Tankersly to arrange for a duel with Tait. "In your visit to Mr. Tait, you will have the goodness to consider your mission as circumscribed within the limits of my note; no equivocal or inky negotiation can be admitted at this crisis; to the point then—The adjustment of the *precise time, place, arms,* and *mode* of *warfare* constitute the objects of your mission, from which I have the fullest confidence you will not suffer yourself to be drawn either by artifice or cowardice—If he wants time give it to him." Tankersly went immediately that evening to Tait's home and delivered the challenge, but Tait declined to give a definite answer as to the time, place, or weapons, which in effect amounted to a refusal to fight. In challenging Tait a second time Van Allen accused Tait of being "disposed to shrink behind an inky curtain of falsehood, malevolence and detraction . . . and least [sic] some false alarm should again drive you to the garret, I shall immediately repair beyond the jurisdictional limits of the state." He stated that he with one friend would go down to Petersburg and cross over the Savannah River to Vienna. "The weapons and mode of warfare shall be of your own choosing—If you are a man of honor or spirit, prove it."

Van Allen with his "one friend" (not Tankersly, it seems) spent the night at Cook's residence, about a mile from Tait's, and the next morning set out early and reached Vienna between 8 and 9 o'clock. There they waited all day until 6 p.m. for Tait to come or to send word, but he did neither. Van Allen had tried in the negotiations (one-sided it seemed) to make it easy and convenient for Tait to fight "on either side of the river, or even in his own yard if he wished it." Van Allen ended up his account of his futile attempt to fight Tait by saying that when he had first refused to fight Tait it was not because of fear but because of Tait's despicable character as established in the court trial, for his "acting in a subordinate capacity, and his being under the influence of those who it is well known make use of you as a tool." Van Allen ended by saying, "Your character has been omitted in this publication for the want of room."[12]

While Tait was avoiding Van Allen, as it seems, or at least not making it easy for Van Allen to find him, he was soon to be relieved of any further annoyance from that quarter, for William H. Crawford now entered the fray. Van Allen had given Crawford ample opportunity, if not invitation, to send him a challenge; but Crawford had refrained, which fact led Van Allen to assume that Crawford would not fight. While the Van Allen-Tait affair was still brewing, Van Allen on seeing Crawford in the Willis Hotel, in Washington, insulted him and challenged him to a duel. Years later, when Crawford was actively in the race for the presidency of the United States, a Georgia supporter observed that Crawford had no quarrel with Van Allen, and Crawford "never gave him any cause of offense. In sending the challenge, Vanallen became a tool of a political party opposed to Mr. Crawford."[13]

On August 7, 1802 this item appeared in the *Augusta Chronicle*: "DIED. Last Monday [July 31], at the house of Col. Thomas Murray, in Lincoln county, PETER L. VAN ALEN, Esq. of a wound he received in fighting a duel with *William H. Crawford*, Esq. on Saturday last, in South-Carolina."[14] The duel took place a few miles below Petersburg, near old Fort Charlotte. Crawford had borrowed a pair of old pistols, which snapped twice while he was trying them out. In later life Crawford always looked on the affair stoically, speaking of it as casually as of any ordinary event in his life. He said that his first shot missed Van Allen, who had made an ugly face at him but on his second shot he pulled his hat brim down from viewing Van Allen's face.[15] Van Allen had the use only of his right eye, having lost his left one "in a drunken brawl" (according to a hostile critic), which loss did not inconvenience him in the duel.[16] Van Allen had come to Georgia from Kinderhook, New York, the home town of Martin Van Buren. This fact led to erroneous assumptions that he was a relative of Van Buren; but it seems that this relationship did exist— a brother of Van Allen's had married a cousin of Van Buren's.[17] Van Allen left a wife and a small daughter and an estate valued at $4,814. Among his possessions were books valued at $200, five horses and colts, a yoke of oxen, and eleven slaves.[18]

Before the tussle between Tait and Van Allen had terminated in the death of the latter, Tait had decided to follow up the part Dooly had played in the early stages of the Tait-Van Allen affair. Van Allen had informed Tait on June 2 that Dooly "gave it as his decided opinion, that from Mr. Tait's standing I ought not to meet him as a gentleman." As has already appeared, Dooly did not want to become involved in duelling in any relationship and soon found it possible to dissociate himself from being Van Allen's second, if, indeed, he had ever thought himself so. Dooly already becoming noted as a wit, according to a tradition had a little argument with Freeman Walker, a well-known lawyer. When it seemed that they might come to blows, several bystanders seized Dooly but only one caught hold of Walker, whereupon Dooly remarked, "Gentlemen, one of you will be sufficient to prevent me from doing mischief; the rest of you had better hold Major Walker."[19]

Tait now wanted to know whether Van Allen had correctly reported Dooly's opinion. Dooly had written a long letter in which he was quite equivocal,[20] and Tait was not satisfied with it. And so on July 26, Tait asked Dooly if he had said that he was not "on the footing of a gentleman." Dooly replied the next day that Tait already knew his opinion and that Tait's demand "will never extract it from me." Dooly rather bellicosely added, "But, sir, I can inform you that no call you can make will effect your object." The latter expression was cryptical, but it seemed to mean that Tait would be unable to maneuver him into a duel. Events were moving fast; on the same day Tait repeated his request for a plain statement: "As your answer seems predicated on the principle that I am already acquainted with the truth or falsehood of Mr. Van Alen's statement and as this is not the case, I trust you will be more explicit on this subject."

On July 28 Tait, who was at Lincoln Courthouse (Lincolnton), wrote Dooly this note: "I shall leave this place within an hour for Elbert, I expect your answer to my note of yesterday." Dooly sent a verbal reply that he had no other answer than what he had already given, and it is evident that he expected the matter to end there. The melancholy news then came two days later that Crawford had killed Van Allen in their duel. This must have been a blow to Dooly and could not have whetted an appetite for a duel in which he was to play a principal part. But Tait was not so affected; he was determined to have satisfaction. On August 4, waiting no longer for word from Dooly, Tait sent him a challenge: "I am reduced to the necessity of calling on you for that satisfaction due to a man of honor." Dr. Bibb, acting as Tait's second, delivered this note to Dooly. Two days later, Dooly, being in Petersburg, wrote Tait that he had called too late for an explanation: "Had you called on me before the challenge and acceptance, or before the death [referring to the Crawford-Van Allen duel], I should have made no difficulty in giving you a written or verbal explanation." But even so, Dooly told Tait that he would advise with Dooly's friends who knew his opinion "on the propriety of now giving it to you." With his spirits now somewhat mended, Dooly curtly added: "If, in the mean time, this should not be satisfactory, you are at liberty to take satisfaction whenever you please; I shall not avoid your company."[21] This expression looked more like an invitation to a fist-scuffle rather than to a duel. One of the witticisms attributed to Dooly was that when a judge threatened to whip him he remarked that there would be no honor in it, "as anybody could do it."[22]

More than three weeks passed without Tait hearing from Dooly, and if neither had tried to avoid the other, at least they had not met on the streets of Petersburg, Lincoln Courthouse, Elbert Courthouse, or on a country road, where Dooly, undoubtedly, would have favored getting whipped in a scuffle rather than killed in a duel. Also Dooly aided by his friends had been busied in seeking appointment to the Solicitor-Generalship of the Western Circuit left vacant by the death of Van Allen. But finally on September 1 Dooly wrote Tait that he had given up consulting with his friends and would have told Tait so "but for the conceived impropriety in an affair of honor, while in nomination for an appointment from the Executive [Governor Josiah Tattnall, Jr.]." Dooly had written this letter from Petersburg, and it would be hard to assume that he had not been conferring with Dr. Bibb, who disliked very much to see people fight duels although he was acting as Tait's friend. But here was something unheard of in the annals of the code duello: a person acting as the friend and second of both principals in a duel. On being asked by Tait to carry his challenge to Dooly, Dr. Bibb with sorrow agreed, mentioning his "high regard for Mr. Dooly, regretting the issue to which the affair was likely to come, and soliciting the privilege of settling it amicably if it could be done." Tait had agreed to this if it was done "compatible with his honor." On the same day of Dooly's answer to Tait (September 1) Dr. Bibb held a conference with Dooly and they agreed on the arrangements for the duel; but without a doubt Dr. Bibb was determined that the duel should never be fought, for he was planning to compromise the trouble.

Tait and Dooly were to go to Barksdale's Ferry, a few miles below Petersburg, and each attended by one friend, they should cross over the Savannah River into South Carolina there to agree where the duel was to be fought. The time was to be September 3, two days after Dooly's note to Tait. At the time agreed upon, Dooly and Tait with his friend Dr. Bibb appeared, but Dooly came alone—no doubt all arranged by Dr. Bibb as part of his compromise measures. In later reporting the affair Dr. Bibb said, "I enquired for his friend, he said he had none, but was perfectly willing that the business should be conducted by me, and mentioned that since making the arrangements, he had informed some of his friends that he had received a challenge, but that they expressed such dissatisfaction to the practice of duelling, as to induce him to avoid a direct application for fear of an arrest."

Now for the duel! When they appeared on the Field of Honor, Dr. Bibb made these propositions to Tait and Dooly: In answer to Dooly's contention that Tait had applied too late for what Dooly's opinion of Tait was, Tait would say that he would have called sooner had he not thought that Crawford would do so and that Tait did make the call as soon after the Crawford-Van Allen duel "as his indisposition would permit." Then Dr. Bibb turning to Dooly: "Whereupon you will say that you never gave the opinion stated by Mr. Van Alen [a statement at variance with the record]. This was agreed to, and the parties shook hands on terms of mutual friendship." This statement was signed by W. W. Bibb and J. M. Dooly, but strangely enough not by Tait.[23] Reporting on the whole affair, Dr. Bibb said that Dooly extended his hand, which Tait "cordially accepted." If the duel had actually been fought and Dooly had needed surgical attention, at Dooly's request Dr. Bibb had agreed to act in that capacity. Dr. Bibb said that he had "acted under the influence of extreme solicitude alone for the welfare of the two gentlemen."[24] Since Tait was the aggressor, it can easily be inferred that Dr. Bibb may not have informed him of all the "back-stage" arrangements that were being made until they were on the Field of Honor.

This affair became famous in the legal lore of the state for many years thereafter, including an element which was entirely absent in the negotiations relative to the challenge and the settlement— it was Tait's wooden leg. Had it not been for Dooly's reputation as a wit and his aversion to fighting, the wooden-leg embellishments would never have been added to the affair and it would have been entirely forgotten. Through some accident in earlier life Tait had suffered a crushed leg and had had to have it amputated. Thereafter he had worn a wooden leg. According to the traditional lore (and there were several versions), when Tait appeared on the battlefield and asked Dooly where his friend was, Dooly replied that he was out in the woods looking for a hollow log into which Dooly intended to place his leg so that he would be on an equal footing with Tait. In the passing of notes resulting in the challenge, according to tradition, Dooly had insisted that he would fight only on condition that Tait agree for Dooly to appear with one leg in a hollow log or bee gum. Tait took this proposition as an insult and threatened to publish him as a coward, to which Dooly replied that Tait might do so "in every gazette in the State, *for he would rather fill a dozen newspapers than one coffin!*"[25]

Political party maneuverings and assassinations were as much back of these challenges and duels as were wounded honors. Duels were convenient ways to get rid of political opponents and party leaders. The Clarkites were behind the Van Allen-Dooly group; and, of course, Tait had Crawford's support. Bibb was not a duellist and, as has appeared, he intervened wherever possible to prevent duels; however, he was a part of the Crawford political faction.

The cause which brought these two leaders into a clash was not long delayed. A vacancy had occurred in the judgeship of the Western Circuit in 1803, and Governor John Milledge had appointed John Griffin to serve until the legislature should meet to elect a judge, at which time Griffin became a candidate for the permanent position. Griffin and John Clark were brothers-in-law, since both had married daughters of Micajah Williamson. Natur-

ally John Clark worked hard for Griffin's election. Charles Tait
was the candidate of the Crawford faction, and Crawford worked
equally hard for Tait's election. Crawford asserted that Clark had
ridden the circuit with his brother-in-law Griffin and had urged
his election, having written to various county grand juries to
recommend Griffin's election. Clark stoutly denied these charges,
but Crawford was successful in securing the election of Tait. The
harsh language Clark and Crawford had been using against each
other was intensified after Tait's election; and now Clark charged
that Crawford had been boosted in his law practice by favors
Judge Tait had bestowed on him.

The result was a challenge which Crawford sent to Clark on
December 6, 1804. Clark accepted, and their seconds immediately
began to make the necessary arrangements for the duel. Captain
Howell Cobb, Clark's second, set the time for the ensuing January and the place "at Fort Charlotte, about one mile below Petersburg, on the South Carolina side of Savannah river." Colonel
Thomas Flournoy, Crawford's second, agreed to the time set,
though he observed that it was a little long after the challenge had
been accepted. But he added, "This however is not so objectionable as the place, as it is known to General Clark, that at or near
the place fixed on, Mr. Crawford lately met Peter L. Van Allen,
Esq. deceased." This reference to the Van Allen affair was a clever
way of unnerving Clark and bringing to his attention the dangers
he would be undergoing in meeting Crawford. Clark caught the
point: "I had no doubt, for the purpose of reminding me of the
hazard to which I was about to expose myself, as Mr. Van Allen,
one of the Solicitors General of Georgia, had, at no very *great*
distance from that spot, in a similar meeting been killed."

Here was the prospect of the state losing the services and leadership of Clark or Crawford or possibly both of them—a tragedy
which a number of gentlemen felt would be a calamity. They appealed to Governor Milledge to appoint a Court of Honor to
bring about a settlement of the dispute. Both men agreed to this
plan, and the Governor was glad to comply. A court of five men
was appointed, who declared that it was their "opinion that both
gentlemen are brave and intrepid, and so decree and award that
they acquit each other of any imputation to the contrary, and that
they relinquish their animosity, and take each other by the hand
as friends and fellow citizens."[26]

Clark was not well pleased with the decision, for he felt that it
was too favorable to Crawford. It was not long before these two

"Kilkenny cats" were at it again. Judge Tait was dragged into the affray by Clark, who charged that the Judge had conspired against him. Clark now called on the legislature to impeach and remove Judge Tait. Crawford played a decisive part in the legislature in decisively defeating the move. Failing in this attempt for vindication, Clark now on December 2, 1806 resorted to challenging Crawford to a duel. The time and the place were set—December 16, "at the High Shoals on the Apalachee on the Indian Territory." The arrangements were worked out in a series of twelve articles; however, a dispute arose over two of them, and that young Petersburger, Dr. Bibb ever ready to compromise duelling difficulties and save lives by truce as well as by his medical skill, was called in to arbitrate the meaning of the two points. He was to be assisted by a Dr. Abbott and a third of their choosing, if needed. With some hesitation Clark agreed but remarked that it was certain that Bibb was "entirely devoted to Mr. Crawford, and under his control." The duel took place with Crawford receiving a graze on his left wrist. He pronounced himself satisfied and refused to continue the fight; and when some months later Clark tried to push Crawford into continuing the duel "to a final issue," Crawford declined.[27]

The conscience of Georgia was rising up against duelling. There were many like Dr. Bibb who were hoping that a stop could be put to this brutal custom of settling personal quarrels and promoting political parties by killing one another. In 1800 the editor of the *Augusta Chronicle* lamented the fact that the civilized world adopted a method of settling disputes, "which violates the commands of God, and sits [sic] at naught the laws of man: And it seems somewhat singular that the crime of wilful murder should be almost universally punished with death, and that the deliberate determination to take away the life of a fellow mortal, carried into effect through the formal ceremony of a duel, should be passed over in silence, or at least winked at by tribunals of justice."[28]

The unfortunate death of Van Allen called forth from "Inimicus Supertitionis" a powerful blast against duelling. "Every instance of a victim to the present fashionable practice of duelling," he said, "is calculated to torture the feelings of humanity, and to cause the cool and contemplative mind to startle at the thought. One would suppose that a practice, taking its rise at a time when the deadly shade of superstition overshadowed the world, would have been long since scouted from a nation presuming to call itself enlightened."[29] In 1809 Georgia passed a law, declaring that anyone "in any way concerned" in a duel "or accessory thereto," upon conviction should be incapable "of holding any office of honor, trust or profit within this State."[30] But so deeply embedded with some people was the custom that for more than a half century thereafter a few duels were being fought.

Although Petersburgers were not promoters of duels they were thoroughly embued with a fighting spirit on proper occasions when the honor of their country was impugned or its dignity insulted. In 1807 when the British warship *Leopard* treacherously attacked the *Chesapeake,* the Petersburgers were ready to march at a moment's notice. In an emotional meeting presided over by old Revolutionary Benjamin Taliaferro, they became excited enough for war against Great Britain. In commenting on this outburst of patriotism the editor of the *Augusta Chronicle* said, "They feel as if they had been at the advanced posts."[31] And when only an embargo resulted there were outcrys in Petersburg against such pusillanimous measures, which did nothing more than stagnate business and trade.

Shaler Hillyer wrote to Oliver Whyte, his friend and former associate in Boston: "I do not think that any thing has happened since the days of '74 that excited so much unusual indignation as this unprecedented attack—the People are ripe for war. They begin to see and feel that national imbecility serves only to invite attack—and Produce National Degredation." He thought that Congress would have to meet soon in extra session, and added, "The Grave of our National honor is already prepared. We stand upon its brink ready to sink to the bottom or rise resplendent." Petersburgers, he said, stood for the most energetic measures.[32] It was doubly easy for Shaler to be indignant at Jeffersonian attempts to ignore insults to his country, for the Shaler family, back in Connecticut, were strong Federalists and had been almost disconsolate over Jefferson's election.

The embargoes and other ineffective measures adopted by the Jeffersonian Democrats finally led President James Madison in June, 1812 to recommend war against Great Britain. Before the end of July, there arrived in Augusta "a detachment of fine looking recruits, under the orders of Capt. [William H.] Jones, of Petersburg," who along with other recruits would soon be on their way to Savannah to defend the seacoast against any attack by the enemy.[33]

Shaler Hillyer put an end to his politics at the water's edge. Patriotism meant everything to him in time of war; politics, nothing. Although he was a New Englander, born and bred, he was greatly disappointed in the soft attitude the Northeast was taking toward the war—actually trading with the enemy and refusing to provide troops. Again he wrote Oliver Whyte in Boston in the summer of 1813: "Do tell me Oliver what your Bostonians mean—Are you Determined on a Division of the Union? Do you mean to bring about a separation of the states. I wish you to Let me know what you think of those things. You know how we are situated in this country & if we are Divided I think it more than Probable that I Shall find it my interest to move Northwardly provided the thing is Done peacably but of this there is no great Danger and I can assure you that I feel more from a Division among ourselves than from Europe combined. You know that I am an enemy to any sett of men who for a moment contemplate a Division. You also know that the Federal Party of your state is composed of a sett of men for whom I have for years contracted a Decided Partiality, but if their object is disunion I must Discard them forever. Let their exertions to federalize the union be confined within the poles of the constitution and they will have my hearty concurrence but if they step one foot beyond that Sacred Boundary, they certainly forfeit my confidence & meet the execration of all Good men."[34] As patriotic as Hillyer was, he still hoped for peace—the war was ruining his business. When the war was little more than a year old he wrote to his New York suppliers, asking "is there any hopes of a General Peace—or a peace with England?"[35]

8

Tobacco and Cotton

THE TOBACCO kingdom was much wider than song, story, and tradition have made it. From its beginning in Virginia it soon spread to Maryland, Kentucky, and North Carolina. Virginians and others were extending its boundaries even in Colonial times into South Carolina and Georgia, and with the flood of immigrants after the Revolution tobacco became the staple crop in this southern Appalachian country from the Fall Line even on up to the foothills.

Jedidiah Morse, known as the "Father of American Geography," wrote in 1789 that the settlers coming into Georgia were turning their attention to raising tobacco, "and the vast extent of land, with a richness of soil suited to the culture of the plant, renders it probable, that tobacco will shortly become the staple of this state."[1] A few years later a South Carolinian noted how the upcountry farmers were planting their small fields of tobacco but that there were no great plantations.

Tobacco seeds were sown in beds in the early spring, and within a week or two they were coming up. They were then transplanted in rows about three feet apart and thereafter they were given careful cultivation and attention. Weeds had to be removed, the soil piled up around the stalks, and worms and caterpillars, removed. The tops were pinched off those stalks not left for seed, thus making "the leaves longer and thicker," and also sprouting suckers were pinched off. When ready to harvest, the stalks were cut off near the ground and carried to the curing house, which was made of logs, with plenty of ventilation. The stalks were hung up on poles spaced far enough apart to keep the leaves from touching one another. Here they were left "to sweat and dry." The leaves were then stripped off "and classed according to their

respective goodness." The leaves were tied in small bundles, with
a leaf or two being used to bind them, and left to air further.
The bundles were firmly pressed into hogsheads or casks preparatory for inspection and the market.[2]

Since tobacco was marketed in casks or hogsheads and such
containers were not open to the view of purchasers, it would be
easy to sell inferior tobacco as first grade. Virginia had early provided that all tobacco for sale should be inspected and graded,
and this system was adopted by other colonies and states later.
Soon enough tobacco was being raised in Colonial Georgia to call
for inspection. A law which the General Assembly passed in 1770
recited that as the "encouragement of the Culture of Tobacco in
this Province will be attended with great Advantages to the back
Settlements . . . where the Lands are particularly adapted to the
same, . . . and . . . in Order to prevent any bad or unmerchantable
Tobacco being offered for Sale or exported," a system of inspection was, therefore, being set up. Three inspection centers were
established (Savannah, Sunbury, and Augusta), where inspectors
should break open all containers and "diligently View and Ex-
amine the same," and if they found the tobacco "free from Trash,
Sand and Dirt" they should stamp every container with the word
"Georgia" and the name of the inspector. Inspectors were paid
six pence for every hundred pounds which they inspected, and
if it should be found that the tobacco was improperly passed as
merchantable, the inspector should be fined fifteen shillings per
hundred pounds, and any person exporting uninspected tobacco
should be fined a like amount.[3]

With the coming of independence, the state began to look to
tobacco as its principal crop in the interior settlements. Since the
cultivation of tobacco was "very considerable and if properly attended to" would "become a most valuable article of exportation," the legislature in 1785 passed an act setting up an elaborate
system of tobacco inspection, using the Colonial statute as a basis.
It set up four inspection centers, continuing Savannah and
Augusta from Colonial times, changing Sunbury to Hardwick (at
the mouth of the Ogeechee River), and in recognition of the
settlements in the upcountry above Augusta, setting up inspection
at "the mouth of Broad River, at Moss's." This last location was,
of course, in the vicinity of Petersburg, which was not to get
started until the following year.

Warehouses were to be erected at these points where tobacco
was to be inspected and stored. The proprietors of warehouses

were to receive one shilling and two pence per hogshead of tobacco stored for a year, and for all tobacco stored for more than
a year the charge was six pence per month. These rates, which
were to be paid by the tobacco farmers, were supposed to make
it attractive financially for the proprietors who were authorized
by law to erect warehouses. Two inspectors were required to be
in attendance at every warehouse from September to June and
for every hogshead "or sack" inspected they should receive one
shilling and two pence. By this act inspectors were to be appointed
by the governor after proper recommendations, and they were
required to break open every container and "without favor or
partiallity" determine whether the tobacco was "good, sound, well
conditioned, merchantable, and clear of trash." If found so, it
should be repacked in hogsheads forty inches in length, thirty-one
inches across the head, and weighing 950 pounds. The casks
should then be marked "sweet scented" or "Oronoko," with various other details as to location, date, and so forth.

"Pickers," who sorted out the tobacco for the inspectors to grade
were to be paid for their services one tenth of the value of the
tobacco saved. All spoiled and rejected tobacco must be burned
in brick boxes some distance away from the warehouse. High
penalties were fixed for any infractions of the rules set up in this
act—as for instances, any inspector who should give a receipt for
tobacco not actually inspected should be judged guilty of a felony
and "shall suffer death . . . without benefit of clergy," and anyone
attempting to carry away any tobacco which had been refused
should for every hundredweight be fined three pounds.[4]

Tobacco was much on the minds as well as in the mouths and
pipes of Georgians and their legislators and led to frequent amen-
dations, clarifications, elaborations, and repetitions of the tobacco
laws. For the relief of small farmers who raised negligible
amounts of tobacco, not enough to fill a hogshead, which must
weigh at least 950 pounds, the legislature in 1787 allowed several
farmers to combine their tobacco to make up a full hogshead and
to be paid on its sale according to the amount they had contrib-
uted. To guarantee better protection of tobacco stored in warehouses because " great quantities of tobacco have been damaged
at some of the inspections for want of good and sufficient shelters,"
all warehouse owners were now held accountable for any damage
to tobacco in their keeping.[5]

In 1791 the legislature repeated the long act of 1785, with several changes. As an eloquent indication of how the raising of

tobacco was sweeping the central and upper part of the state, eleven new inspection centers were set up, including Lexington and Washington in the Upper Broad River Valley. A new warehouse was designated at Petersburg on the land of John Oliver. The judges of the Inferior Court were now to appoint the inspectors; the length of the hogshead was increased to forty-nine inches but the distance across the head was to remain at thirty-one inches; the inspectors were to receive two shillings per hogshead inspected instead of the one shilling and two pence in the former act; the hogsheads must now have six good strong hoops around each one; the brands must be labeled "Sweet scented, leaf," "Stemmed," and "Oronoke, leaf," and the word "Georgia," in letters one inch high must be marked on every container. The period when the warehouse must be open for the inspection of tobacco was changed from September to June; it now must be from October to August.[6]

The two main types of tobacco, Oronoko (Oronoke) and Sweet Scented, differed in that the former grew best on rich bottom land and had a longer and more pointed leaf, while the latter thrived best on sandy loam upland soil and was milder in flavor. Oronoko was generally marketed unstemmed.[7] By later legislation Georgia inspectors were required to grade tobacco into "first, second, third, and fourth qualities."[8] When competent inspectors could not be found in some counties containing warehouses, the law allowed the justices of the Inferior Courts in several counties to act together in selecting inspectors without regard to county lines.[9]

Raising tobacco was long in subsiding after other crops began to engage the attention of farmers and planters. As settlements extended farther up the Savannah River and inland, more tobacco inspection warehouses were authorized, in Athens as late as 1841 and on across the mountains to Rome in 1842.[10] From early times, South Carolina had inspection centers on its side of the Savannah River, having authorized in 1784 an inspection "at the most convenient place at or near the head of the navigation upon Savannah river."[11] In the course of time various changes were made in the charges for storage and in the fees of inspectors and pickers.[12]

The strategic location of Petersburg made it the most important inspection center above Augusta. The Inferior Court of Elbert County regularly appointed the inspectors for its warehouses and there was no dearth of applicants. At one time one of the inspectors was Joel Crawford, a brother of William H. Crawford.[13] There were several warehouses in Petersburg with the principal

ones in 1797 being John Oliver's and William Watkins'. Now
and then warehouses changed ownership, though the original
establishment of all warehouses had to be authorized by law. In
1801 John Oliver sold his warehouse to LeRoy Pope for $2,000;
the next year William Watkins sold his warehouse on Lot 35 to
John Oliver for $1,500; and in 1804 LeRoy Pope sold his ware-
house back to John Oliver for $1,450—there must have been some
other consideration in this last transfer, for Pope was too good a
businessman to loose money on a deal.[14]

It was of primary importance that tobacco be honestly and
correctly inspected and graded, for the economic well-being of
whole regions depended on the reputation of their tobacco. But
with all the minute regulations provided by law and punishments
even to the infliction of death for violations, still there were complaints about poor inspection from which Petersburg was not to
escape. In 1799 the Grand Jury of Elbert County presented a
grievance that the warehouses in Petersburg were not kept in
good order.[15] Complaints probably arose from the fact that at least
one of them was not "enclosed,"[16] a situation which allowed rain
to blow in and injure the tobacco. A person commenting on the
tobacco trade at this time charged that the inspection at Petersburg was not being properly done at one of the warehouses,
"which will be highly injurious to that growing and commercial
town." Some tobacco had been passed "that was not worth its
freight to market." He added that " 'tis well known that no part
of Georgia does, or can furnish better tobacco than some that
comes to the town of Petersburg." The bad inspection at one of
the warehouses would ruin the reputation of all.[17]

Because some bad Georgia tobacco was being received at
Charleston, there was a tendency there to discount all tobacco
from that state. Ferdinand Phinizy, now merchandizing in both
Augusta and Lexington, answered, "I cannot bear to hear every
man abused for those that perhaps have done wrong." But he
added that it was certain that some tobacco had "been very badly
inspected, and others damaged by water before it got to Charleston (particularly the Petersburg and other inspections in the
country)."[18] By 1816 when Georgians were less interested in raising tobacco but were still producing some for sale, it was generally
agreed that Georgia tobacco was much less desired and sold for
much less than Virginia tobacco. The reasons Georgians gave for
this situation were that the planters did not give as close attention
to curing and packing it and too many of the inspectors showed

a "total want of principle and competence." Some of the tobacco was so green that it could not withstand the voyage to Europe.[19]

Georgia's early market for its tobacco was in Europe. In 1792 the state exported 5,471 hogsheads.[20] Some of it went through Charleston, but probably most of it went down the river to Savannah. In 1789 there were agents for buyers of tobacco who said they were chartering a ship to take it to England. They would sell the tobacco there for a commission of 5%, buy goods there for a like commission, and insure it all for 5%—making 15% for the whole transaction.[21]

The common way of transporting tobacco to Petersburg and other river ports was by a method known as rolling. A rod should be inserted through the hogshead and fastened to wheels on each end—the wheels being high enough to lift the hogshead a foot or more off the ground—and with two shafts attached and a horse hitched between the tobacco was rolled to market. Ridge roads were used to avoid crossing streams by fords, and where bigger streams had to be crossed, ferries or bridges were used. The road from Washington, Wilkes County, to Augusta crossed Little River on a bridge, and the fee for rolling a tobacco hogshead across was twenty-five cents.[22] Of course, most of the tobacco which reached Petersburg went down the river on boats; the rate which merchants paid was $8.00 per hogshead.[23] Petersburg merchants generally sold their tobacco in Augusta or left it with factors there but some sent it on to Savannah.[24] However, Petersburg tobacco boats went no farther than Augusta.

There was a great clamor for tobacco by Augusta merchants. All were anxious to pay the "highest price," such as George Barnes & Co., who ran the advertisement in the city paper: "The highest price in Cash will be given by the subscriber for TOBACCO."[25] Tobacco came to be almost as much a medium of exchange as it had been in early Virginia; the Grand Jury of Elbert County presented it as a grievance that tobacco and tobacco warehouse receipts and notes were not made receivable for public taxes.[26] In 1792 a person sold a slave for 6,000 pounds of tobacco.[27]

Of course, tobacco in the leaf had to be manufactured for consumption, and that used in Georgia was to some extent manufactured in the state. Certainly for that brief period from 1786 onward to the establishment of the Federal Republic in 1789, manufactured tobacco from abroad was taxed $1.00 a pound on entering the state, according to Georgia's tariff law passed on February 13, 1786.[28] It should be inferred that some tobacco was manufactured in Petersburg, for Shaler Hillyer of the merchant firm of Hillyer & Holt wrote in 1808 that he had a quantity of "manufactured tobacco," which he would like to exchange for sugar, coffee, rum, and other merchandise. He had 2,000 to 2,500 pounds which he would like to exchange.[29]

Manufacturing tobacco at this time meant converting it into chewing tobacco, "Negro head and pig tail" being varieties;[30] "Rappee Snuff," manufactured in Augusta and for sale at 62½ cents per one-pound bottle, "highly approved of" by competent judges;[31] and smoking tobacco, which required little processing for most smokers beyond crushing the dried leaves in the palms of their hands—and some chewers probably did the same. Chewing tobacco was sold "by the keg" or in smaller amounts.[32]

The price of tobacco in the leaf varied widely. In 1801 "Petersburg Inspected Tobacco" was rated at 7 cents a pound in a court suit.[33] Its price on the market fluctuated from 3½ cents to 4½ cents until 1811 when it dropped to 2 and 2½ cents a pound.[34] This latter low price was brought on by the unsettled conditions leading up to the War of 1812, but it increased until the end of 1815, when it reached from 6 to 7 cents. The next year, influenced by the effects of peace, the price jumped to 14 cents; however, it then began to recede until in 1821 it was down to 3¼ to 4¼ cents.[35]

Long before this time, tobacco had ceased to be the principal crop among the farmers and planters of the Petersburg region and the Broad River Valley. Of course, the foremost reason was the rise of King Cotton, but even without the interference of His Majesty, there were factors and forces which were making hard sledding for tobacco. There was the progressive losing of the European market, both from competition abroad and from the increasing import duties. In Great Britain these duties rose almost to $1.00 a pound at certain times but were generally lower, however, still practically prohibitive. France also imposed high tariff rates. The commercial turmoil during the Napoleonic wars was a great hindrance to the exportation of tobacco. Almost as great a deterrent to the cultivation of tobacco as the rise of cotton was the effect tobacco had in exhaustion of the fertility of the soil.

Cotton was not unknown to Georgia from early Colonial times, for it had been scatteringly grown from Virginia to Florida even though it was nowhere a staple crop for money either on the domestic market or for export. It was sometimes grown in yards as an ornamental plant and its fibre was mixed with wool as a filler in homespun cloth. This was the variety of cotton which came to be known as short staple, upland, or green seed. In the late 1780's another variety came to Georgia from the Bahama Islands, which received the name of Sea Island from having been first grown on St. Simons and other coastal islands. It had long staples and black seeds. This cotton first entered world trade and was soon to flourish as raw material for the cotton mills of England, made possible about this time by the inventions of Richard Arkwright, James Hargreaves, Samuel Compton, and Edward Cartwright.

As Sea Island cotton could not be produced except on the islands and on the coast for about thirty miles inland, it was of no interest to Georgians of the interior, who were forced to depend largely on tobacco as their staple crop. Sea Island cotton became a principal crop on coastal plantations because the fibre, which did not cling very tenaciously to the seed, could be easily separated by small machines or gins (as all cotton machines soon came to be called), which could be run by the foot or hand; but these machines could not be used on upland cotton because the fibre of this variety was short and clung very closely to the seeds.

For a long time people with a mechanical turn of mind had been experimenting with contraptions that could separate the lint from this upland cotton seeds, which for the most part was being laboriously pulled apart by hand; as long as this method had to be used, cotton could never be of much value as a crop. In India, where some cotton was being produced, a small roller machine was used with some success. In 1788 it was reported that South Carolina planters were "making experiments in the culture of cotton," because "they have got *the gin,* or machine for cleaning it, by which the profit of raising it must be much increased."[36]

All of these early gins used a set or two sets of rollers. Joseph Eve of the Bahama Islands had a model going by 1790 consisting of rollers with teeth instead of grooves characteristic of other types.[37] However, it appeared to be more useful for Sea Island cotton than for the short staple of the uplands, though it was being advertised in Augusta. The common type of the small roller gins allowed some seeds to go through with the lint if the rollers were very far apart, but if they were put closer together they cracked some of the seeds which went through with the lint.

About the time when talk about gins was uppermost and excitement was welling up over the possibilities of cotton becoming the miracle crop for the South, Eli Whitney appeared on the scene in 1792, coming as the guest of Mrs. Nathanael Greene, the widow of the Revolutionary hero, at her Mulberry Grove plantation a few miles from Savannah. Whitney soon caught the contagion, and being long interested in mechanical devices, he developed resplendent visions of great wealth if he could make a gin which would avoid all the little defects in the various types floating around. He became so excited with the prospect that he became very secretive, not writing back to his father in Connecticut until April, 1793, even though he had come to Georgia the preceding year. When he did write, his letters were somewhat rambling; however, he made plain that he had been told by gentlemen at Mrs. Greene's home that if a machine could be invented which would clean cotton rapidly, "it would be a great thing both to the Country and to the inventor."[38] Finally when he told his father about his invention he added that he did not want any news of it to be given out to anyone "except my Brothers & Sisters," and they should keep it "a *profound secret.*"[39]

Although Whitney declared that he had never seen a gin until three months after he had completed his invention, it was similar to gins that he could hardly have escaped from seeing in that it had the customary rollers. The difference was that instead of making grooves in the rollers he inserted wire teeth in one roller and brushes in the other to pull the cotton loose from the teeth—and this was the basis on which he got his patent. The patent was applied for in November, 1793, and not until March of the next year had the application been passed on to the final grant. Patents ran for fourteen years.[40] Phineas Miller from Connecticut, originally having been engaged to tutor the Greene children, now the overseer of Mrs. Greene's Mulberry Grove plantation and later her second husband, became a partner of Whitney's in the gin patent and in promoting the gin business over the state and throughout the cotton-raising South.

Immediately after the patent had been granted, Miller inserted advertisements in the newspapers of the state that he would gin "in a manner equal to picking by hand, any quantity of the green seed cotton." For five pounds of cotton in the seed, he would give one pound "of clean cotton fitted for market." For the convenience and encouragement of cotton planters he was planning to erect gins widely over the state.[41] This announcement made plain that Miller and Whitney were not building gins for sale. Instead, they would retain possession of all gins and would exact tolls as was the custom of grist mills. The toll was too high to please most cotton planters, for five pounds of seed cotton would produce one and two-thirds pounds of clean cotton, showing that for every pound of clean cotton the planter received, the gin owners would receive two-thirds of a pound. This toll would amount to Miller and Whitney receiving two-fifths of the whole cotton crop of the South.

Whitney went to New Haven, Connecticut, to manufacture the gins, and Miller began scattering them over the state at strategic locations, to be run by horse power, ox power, water power, or even by hand power for the smaller ones. By 1796 there were thirty gins in various parts of the state.[42]

The coming of the cotton gin was the forerunner of storm clouds ahead for Petersburg. The town had been born of tobacco and was cradled in tobacco warehouses supplied by the rich lands of the Broad and Savannah river valleys. Now there was arising a contest between the cotton gin and the tobacco warehouse, and the gin was destined ultimately to win out. One of the first of the Miller and Whitney gins was located on the outskirts of Petersburg, to be run by water power, probably on Broad River. It had hardly been set going before a flood washed it away, but it was soon rebuilt. The gin could either be set on a flat in the stream itself or made to straddle a canal. In either case, the power was generated by a barrelled-shaped wheel about four feet in diameter and as long as fifteen feet (to turn more than one gin), lying horizontally flat on the water.[43]

A tradition that grew with age firmly held that Joseph Watkins, who resided on his plantation near Petersburg, was the first inventor of the cotton gin, and was using it on his plantation when he was visited by the frustrated Eli Whitney, who on seeing it went back to Savannah and soon developed his model which he patented. Watkins, according to the story, was urged to sue Whitney, but having no desire to engage in a controversy he never asserted his claim, or as Hugh N. Starnes, about a century later, said, "but as he was a planter of large means, who pursued the study and application of mechanics more for amusement than profit," he always refused to act. Pursuing the subject further, Starnes said, "Truth is inevitable and relentless; and, while the position of an iconiclast is unenviable, history must be preserved. All that is here stated regarding Joseph Watkins, can, upon demand, be thoroughly substantiated."[44]

This tradition raises the point that it is a singular fact that Miller and Whitney never sued Watkins for infringing their patent, for his gin was of the same mechanical devise as Whitney's. It might be suggested that Miller and Whitney did not sue because it would be brought out in a suit that Whitney had copied Watkins; or it could be said that the tradition was groundless and that Watkins never developed a gin at all. But the fact still remains and raises another question and some confusion, that "Robert Watkins of Petersburg" did publish in 1796 that he had invented a "Machine for cleaning cotton by Rollers," and that a model of it could be seen in Petersburg soon, and a little later at Augusta. Rights or shares were being allotted to every county in Georgia and South Carolina, six to each county at the price of $60 a share. The purpose in owning a share was to give the purchaser the right to make as many of these gins as he pleased, however, none could be moved out of the county. The gin was very easy to make, "the whole expense of making one is very trifling; [and] two or three persons are sufficient for attending one of any size." Anyone knowing the use of carpenter's tools could do the wood work, and any blacksmith could hammer out the iron needed. Watkins promised that three or four disinterested gentlemen would be allowed to see the machine in operation and if they certified that it did the work, then the purchasers of shares "must pay the money before they can see it."[45]

Two months later Watkins published a testimonial signed by four gentlemen, including William Longstreet of Augusta, stating that they had tried the machine and "we conceive its construction simple, and well calculated to clean Cotton with great expedition, without any injury to the staple." Furthermore Watkins' invention "appears to us new and ingenius, may become of great utility to the public, and well deserves their attention."[46] Watkins' publications lends proof to the tradition that there was a Watkins gin, but the time of the announcement of the invention was after the Whitney patent, and the name signed was "Robert Watkins of Petersburg," and not Joseph Watkins. However, there is this possible explanation, that since Robert Watkins and Joseph were brothers, Robert might have been acting for his brother, and in the light of the traditional modesty of Joseph, announced himself as the inventor.

Since Miller and Whitney were so grasping in their high toll rates, since it was so easy to make the simple Whitney gin either with or without the wire teeth attached to the rollers, since already gins were being made before Whitney's was patented, and since there was no likelihood that the Whitney gins would be in sufficient supply to take care of the large cotton crop anticipated for 1794, various people, besides Watkins, set to work making gins of their own, some to be patented and others not. Before the end of the year (1796) William Longstreet, who was one of those gentlemen who had so highly recommended Watkins' gin, now announced that he had invented a gin "whereby the art of ginning by rollers is reduced to the greatest simplicity," and it would be sold "upon the most liberal principles." He had a statement signed by eight gentlemen, certifying that they had "attended to the performance" of the gin, that it was an entirely new constructed cotton gin, and that in simplicity, expedition, and durability, "it excelles, in our opinion, any thing of the kind now extant." They stated further that the rollers could be "arranged to move with less friction, or in a less space."[47]

Watkins had announced that he was selling the right to make his gins. Longstreet proceeded on a different principle in that he would sell his gins for $150 apiece. Both of these methods differed from Whitney's, for he was not selling his gin at all, but later he offered to sell rights to the gin, and a few states bought them. Longstreet was liberal in his terms, giving eighteen months time in which to make payments. With an indirect reference to Whitney, he added that "this invention is not intended for private benefit only." He had applied for a patent and expected it to be granted within three or four months. This gin would clean from 80 to 100 pounds a day of green seed cotton and twice that of black seed.[48]

Now "Robert Watkins of Petersburg" put in a word. He charged that Longstreet, after having seen the Watkins gin and certified to its value, proceeded to copy it and claim it as his own. Watkins declared "that the invention is none of his, that he has no right to dispose of it," and he warned all people against dealing with Longstreet. Denying that his gin was a copy of Watkins' gin, Longstreet produced a statement from a John Catlett asserting that Longstreet had shown him a model at least four years ago constructed on the principles as the present one. Longstreet added that his gin and the Watkins gin were "as different from each other in their principles, as it is possible for two roller gins to be, except their both being worked by coggs."[49] Six months later Longstreet announced that he had improved his gin to where it would clean 120 pounds of cotton daily and the price would now be $120. He expected to scatter his gins all over Georgia and South Carolina in sufficient numbers to "clean a considerable part of the crop of cotton now growing."[50] He announced that one of his gins being fed by one person had cleaned in eight days 598 pounds of cotton.[51]

There seemed to be no end to the cotton-gin inventors who entered the lists with their machines. Hodgen Holmes of Augusta, who could not even write his name but was a clever mechanic, received a patent on a gin he had constructed in 1796, differing from Whitney's by having saw teeth instead of wire, and on this basis the patent was granted.[52] Then there was Edward Lyon, living near old Wrightsboro, who made and sold gins more like Holmes' than Whitney's.[53] In December, 1796, John Currie, living "near the Shoals of Ogeechee," announced that he had invented a gin with a variety of rollers which "may be made to feed themselves," and anyone wanting one of these gins must make payment "before the model is seen; and if the gins, on trial, are not superior to every other plan that has yet appeared, it shall be returned."[54]

Whitney had apparently set the style for secrecy among these gin inventors, until they could secure patents; and before the contest died down about a dozen patents, including Whitney's, had been secured.[55] It became a stock story that spies dressed in women's clothing were able to get permission to see models and that they thus stole information from one another. Tradition has this and various other forms of skulduggery and deceit being used: that Lyon dressed as a woman saw Whitney's model; that Whitney went to Petersburg and that Joseph Watkins in entertaining him as a gentleman should, showed him the Watkins gin; that shortly before Whitney's model came out, a person dressed as a woman was allowed to see Longstreet's gin; that Whitney's shop at Mulberry Grove plantation was broken into and his model copied.[56] Relative to the story of Whitney's shop being broken into, it was stated by D. A. Tompkins, a competent authority, that as to its truth "there is not a word in the voluminous records of evidence in the infringement suits, extending over 13 years."[57] And the women stories seem to be equally devoid of fact.

Whitney was in part, at least, the architect of his own misfortunes. His greedy attempt to rob the South of almost half of its cotton crop by exacting high tolls was at the bottom of his troubles, as also were the facts that gins were very simple to make and were being made about like the Whitney model, though less effective, before he came to Georgia, and that his gin was little different from them. Unfortunately Miller had got mixed up in the Yazoo land sales, which were held by most Georgians to have been fraudulent and were resented with high emotions; it was easy enough to transfer this hostility to the Whitney gin. Also the fact that Holmes had been granted a patent in 1796 was considered proof that Whitney's pretense to originality was a fraud, as outrageous and far-reaching as the Yazoo Fraud. Georgians did not like monopolies, and Whitney's monopoly was liked least of all, for it was an attempt to rob the planters of their fair chance now to become wealthy raising cotton.[58] Governor John Milledge in 1803 denounced the Whitney patent in his message to the legislature, and a joint committee of that body responded with a report in which it declared "that monopolies are at all times odious, particularly in free governments, and that some remedy ought to be applied to the wound which the cotton gin monopoly has given, and will otherwise continue to give, to the culture and cleaning of that precious and increasing staple."[59]

Miller and Whitney took to the courts for the protection of their patent, and in the course of a few years they had instituted more than sixty law suits,[60] most of which they lost on the grounds that their patent was not being infringed. For example, Archibald and Thomas Stokes, Petersburg merchants, announced that they had given a note to Miller and Whitney in 1800 "for the privilege of running the Saw-Gins; and as it appears that they were not the proper Patentees, we are determined not to pay said note."[61] Robert Watkins of Augusta was the council for the defense in many of these suits, and he often entered counter suits against Miller and Whitney for court costs, winning them in such amounts as $8.33, $9.88, $15.33, and $16.53.[62] In 1803, in the midst of his troubles, Whitney wrote: "I have a set of the most depraved villains to combat and I might as well go to hell in search of happiness as to apply to a Georgia Court for justice."[63] Whitney's patent ran out in 1808; and he could now look back on blasted hopes of making almost as much money ginning cotton as Southern planters would make in raising it. He wrote Robert Fulton, another inventor, who fared little better with his steamboat than Whitney had with his cotton gin, that his invention was new and was not made up of anything previously known.[64]

Even without the impetus which Whitney's gin gave to the production of cotton, planters were becoming excited over the prospects of growing this crop, and whether Whitney had come to Georgia or not, out of the various models floating around someone would soon have devised an efficient machine to clean cotton. Since little was known concerning the best methods of raising the crop, notices were appearing in the newspapers before it was generally known that Whitney was working on a gin, calling for the help of persons "acquainted with the culture of cotton."[65] And what little cotton there was on the market was eagerly sought after, being put on the basis of tobacco as a medium of exchange as early as 1793; for example, a bookseller announced that he would exchange books for cotton.[66] Articles were soon appearing in newspapers and almanacs on the best methods of planting and cultivating cotton. As the cotton kingdom began to extend beyond the river bottoms and hardwood lands calls were going out for persons who had "a proper knowledge of the cultivation of Cotton on good Pine Land."[67]

As early as 1788 people were begging for cotton seed and offering to give "a generous price,"[68] and this year it was announced that South Carolina planters were "making experiments in the culture of cotton."[69] By the early 1800's cotton bales or bags were crowding against hogsheads in tobacco warehouses, and the price of the staple was soon being listed with that of tobacco. In 1803 it was reported that the cotton crop was "most excellent and abundant."[70] A few years later a Federal judge had occasion to say, "Individuals who were depressed with poverty and sunk in idleness, have suddenly risen to wealth and responsibility. Our debts have been paid off. Our capitals have increased, and our lands trebled themselves in value."[71]

Cotton was soon on the mind of everyone, including the rhymester:

> De little bee suck de blossom,
> De big bee make de honey.
> De nigger make de cotton,
> And de white folks tote de money.[72]

Travelers passing through the upcountry were soon noting that the planters and farmers were turning away from tobacco to plant cotton. A writer three-quarters of a century later made this romanticised description of what was happening in those early times: "Broomsedge and sassafras disappeared from the fields, and the new grounds smoked in the early spring, and the cheery song of the laborer amidst the fallen forest trees rose on the frosty air, as acre after acre of virgin soil was reclaimed to whiten in season [the fields] with its tribute of snowy fleece."[73]

Just as Georgia had deemed it necessary to set up methods for the inspection of tobacco, it appeared equally necessary to inspect cotton. The reputation of the state for its merchantable products should not be allowed to suffer. The production of cotton had made such a deep impression on the lawmakers by 1796 that they set up a system of cotton inspection whereby all cotton before it should be passed to the market should be "well ginned and cleaned, so as to be made good merchantable cotton." The inspector had to stamp his name on the bale after the words, "Inspected by me," and it must also bear the planter's name and the word "Georgia." The inspector's fee was one-eighth of a dollar for every 100 pounds to be paid by the owner of the cotton. After inspection the cotton should be stored in a safe dry place until the owner called for it and paid 10 cents per 100 pounds warehouse rent.[74]

This act must have produced a great outcry as an unneeded interference with the marketing of cotton because the bales could be easily inspected by any buyer. Early the next year the legislature repealed the law, stating that it had been "found in its operation not competent to the objects proposed, by no means beneficial to the interest of the State, and an unnecessary burthen on the planters of that article."[75] The custom soon grew up among merchants who bought cotton from the planters to deduct two pounds from every bale and to exact further charges for weighing it. Declaring that this custom operated "injuriously to the people of the State," the legislature in 1806 forbade any deductions from any "bale, bag or package of cotton" and any charges of more than six and a quarter cents for weighing it.[76]

The legislature also found it necessary to regulate the operations of cotton gins in relation to their disposal of the seeds. As no use in the early times had been found for cotton seed except for planting, they were thrown out in heaps to rot or be eaten by livestock. In either case they were considered a nuisance, and to abate it the legislature in 1803 required all gins in any town or village or nearby to "enclose the seeds in such a manner" as to prevent stock, "especially hogs from eating them," and they should be kept dry or removed out into the country "to prevent all the unwelcomed effects resulting from the stench and vapours arising from the seed, in their putrid state, if suffered to remain in heaps," and when they were removed out into the country still they should be enclosed to prevent stock from feeding on them.[77]

The repeal of the cotton inspection law led to bad results. Small rocks and gravels seemed to have been purposely placed in cotton bales by some planters. Now and then seeds, pieces of the hulls, enclosing bowls, and fragments of stems got accidently mixed in. Governor James Jackson called the attention of the legislature to "the deceptions in the package" of cotton, and asked the legislature to do something about it, for the reputation of Georgia cotton was suffering and the price was going down. However, that was not all, for "such infamous practices tend to stamp on our character as a people a total want of honor, justice, and morality."[78] The legislature did nothing. Certain evil practices continued and the next year an Augusta newspaper editor reported that twenty bales had been received in that town, unmerchantable because they had quantities of seeds mixed in. This "fraud ought not to pass unpunished," he argued.[79] The situation which was now left to the consciences of the planters, assisted by inspection by cotton buyers, gradually righted itself. And even the rhymester came in to add this bit of help:

> Your Corn secur'd, your Cotton GIN with care,
> Make tight their roofs, and where they need it, mend,
> Your Corn and Cotton houses, now attend,
> The price will compensate for packing fair.[80]

In the progress of time, cotton was packed and marketed in varying shapes, sizes, and weights, and referred to as bales, bags, and packages. In the infancy of the crop, before the appearance of gins, it was packed in bags of about 150 pounds each.[81] Miller and Whitney packed their cotton in bales weighing from 260 to 320 pounds each.[82] Some of the cotton came down Broad River to Petersburg in round bales about two feet in diameter and seven feet long, one lot of seven bales weighing from 274 to 340 pounds each.[83]

Petersburg had started out as a tobacco inspection town and its first business prosperity had come from the tobacco trade, but now that cotton was a booming crop, in sharp competition with tobacco and destined ultimately to displace it in Petersburg, in the Broad River Valley, and in all the rest of upper Georgia, it was to the interest of the town to get into the cotton trade as far and as quickly as possible. For the year the inspection act of 1796 was in force, Petersburg became an inspection center for the upper part of the state; and John Oliver was appointed inspector, no doubt carrying out his brief career as inspector in his tobacco warehouse. The price of cotton varied as widely as that of tobacco, but it was always considerably higher. By 1800 Petersburg merchants were trading for as much cotton as might be brought down the Broad and Savannah rivers and from the intervening hinterland by wagons. Petersburg merchants were paying from 25 to 28 cents per pound at this time, but the price dropped for the next few years and until Congress passed the Embargo Act in December 1807, cotton was selling on the Petersburg and Augusta markets from 15 to 18 cents per pound. In December 1806 a cargo of seventeen bales from Petersburg sold on the Savannah market for 19½ cents. Even with the gins at work, cotton could be sold in the seed on the Petersburg market. LeRoy Pope agreed in 1803 to pay Memorable Walker 2½ cents a pound for all the cotton he might bring in "as fast as he could get it out of his field in good Merchantable order to be delivered in the Town of Petersburg."[84]

Throughout the period of the Embargo (1808 to early 1809) the price in Augusta was from 8 to 10 cents; and the planters in and around Petersburg were allowed a fixed price for cotton stored there, with any increase when the Embargo was repealed. Shaler Hillyer, who had now moved out of Petersburg to the plantation of his father-in-law, John Freeman, shipped his cotton to New York and Boston (coastwise traffic being permitted under the Embargo regulations) on a basis of a fixed price of 16 cents per pound with any increase to be added when trade loosened up. But many planters preferred to keep their cotton on their plantations while awaiting a rise in price.[85]

The repeal of the Embargo took place in early 1809 to be superceded by the Non-Intercourse Act, which cut off trade with England and France but left it open to the rest of the world and would restore trade to either England or France, depending on which nation removed its objectionable restrictions on American trade. In this period of uncertainty, planters expected the price to go up, and the rumor was soon out in Petersburg "that cotton has been sold in Augusta for *15 cents*."[86] The belief was that the difficulties would soon be settled with England, but Hillyer soon came to the conclusion that "the state of the world" was such that the price of cotton might never reach what it formerly was, for with the repeal of the Embargo the price had not risen.[87] In fact, during the ensuing few years leading up to the war with England, which was declared in June of 1812, the price dropped to 6 cents. Hillyer was able to get 6½ cents a pound on eight bales which he sold in December of 1812.

The war was not going to last always, and to those with a speculative mind this period opened up visions of immense wealth to be made by buying up cotton at bottom prices and holding it until peacetimes. Hillyer saw this possibility and he tried to borrow from $7,000 to $10,000, stating that he had "an open contract for cotton which I can make very profitable if I can obtain money."[88] He could buy cotton in the Petersburg region for 6 cents and send it to Oliver Whyte in Boston.

By the fall of 1814 cotton had jumped to 16 cents in anticipation of the war ending soon. The Senate ratified the Treaty of Peace in February 1815, and the price of cotton began advancing. By summer it was 19 cents, and the "price of Cotton is still advancing in our market," reported the *Augusta Chronicle*.[89] With the new crop coming in during the fall, the price jumped to 21½ in Augusta and went up to 26 cents in New York.[90] In October it reached 26 cents in Petersburg and Augusta, and continued at that rate until the spring of 1816 when it was quoted at 30 cents. Hillyer, who had not been able to borrow the money to carry out his wartime speculation, which would have cleared him of all his debts, still had the foresight to plant a large cotton crop. In July (1816) he wrote to his friend and factor in Boston, Oliver Whyte, that "great indeed is the Cotton fever in this Country, and I should not be at all surprised if corn was to rise to one dollar a bushel."[91] The next year he planted 85 acres in cotton.

Cotton prices continued high for the next several years, reaching even 31¼ cents in the fall of 1817; but with panicky conditions developing in 1819, the price dropped to 16 cents, and by the spring of 1821 it was down to 11 cents. With the cotton depression on, Hillyer wrote that the "great fall of Cotton in Georgia has had the effect of depressing the price of every article offered for sale, among other things Negroes have fallen at least 25%."[92]

Georgia manufactured little of the cotton it raised; some of it went to the North to be manufactured, but a great amount was exported. In 1820 the whole South exported 127,860,000 pounds.[93] According to a tradition, which is wholly erroneous, the first cotton mill in the South was erected in Petersburg.[94] It is very unlikely that there was ever a cotton mill there, but a few miles above Petersburg, there was in operation a cotton factory on Broad River in the late 1840's which ran 5,000 spindles and another on Beaverdam Creek, which flowed into the Savannah not far above Petersburg.[95]

Cotton and tobacco were the so-called "money crops," but, of course, agriculture was not limited to them alone. There was, at least, one other "money crop," which was early tried in the Petersburg-Augusta region, and raised with some little success for a short time—indigo. In 1787 Thomas Cole announced that he had indigo seed for sale, saved from last year's crop;[96] and those planters who knew how to grow it now and then published information on the subject.[97] Many of the planters around Petersburg raised flax in small quantities, which could be spun into "beautiful sewing thread"[98] and also be made into ropes and bed cords, some of which were manufactured in Petersburg. There was, of course, small grain raised for food and feed—wheat, rye, buckwheat, corn, and barley, for which there was a market in Petersburg and in Augusta[99] (anything which Petersburg traders bought could be easily floated down the Savannah to the Augusta market). And practically everyone had a kitchen garden to produce everything expected from such a place, and often extensive enough to provide Irish potatoes and especially the delectable sweet potatoes. There were fewer fruit orchards than gardens; however, anyone growing more peaches and horse apples than needed for home use could find a ready market in Petersburg and in the down-river markets at Augusta.[100]

Next to cotton and tobacco in importance was corn, a crop which was basic for home food and feed for livestock, and for which there was always a local market for surpluses. The price of corn was reflected little in international trade, for little or none was exported, but in the general economy corn had to take its place. When the price of cotton was low in 1809 and selling for 10 cents per pound, the price of corn sank with it to 37½ cents per bushel. Even though in 1811 it was up to 75 cents, throughout the war period (1812-1815) the price was from 50 to 56 cents. In June of 1815 corn took a spurt to $1.00 a bushel, which continued for only a short time, for during the next few years it was 50 to 75 cents per bushel. The panicky years from 1819 to 1821 pushed the price down to 37½ cents; however, in December of the latter year corn was bringing $1.00 a bushel.[101]

Even with the amount of corn being raised, the cotton surge at times invaded the lands which should have been given over to corn. The cry was raised which was to be heard for the next century, that more food and feed crops should be raised, and especially corn. In 1807 an agricultural reformer recommended to planters "to raise more corn & less cotton; for he thinks that a man well cloathed, but with an empty belly does not look or feel so well."[102]

Some of the principal Petersburgers owned plantations, and though considering themselves townsmen and spending much time in Petersburg on business interests, they lived for the most part on their plantations. A plantation without slaves was hardly to be thought of and certainly not to be successfully run. And no Petersburger of any standing could get along without a few household servants and several slaves to help in any business he might be conducting. Hillyer owned a dozen or more on his plantation up Broad River, and many years later, in 1860, when Petersburg had become more of a cotton field than a town, Drury B. Cade owned 59 slaves.

With the need Petersburgers had for slaves as household servants and with the demand of planters for slaves to work in their cotton and tobacco fields, slave-trading became a part of Petersburg's business activities. In 1797 the firm of Pope and Walker, merchants, bought twelve slaves for $3,200, consisting of eight girls, Betty, Sally, Hager, Vina, Amy, Silvey, Tenny, and Lilla; and four boys, Mingo, Phill, Toby, and Sander.[103] Probably these were sold in town as household servants. In 1805 John Manning advertised in the town newspaper: "AFRICANS. Likely young Africans for sale, either for Cash, Tobacco, Cotton, or on credit for approved notes."[104] The newspaper editors had a slave for sale, who had been raised near Louisville, now being offered for sale "not in consequence of any failing more than is incident to his species. None but a person who, it may be presumed, would treat him as a rational being, need make application."[105] Thomas Bibb, brother of William Wyatt Bibb and destined to be the second governor of Alabama, announced at this time that he had "a few Likely Africans for Sale," among them being a boy about thirteen years old, who had been in this country about a year but "speaks pretty good English, and of an excellent disposition." Bibb offered to take in payment "Cash, Cotton or Approved Notes."[106]

Hillyer had a prize slave named Bob, whom he was thinking of selling but he hardly knew how to proceed. He had been offered $1,000 for Bob by a person "who would have made him a good master," but Bob vetoed the deal. Hillyer said that he "would not sell him to a man that I think would treat him ill," and he had come to the conclusion that Bob was satisfied where he was and would not agree to being sold. Hillyer said that he had hired out Bob at times for $12.00 a month.[107]

All slaves in and around Petersburg were not as satisfied with their masters or their stations in life as was Bob. LeRoy Pope advertised in several newspapers that his slave Emanuel, who had been bought in Alexandria, Virginia, by Farish Carter, had run away, and he thought might be trying to get back to Virginia. He offered $20.00 to anyone who would bring him back to Petersburg.[108] John Ousley wanted information from anyone who might have seen his slave, "a negro wench named Henny, about 5 feet high, a large lively eye, a plump round face and a small foot." She sometimes called herself Fanny. Ousley thought that she might be hiding around LeRoy Pope's plantation.[109] Another runaway got as far as Augusta, where she was taken up and lodged in the Richmond County jail. She said that her name was Juno. She was "about 24 or 25 years old, and is pregnant, says she belongs to Major Oliver, of Petersburg."[110] In addition to slaves, there were a few apprentices in Petersburg, who being no more satisfied with their lot than were some of the slaves with theirs, ran away and were pursued by the offers of rewards ranging from "six and a quarter cents" to $10.00, the latter reward being offered to anyone bringing back Henry McBride, "somewhat cross eyed."[111]

There was, at least, one free Negro in Petersburg around 1800, Thomas Evans, who was "up and about" sufficiently to engage in a few real estate transactions. In 1800 he bought from Memorable Walker a twelfth of Lot 79 for $30.00. Three years later he sold one sixth of Lot 20 for $120.[112] Infrequently some Petersburger recorded in his will freedom for a slave or two.[113]

9

Merchandising and Other Businesses

PETERSBURG started out as a collecting, inspecting, and shipping center for tobacco. As it grew and prospered it never got far away from a trading town, whether it be in tobacco, cotton, the minor products of the fields and forests, or in supplying the townsmen and the countrymen of the outlying regions on both sides of the Savannah and Broad rivers with all the importations their hearts desired and their purses allowed. Evidently the center and almost the whole circumference of business activities were collection and distribution. Merchants flocked there from as far away as New York and Boston to set up businesses in which their activities extended from selling a villager a paper of pins to sending a boatload of tobacco to Augusta or Savannah or a shipload of cotton to Boston. These businessmen ran what a century later would be called department stores and they acted as financial agents and factors for the planters of tobacco and cotton even as they themselves had their factors in Augusta, Savannah, New York, and Boston.

There were merchants both great and small, varying in number but always in a good supply. There was much competition among them, some long-lived and some short, consolidations and dissolutions, and associations with other firms in Augusta and Charleston. Among the Petersburg merchants operating before 1800 were Thomas C. Russell & Nathaniel Rossiter, Roundtree & Taylor, Archibald & Thomas Stokes, James Holliday & Company, Matthew Hill & John Jackson, Littlebury & Whitfield Wilson (firm dissolved in 1800), a Gantt firm by a gentleman from Maryland, and Oliver Whyte from Boston.[1]

Additionally, LeRoy Pope, who could not resist any business opportunity that came along, was early engaged in merchandizing.

Furthermore, as early as 1798 he and Memorable Walker (both already established as merchants) bought of Joseph Groves (Graves?) a Petersburg lot for $1,500.[2] This transaction indicated that they were engaging also in the real estate business (being "realtors," according to a term later coined), supported by the additional fact that the next year they sold a lot to William J. Hobby, an Augusta merchant out of Connecticut and soon to become a newspaper editor. They were also buying a lot from the merchant firm of Archibald & Thomas Stokes.[3] This same year Walker dissolved his connection with Pope and formed the firm of Memorable & James S. Walker. Pope now entered the firm of James Holliday (sometimes spelled Halliday) & Company. This firm was dissolved in 1800, and Pope announced the same year that he had "once more embarked in the Mercantile Business with Alexander & John M'Clure of Charleston under the firm name of LeRoy Pope and Co."[4] This firm lasted only three years;[5] however, Pope was still merchandizing in 1806, and probably he had such connections as long as he remained in Petersburg.

The Stokes brothers, Archibald and Thomas, besides the main business of their mercantile firm were, like LeRoy Pope, dealing in Petersburg lots. In 1801 Archibald sold to Thomas Lot 82 for $1,000,[6] for now their firm was dissolved, and Archibald announced that he would continue the business of the original firm and that he had "a handsome assortment of Goods."[7] Thomas now doing business alone seemed to have had more than the usual troubles which beset merchants, though as was the custom he announced on occasion the arrival of new goods, listing them in great detail, especially such appetizers as a hogshead of Jamaica rum, a barrel each of sherry wine and Philadelphia ale, and a few dozen bottles of London porter. His main trouble was collecting the debts owed by his indulged customers.[8] With his patience wearing thin he warned in August, 1805, that "*that* which is due him he must and will have. Those who come forward and pay their accounts, before the first day of December next, like honest *Men*, will receive his thanks; but those who neglects this *little hint,* may certainly expect another, which will be attended with some expense to them."[9]

Besides finding it difficult to collect his debts he was unfortunate otherwise. While he was visiting in Augusta in 1808 a thief made away with some of his belongings, and in an attempt to recover them he inserted this notice in the *Augusta Chronicle*: "39 Lashes Reward. Stolen from off my horse, on Saturday Evening the 13th inst. at Mess'rs Harrison and Hamilton's Rack, a pair of Saddle Bags, Containing one Coat and two pair of Pantaloons somewhat worn, three Cravats, two Shirts, one Pair Socks, and one fancy Vest, one white do. with sundry other Cloathing not recollected. Any Damned Rascal that stole them, shall receive the above Reward, or Twenty Dollars to any Gentleman giving information thereof, to be paid on sight, by Thomas Stokes."[10] The same paper which published this announcement published also in late May five years later this item: "Departed this life on the 21st inst. Mr. Thomas Stokes, of Petersburg, Georgia.—He was unfortunate, but lived and died an honest man."[11]

Archibald was more fortunate both in business and longevity. He continued as a merchant, passing through several co-partnerships, such as Stokes, [Nicholas] Pope & Company, Stokes & Sayre, and Stokes & Taylor, continuing on down into the 1820's and being the merchant of longest standing in the history of Petersburg.

Two other merchant brothers, associated in one way or another with Petersburg, were William and Beverly Allen. It seems that they never ran a mercantile establishment in Petersburg, but William began dealing in town lots as early as 1794 and continued for a half dozen years and more;[12] earlier the two brothers were merchants on Beaverdam Creek, a few miles in the interior, where they were able to catch country trade before it could reach Petersburg.

Before joining his brother in the mercantile trade, Beverly Allen had had a varied and somewhat notorious career. Being six feet tall, of a commanding appearance, with a melodious voice and an ardent temperament, he was the perfect type to carry religion to the frontiers. He first came to notice in Chatham County, North Carolina, as a Methodist preacher, where Bishop Francis Asbury noted in 1780 that he met "brother Allen—a promising young man, but a little of a Dissenter." Allen accompanied the Bishop on some of his journeys,[13] and in 1783 he settled in Salisbury, North Carolina, long enough to establish Methodism there. Two years later he was appointed to introduce Methodism into Georgia, but on entering South Carolina he began preaching there and did not continue into Georgia, though it is probable that he did some preaching there later. He became a great favorite with the masses, but his powerful influence got him into some sort of trouble, which led Bishop Asbury to state in 1786, "I was grieved at Beverly Allen's Conduct,"[14] and in 1791 the Edisto Circuit in South Carolina expelled him from the ministry for a "flagrant crime."[15]

Now out of the ministry, the following year he joined his brother as a merchant, and the two were soon supplying their store with merchandize from Charleston. In early January, 1794, they went to Augusta for additional supplies, but instead of paying up their debts to former creditors they began dealing with others, whereupon the former creditors sued out a writ for the arrest of the Allens. Robert Forsyth, the Federal marshal and the father of the John Forsyth of future greatness, in attempting to serve the writ was shot and killed by Beverly.[16] When news of this crime reached Bishop Asbury he was greatly shocked: "Poor Beverly Allen, he has been going from bad to worse these seven or eight years—speaking against me to preachers and people and writing to Mr. [John] Wesley and Doctor [Thomas] Coke, and being thereby the source of most of the mischief that has followed . . . is now in jail for shooting Major Forsyth through the head." For nine years, Asbury continued, he had been doubtful of Allen's integrity, but "I pity, I pray for him—that, if his life be given up to justice, his soul may yet be saved."[17]

Allen was placed in the Augusta jail, but soon broke out. In announcing the news, the *Augusta Chronicle* noted that he was "the once so celebrated Methodist preacher, well known in that character in many parts of the Union—nearly six feet high, smooth speech under a thin cloak of sanctity, and about 40 years of age. The apprehension of this man will be liberally rewarded by the respected inhabitants of Augusta, besides the approving voice of every good character in America."[18]

Allen was soon caught and lodged in the Elbert County jail, but so popular was he among his countrymen that a mob of two hundred people stormed the jail and freed him.[19] Beverly fled to the frontiers of Kentucky, where the law made no effort to follow, and there according to varying reports he entered the ministry again (or became a physician), living to be 90 years of age.[20] William Allen continued a respectable member of the Elbert County community. He held his brother in grateful rememberance and named one of his sons Beverly. This Beverly lived until 1846 and was buried on a knoll overlooking Beaverdam Creek in a community which bore the name Beverly into the twentieth century.

As long as Petersburg lasted, its chief prosperity lay in merchandizing. Stores came and went: Wash and Jones (Thomas Wash and William Jones), Robert S. Sayre, Robert Thompson

("Old Blue"), Oliver & Watkins, John E. Stokes, Robert & John Bolton, John I. Smith, William Patterson, and on and on the numbers grew and faded. In 1804 there were nine stores serving Petersburg and the surrounding country and business was so brisk that they were unable to handle all of it, making it necessary for some prospective customers to go to Augusta. In 1804, a Petersburg merchant in writing a North Carolina friend remarked, "Another such season will revive the buildings of Petersburg altho the little stores in the Country draw off much of our cotton trade."[21] Although there was little competition from Lisbon and Vienna, yet in the latter town, Charles W. Wittick & Company carried on an extensive business for many years, certainly as late as 1826, and at this time they had a branch in Petersburg.[22]

Somewhat akin to merchants were vendue-masters, later called auctioneers, who sold articles at public outcry to the highest bidders. They were strictly regulated by state law. Petersburg was awarded one in 1797.[23] They were given authority "to set up and expose to sale by public outcry and vendue, all and any houses, lands, ships and vessels, goods and wares, and merchandize and property whatsoever." They should pay the state 1% of their gross sales, and they should receive for selling houses, lands, slaves, and ships 2½%, and for all other items, 5%.[24]

If not the chief businessman in Petersburg, Shaler Hillyer was close behind LeRoy Pope who might well have carried that distinction, for certainly after 1810, when Pope deserted Petersburg for Alabama, it could hardly be said that Shaler had a rival— though he did precede Pope out of Petersburg by moving up Broad River a few miles to a plantation. However, Shaler always maintained important interests in Petersburg as much as if he lived within its corporate limits.

Shaler Hillyer was born in Granby, Connecticut, in 1776, and when he became of age he made a trip to Boston, where he met Oliver Whyte, a young man who had established a store in Petersburg. Whyte persuaded Hillyer to become a clerk in his Petersburg store. After arranging his affairs in Connecticut, Hillyer set sail for Savannah in 1799, and from there proceeded to Petersburg by land.[25] His clerkship soon developed into a co-partnership with Whyte. The constant necessity of prodding customers to pay their store accounts, which often called on the law for help, led Hillyer to become a lawyer—a "collecting lawyer," who never entered into general practice nor lessened his interest in merchandizing.[26]

Growing weary of Petersburg and merchandizing conditions

there, Whyte in 1805 sold out his ownership in the store to Hillyer and returned to Boston,[27] but his interest in Petersburg and Hillyer never dimmed even to the end of Hillyer's life, for two reasons. The two reasons were first, Whyte immediately announced that he was offering his services to the Petersburg trade "in the Commission line,"[28] and second, the debt (said to be $20,000) which Hillyer owed him was long in being paid, though for the rest of his life he devoted the profits of his businesses to paying it—both always remaining on the most correct and friendly terms, socially and financially.[29] Hillyer sent Whyte cotton on his own account and on commission for his customers, frequently acting as a collector for notes and judgments owned by Whyte.[30] Now and then Whyte made visits to Petersburg and was entertained by Hillyer at his "Poplar Grove" plantation home.[31]

Before moving to his Poplar Grove plantation in 1807 Hillyer had become much discouraged with the way his business was progressing in Petersburg. He wrote to Whyte in November, 1806, that he had lost more than $2,000 in "Bad Debts," and that he had tried to sell out: "If I could get rid of my Possessions in Petersburg I would quit business," and he doubted that he could get $800 for his store lot and house. Yet during the year he had sold at wholesale $3,500 in supplies and at retail $2,733. Ending up in a more hopeful spirit he said, "My business is tolerable good—and I may by continuing make Something for myself."[32]

In moving to the plantation he intended to set up a store there and retail an assortment of goods: "I am *Sick very Sick* of selling goods in the country by whole sale and am I think finally cured of the credit killing *eppedemic*." There he could engage also in planting activities and some factoring for the bigger planters until he could get out of debt, "When God preserving me and mine I intend to move Northward."[33]

Living on a plantation gave him a quieter life and more time to catch up on his correspondence, as well as "more leisure than formerly and being more secluded from the 'calls of social friendship' than when in Petersburg."[34] Having about forty slaves, inherited from his father-in-law, John Freeman,[35], he could engage in extensive planting, which he directed mostly into cotton. To add to the grazing offered by the native wild grasses, he ordered from the North white clover seed, timothy (called also "herd grass"), and blue grass ("By the Yankeys [called] English Grass," Hillyer observed).[36]

For a short time he established a partnership with John Saunders Holt in the mercantile business under the firm name of Hillyer & Holt; and the assortment of goods which was offered for sale indicated a clientele of enlightened taste—good sherry wine, Malaga, Jamaica rum, chocolate, cinnamon, ginger, and all that "assortment of Fashionable Fancy Goods" for men's and women's wear, so often announced by merchants. Supplies especially for the plantations were "good cargo pork" at $10 a barrel (for slaves), middling pork at $11, and prime pork at $12, also "Patent Riveted Hoes of a superior quality," not to mention many other items.[37]

Never deserted by that New England business imagination and acumen and yet never quite successful in business, Hillyer was soon the originator and moving force in a mercantile adventure which he thought was based on a firm foundation and had every reason to succeed. In a letter to Whyte which he wrote in 1809 Hillyer gave a hint that "there is a prospect of my forming a connection in Trade on a permanent and extensive plan"; and in another letter which he wrote Whyte he was more explicit, saying that the planters in the regions around Petersburg, embracing several counties, were "about associating themselves into a Mercantile Company."[38] This firm was organized on August 4, 1809. Its president was William Barnett, physician, former sheriff of Elbert County, and later a member of Congress. Hillyer was one of its two directors. The firm was captialized at $30,000, with the promise of going to $100,000 if desired. Stock in the firm was offered to planters and others at $50 a share. Originally the number of shares was 225, but within a year they were increased to 600. No one living more than twenty-five miles from Petersburg could be elected president or director.[39] The name of the firm was Petersburg Mercantile Company, and its store was called the Planters Store. Although its headquarters and main establishment must be in Petersburg, it was allowable to erect one or more branch stores out in the country.

Hillyer was enthusiastic over his new venture. Within less than a year it had made a profit of $5.33 on each share, and he was anxious to have Whyte to take twenty shares. Explaining further the purpose of the firm he informed Whyte that "a number of the planters in the neighborhood have associated themselves together for the purpose of carrying on trade in Petersburg for their mutual advantage." Already (in early 1810) $12,000 had been subscribed, business having begun "last fall" with a small stock of goods, and sales were "equal to our most sanguine expectations." In promoting a firm financial standing with suppliers, Hillyer stated that the company's credit would not be extended "beyond our real and substantial capital." Stockholders in the company were "some of the first rate planters in the up country . . . of undoubted credit as individuals." the "novelty of our Company" should not create any doubt as to its responsibility.[40]

Since the Petersburg Mercantile Company was Hillyer's creation its promotion and management fell to him. To cater to planters' wants he saw to it that there was a good selection of planter supplies. He was soon ordering 500 pounds of "good iron suitable for Plantation use," which blacksmiths would pound and weld into whatever was needed, and out went an order to Augusta for 200 bushels of salt which provident planters would use in curing and preserving pork instead of having to buy it. He wanted the salt sent in good, strong four-bushel sacks, which could later be used as "Mill Bags." Of course, there were many other items which the Planters Store constantly kept.[41]

Much of Hillyer's trade went overland to and from Augusta in wagons, and what he had to sell was for the most part cotton and whiskey, both of which he received in trade from planters or by acting as their factor, and some of which Hillyer himself supplied. In early 1813 on sending a wagon load of whiskey to Augusta he noted that this "is my first attempt this year. I am told that twill bring $62\frac{1}{2}$ cents [per gallon] but you must sell without storing if twill bring 50. Do the best you can with it. The casks you will reserve if possible as they are an article Difficult to procure."[42] A little later he sent five casks of whiskey, consisting of 277 gallons, all on one wagon. This year Hillyer put up a distillery "on the New plan," which he described in some detail.[43]

By mid-summer of 1813 the Petersburg Mercantile Company failed and Hillyer bought its assets including debts owed to it assuming the debts it owed, most of which he thought would be good. Now for the next few years he had the task of trying to collect these debts but he had little success.[44] He continued to run the store on his plantation, which must have been an important part of the Petersburg Mercantile firm's organization. Living on his plantation up Broad River, he was often associated with legislation dealing with that river. In 1809 he was appointed one of the commissioners to view Broad River and to prevent and remove obstructions in the river;[45] the next year he was one of the incorporators of the Broad River Navigation Com-

pany, as previously noted,[46] and in 1815, he was appointed one
of the commissioners to improve navigation on Broad River and
charge a toll.[47]

As has already amply appeared, the Petersburg merchants pro-
cured their supplies in Augusta, Savannah, and Charleston, in the
South, and principally in New York and Boston in the North;
but Hillyer also dealt sometimes with Seth Craig & Company in
Philadelphia. Although Hillyer had considerable dealings with
Oliver Whyte in Boston, he carried on more extensive operations
with New York firms, among them being Moses Jarvis & Company, Brisbane & Brannan, Clendenning & Adams, Abram R.
Lawrence & Company, George Newbold, W. &. C. M. Slocum,
John & George Tredwell, Benjamin & Joseph Strong, Robert H.
Bowne & Company, and Wright & Tibbals. Generally a friendly
and personal relationship existed with these suppliers and factors,
for such extensive merchants as Hillyer and the Stokeses often
visited them to make purchases on the spot. Trips were made by
sea almost invariably, starting either in Savannah or Charleston.
In making a trip to New York in 1806, Hillyer went to Augusta
and then on to Savannah, requiring three days for the latter part
of the land trip, and he wrote his wife Rebecca "no accident happened to me on the road."[48] The close personal friendship that
existed between Hillyer and his Savannah factors Beggs & Groves
is reflected in a letter which he wrote to Groves when he heard of
Beggs' death: "We may lament, but we cannot restore. It is a
state that awaits us all. A little more Bustle & noise seems allotted
to you & me in this world but we shall soon take the road friend
Beggs has gone."[49]

One of the merchandizing Stokes family, Armistead Y., in reporting to his brother on a trip to New York in 1821 to buy
supplies for his Petersburg store, mentioned that he had arrived
"after a passage of 11 days from Augusta," not indicating whether
he boarded the ship in Charleston or Savannah, but most likely
in the former port. His trip was not the usual one to New York
harbor, for he passed up the Delaware River and was entranced
by its scenery: "During my passage of the delaware, the most
beautiful river in the world, every vale a vilage & every Hill
abounding with cotages. The sun sunk behind the embatled
clouds leaving there illuminated points tinged with a thousand
colours and as these changed, first deepning & then fading, the
evening Star appeared in the blue Sky trembling above the dark
clouds which appeared like some extensive forest stretched along

the Horizon; then add the Swift Passage of the steam boat it gave a silent and solitary majesty to every object around particularly situated as I was without any acquaintance on board."

In New York he shopped around among suppliers and soon completed his purchases, amounting to $7,000 "at very fair prices." He expected to make a profit of from 70% to 90% on these goods "and sell much lower than usual."[50]

As an index to how people lived in Petersburg in the later 1700's and early 1800's a partial list of what merchants bought and sold, slightly repetitious of items already mentioned, should be useful. The merchant could probably take care of anything a person wanted or had to sell, whether it be fresh venison at 50 cents a quarter, new goose feathers for feather beds, horses (from $145 to $230 apiece), "fowles," furs (grey fox at 32 cents apiece, raccoon at 25 cents, wild cat at 32 cents, otter, muskrat, beaver, and other "little folks of the fields and forests"), or Indian blankets.

For clothing and accessories (man and woman), a merchant could supply almost any taste: silks, "lustrings and pelongs," linens, satins, nankeens and osneburgs (for slaves), platillas, bombazette, cassimere, corduroy, velveteen, muslin, calico, silk florentine, "superfine blue cloth," lace, lady's hats, hair ribbons, hair powder, "white pic nic gloves," lady's long gloves, lady's kid skin gloves, lady's silk gloves, tortoise hair combs, fine tooth combs, ivory and horn combs, lady's cotton hose, broad rib stocking, lady's "plain and lace clock hose," veils, Leghorn and willow bonnets, muslin shawls, yarn, pomatum (a dressing perfume), vials of bergamot, "diaper tape," "nuns thread," brass thimbles, pen knives, small scissors, white thread, girl's hats, umbrellas, and other items.

For men's dressing wants, the merchant had: suspenders, "swandown vests," Cashmere vests, "overals," boots, half boots, cuff links, razors and shaving boxes, beaver gloves, plated knee buckles, jack knives, snuff boxes, bandanna handkerchieves, and other articles "too tedious and numerous to mention."

For his kitchen and dining room the Petersburger could buy almost anything he might want: salt, pepper, coffee, tea, ginger, brown sugar, allspice, "best Northward Cheese," tea kettles, carving knives, "jappanned sugar boxes," "Dutch ovens" (for the outside), pewter plates, coffee mills and pots, iron pots, frying pans, earthen plates, milk pots, gallon measures, cream pots, "baking dishes," all sorts of cutlery, silverware, linen tablecloths, and so on.

For refreshments with alcoholic contents there was a variety of wines, rums, porters (a mixture of ale and stout), and whiskies of local manufacture. To relieve small aches and pains too trivial to demand the attention of a physician, and to provide chemicals for other needs, the merchant had: "camphire," smelling salts, "bottle bitters," British oil, "batman drops," glover salts, brimstone, copperas, white lead, salt petre, lime, linseed oil—and many drugs which a sick person able to be on his feet could get by going to a physician's office.

For various amusements and pastimes a person could buy jewsharps, playing cards, gun powder, buck shot, hawk-bill knives, fishing lines, and fish hooks. And for barnyard and plantation use, the merchant could supply anything needed: hoes (weeding, hilling, and broad), riding chairs, rope, whips, saddles and saddle bags, bridles, lady's saddles, curry combs, surcingles, horse brushes, horseshoes, hand and claw hammers, rasps, drawing knives, rat-tail files, carpenter's squares, blacksmith's bellows, plows, plow lines, cradle sticks (for reaping cradles), nails, chisels, gimlets, funnels, hinges, screws, gun locks, and many other hardware items.[51]

Such were some of the items which entered into the lives of the Petersburgers and their neighbors in the surrounding country; a quarter century later Petersburgers and their neighbors would be buying the same necessities and conveniences, but there would be some progress in the fineries and elegancies which they had taken on. Silks more than ever would be in style. Ladies would now be dressed out in "elegant white lace veils" ($8.00); "elegant silk shawls" ($6.50); white silk hose ($3.00) or blue silk hose ($2.50); they would be carrying a silk purse containing a phial of "Oder of Roses," an "elegant parasol" ($5.00), and an "elegant feather fan"; and they would be wearing gold earrings ($10.00), gold necklaces ($6.90), and gold breastpins ($10.00).

A gentleman might be seen riding a $250 horse, on an "elegant saddle" ($24.00), with a "loaded horse whip" ($2.50), and carrying a $7.50 pocket pistol and an "elegant gold watch," for which he paid $150. If on foot, on special occasions he might be wearing an "elegant sword" attached to an "elegant sword belt," and if he wanted a "military feather" in his hat, it would cost 50 cents. To enliven himself, he might drink Madeira wine at $2.50 a gallon or rum at $2.25. Whiskey could be got for $1.25 a gallon. If he smoked it would be Spanish segars at 25 cents a dozen or Petersburg-manufactured tobacco at 50 cents a pound. Those who chewed paid 12½ cents for either a plug or twist—undoubtedly large size. For the river, boat poles could be bought for 18¾ cents apiece. And fishing lines would cost the same price apiece, while three dozen fish hooks would cost only 12½ cents. Children wishing to play marbles could buy them for 12½ cents a dozen.

Blue was the most stylish color, whether in lady's hose, cloth, or chinaware. Elegant blue cloth cost $9.00 a yard, but "Super Blue Cloth" sold at $13.20 a yard. An "elegant sett blue dining ware" could be bought for as little as $30.00. Cut glass goblets cost $12.00 a dozen, and a dozen silver table spoons cost the ladies of Petersburg $40.00. Two dozen "elegant fancy chairs" cost $84.00. A set of "elegant shovel and tongs" cost $6.50, while $20.00 was necessary to buy an "Imperial rug." "Elegant gold luster pitchers" and bowls, which must always be accompanied by "transparent soap" costing $5.50 a pair.

School children could buy at a Petersburg store primers, spelling books, dictionaries, and slates. Merchants had for sale also writing paper, dutch quills, ink stands, ink, and ink powder. No household was any more complete without an almanac than without a Bible, and Petersburg merchants could always supply both, the almanac selling for 18¾ cents around 1820. Large family Bibles were supplied at $10.00 apiece. Morse's *Geography* and the *Columbian Orator* were $1.00 each and the *Life of Franklin* was $1.12½. *Erasmus* could be had for 56¼ cents. There were other books for sale, generally of a religious and moral character, as *American Moralist, American Preceptor,* and Watts *Hymns.*[52]

As it has been previously noted, Petersburg was an excellent trading center for varied merchandise unequalled in Georgia north of Augusta and drawing customers from far up the Broad River and across the Savannah in South Carolina. The Calhouns were regular customers for "elegant" goods,[53] and Moses Waddel, over in his Willington school community, came frequently to trade at the Petersburg stores. George Cook and John Dooly from across the Broad River in Lincoln County came to trade and engage in law business, and old Elijah Clarke from over in Wilkes County could now and then be seen on the streets of Petersburg up to the very year of his death in 1799. On May 6th he settled up his debt at a Petersburg store "in full 6.00."

Petersburg merchants acting as factors for planters in the surrounding country marketed their cotton and tobacco for them and supplied them with their general plantation wants. But often these Petersburg merchants had for themselves factors in the large trading centers in both the South and the North so that between the planter and the final purchaser there might be two or three middlemen, each exacting his commission. The merchants generally expected ninety days credit in what they bought in these factor transactions where they did not pay with products, but when they did send products to their factors and did not take merchandise in return they wanted payment immediately. In 1806 Hillyer sued a factor who sold three hogsheads of tobacco for him but did not remit the proceeds.

Acting as factors for planters in the first instance these Petersburg merchants were in reality engaging in barter trade. There was considerable barter trade every day with the small purchasers, who brought in fowls, vegetables, and other country produce. Merchants often advertised their wares "for cash, cotton and tobacco."

The merchant always needed a clerk or two, unless his business was very meagre. A successful clerk needed training and advice in how best to handle his customers. Probably then there was no slogan such as "The customer is always right"; but a clerk must be polite and conduct himself in such a way as to lead the customer to want to come back without being begged to do so. There was brisk competition among Petersburg merchants, making good clerks, therefore, doubly important.

A Petersburg merchant in 1818 looking for someone to replace a clerk who had returned to his New Jersey home explained to a young man whom he was trying to interest in the position the duties of a clerk and the opportunity that would come his way in advancement. The salary to begin with would be $150 a year, "merely to keep you in good clothes." He would be given instruction in bookkeeping and in the general duties of a clerk. Anyone wanting to become a merchant should start out as a clerk, "For no man can Learn to Navigate a ship unless he has been *first* a sailor, nor no man can command an army unless first a Soldier nor no man can be a merchant & know his business & be capable of teaching others, unless he is first a Clerk, & goes through all the difficulties and hardships (as young men please to call them) which naturally attach themselves to that business, for a man to suppose that he can be a merchant & succeed will be at the *start* without complete knowledge of the business is absurd, as your Father & myself can both testify. I can give you more information in six months than I had at the end of three years. My wit was bought at a very dear rate."

Everyone must be at work by 9 o'clock in the morning, and there must be no gambling or sitting up late. "You must assist in cutting your wood, Drawing your water, making your fires, sweeping your store," and in getting everything in order before breakfast. "This is a good morning employment & good for your health." In the evening the bookkeeper never quits "until the work of the previous day is copied." "The *secrets* of our *business* & family are always to be kept inviolate, [and] . . . every principle of *honour* & *honesty*" must be respected—"no cheating any one out of any thing, and more particularly the ignorant. I would view one of my young men in a most contemptuous light who would cheat an ignorant person or a poor Negro out a 3½d, because such is ill gotten gain."[54]

The bane of a merchant's existence was giving credit to his customers which in the absence of a sufficient supply of money scattered among the masses was looked upon as a necessity. Credit was the prime cause of the failure of merchants, who frequently belabored their customers to pay up, as unfortunate Thomas Stokes had done,[55] and frequently with no more success. Sometimes the refusal or delay in settling store debts, as well as others, was based on a dispute as to the correctness of the amount demanded. Rather than bring suit in the courts, there was a legal method in use to bring about a settlement. The Superior Court now and then, and frequently in the 1790's and early 1800's, would refer the dispute to a set of arbitrators whose decision would be final. As an example, the Elbert County Superior Court referred the dispute of Abram Colson and Jacob Bugg against E. Ragland to these gentlemen: Benjamin Taliaferro, Thomas Wooton, Thomas C. Russell, and LeRoy Pope. They met in Petersburg, went over the account in dispute, and found that Ragland owed Colson and Bugg 54 pounds, 3 shillings, and 9 pence.[56]

Threats of war with England, embargoes disrupting trade, and prices of cotton and tobacco approaching the vanishing point made economic conditions in Georgia calamitous. To help the debtor class, to which most people belonged, the legislature began passing stay and alleviating laws. The first came in May, 1808, which stayed any execution against any debtor until the following Christmas if he should give security for the amount of the judgment and costs.[57] Supposing that conditions had improved a little, the legislature in December, 1808, continued its alleviating policy by staying any judgment if the debtor gave good security for the debt and paid one third of the amount and of costs. This law was to continue in force until Christmas, 1809,[58] but since conditions did not improve, the legislature in December, 1809, continued the

law until Christmas, 1810. Where a third had been paid before
Christmas, 1809, the next third would not be due until May 1,
1810, making the final payment due before Christmas, 1810.[59]
With the outbreak of war in 1812, so great were the economic
uncertainties that the legislature passed a law in November (1812)
withdrawing the right of a creditor to issue any civil processes
against property unless the debtor was about to squander it. Then
a judgment might be secured, and if the debtor was about to leave
the state the execution of the judgment might be made.[60] To protect the solvency of banks, the legislature the next year allowed
them to sue, get judgments, and levy on property.[61] In 1814 debtors were allowed a year's grace if they gave good security, but no
soldier could be sued while in the service and within six months
thereafter.[62]

Petersburg merchants were hard hit by these laws. Hillyer wrote
to his friend Whyte in Boston that the Georgia stay law had
"stopped all proceedings" in courts for the collection of debts.
"This procedure, as *oppressive* as *immoral,* has quieted the fears
& I might add the *consciences* of the debtors so that no more ex-
ertion is made for the settlement of accounts by them. Where this
demoralizing principle will end, God only knows." He wished he
could meet all of his debts to Whyte but "the untoward circumstances of the country—added to the wicked proceedings of the
Legislature have interfered."[63] A little later in 1809 Hillyer wrote
that the "times for collecting money in this country are more distressing than I have ever known them. Legislative interference
still prevents our collecting money by law."[64]

In 1810 Hillyer gave a little description of the way in which
the law worked. Debtor—"Mr. what do you intend doing with me
about [what] I am due you?" Creditor—"If you don't pay me I
am ruined." Debtor—"Well I never saw money so hard to get in
my days. I mean to pay all I owe. I don't think any better of the
thirding law than you do. I am determined that I will third no
more. I am above it. If you can wait till Christmas I will pay you
every cent." Relying on such promises, the creditor waits, but no
one pays him a cent. He then sues, but it is too late to collect the
one third for that year. Hillyer declared that he was going to sue
every one of his debtors possible.[65]

The bustling town of Petersburg had, of course, to provide its
people with services other than the buyings and sellings carried
on by the merchants; however, none of the needed little occupa-
tions approached merchandizing in extent and importance. There

was a tan yard which provided leather for the cobblers and harness-makers; Jeremiah Burdine engaged in cabinet-making; and blacksmiths would shoe a horse for $1.25 in 1799. Jane Rucker, a seamstress, in 1806 inserted a notice in the Petersburg newspaper soliciting further business and correcting certain reports which had been going the rounds: "She hopes for a continuation of those favors, assuring . . . [the public] that her work will be inferior to none, fashionable and at the most reduced prices. Punctuality and dispatch will be strictly adhered to." She was publishing this notice because a rumor had been started that she said, "I did not mean to take in any more work, that I could live without it, and that I stood in no need of any." She wished to inform the person who started the report "that I stand in as great need of work as the most indigent of my neighbors, and have ever been anxiously bent on industry which I mean to pursue to the termination of my days."[66]

James Pace, the town tailor, had difficulty collecting what was owed to him. Inserting a notice in the town newspaper in 1806, headed "Help the Needy," he added, "The Subscriber only asks for that he has earned."[67] As this plea did not seem to awaken the consciences of his debtors, six months later he published this reminder: "I Find it High Time to Speak Plain. For the last time, I sincerely request my debtors to make the most speedy payment, . . . as I am determined to give no longer indulgence."[68]

Outside of Petersburg and yet not very far away were several kinds of extractive industries, in addition to plantations, which secured their power from the Broad and Savannah rivers and from their many small tributaries. Grist mills were early coming into prominence, especially to grind wheat for the neighborhoods, any surplus being sent down to Petersburg and Augusta. According to a law passed in 1786 the toll exacted from customers bringing their grain to be ground for their own use was one eighth "and no more," and the miller was required to grind as much as five bushels out of every lot brought, in the order received.[69] Since most mills ground flour also on their own account it was necessary to buy the grain from wheat farmers. A miller on Broad River near Petersburg was advertising in the Petersburg paper in 1805 an offer of $1.25 a bushel.[70] Another mill on Broad River, five miles above Petersburg, was advertising its flour as "not to be equalled or excelled."[71] The minimum daily grinding capacity for the ordinary grist mill was 150 bushels a day.

The political philosophy of the day in Georgia required gov-

ernmental inspection and regulation of any important manufactured and processed article which reached the market for sale.
In 1801 Petersburg was made an inspection point where flour was
to be graded into first, second, and third qualities, with the number marked on every barrel by an inspector, who was to be paid
twenty-five cents a barrel by the owner of the flour.[72]

For the inspection of flour, in December, 1811, the legislature
passed a much more elaborate act which was to go into effect six
months later and to apply only to Petersburg and four other
towns—Savannah, Augusta, Darien, and Milledgeville. As these
were the main towns where flour was received in extensive trade
and also used for exportation, the flour intended for all the rest
of the state was presumably to be free from inspection—thus re-
lieving flour for toll customers from this burden since it was for
their own consumption. Also the inspection did not apply to the
flour which the many mills scattered over the state were producing
for sale elsewhere than in the inspection towns. According to this
act the Inferior Court in each county concerned should appoint
"a person of good repute, and who is a skilful judge of the quality
of flour." To be merchantable all flour should be "bolted wheat
flour . . . and of due fineness, and without any mixture of coarser
flour, or the flour of any other grain than wheat." The flour
should be packed in barrels and half-barrels of 27 inches in length
and bound with at least 10 hoops, weighing 196 and 98 pounds
respectively—specified fines being charged against the miller for
any shortages. The inspector should bore into each barrel "from
head to head, with an instrument of not more than three quarter
inch in diameter." He should plug the hole and mark on the
barrel with the name of the inspection town and the quality of
the flour, as "Superfine, Fine, Middling, and Ship stuff." Before
sending the barrels to the inspection town, the miller must "brand
his name on each and every barrel."[73]

The legislature had a difficult time making up its collective
mind on the inspection of flour, for the act had been in effect
only six months when this body, finding the act did not "answer
the purposes for which it was intended," repealed it in December,
1812.[74] But the next year (November 22, 1814) stating that "experience has shown that the establishment of flour inspections,
under proper regulations, will advance and promote the interest
of this state," the legislature repassed the original act with almost
identical provisions, except that it applied only to Petersburg,
Augusta, and Savannah.[75] Later Darien was added.[76]

As early as 1813 Shaler Hillyer became interested in the manufacture of flour, having already as a merchant been engaged in the flour trade. This year, he sought a contract to deliver 500 barrels in Augusta by Christmas. He was soon inquiring in Augusta for the necessary machinery for setting up "a merchant mill" on Broad River near his plantation home, agreeing to swap cotton for it.[77] Two years later (in 1815), as has been previously noted,[78] he induced the legislature to grant him permission to build a dam across the river at Muckle's Ferry Shoals. By the middle of the next year, he had constructed his dam, built his mill, and had it in operation, shipping "real Superfine" flour down to Augusta.[79] During the first winter and spring after he had constructed his dam it had withstood all the floods and freshets customary for that time, but an unusual freshet in May washed away his dam and put a total stop to his grinding. Since he needed his slaves in the fields about this time he did not replace the dam for a month. By 1818 his dam and mill had cost him about $8,000.[80]

The other extractive industry which was of importance to Petersburg was lumbering. True to its ever-watchful eye over the good name of Georgia products, the legislature early provided for the inspection of lumber. Wherever there was waterpower, it was easy to set up sawmills, and soon many were buzzing and humming on the streams around Petersburg. As inspection of lumber was intended primarily for that which was being exported, Petersburg was only an assemblying point for lumber being shipped down the Savannah River. After specifying that all scantlings and boards must have square edges and be "free from worm or knot holes," the law gave greatest attention to staves used in making barrels, hogsheads, and pipes,[81] which were a standard article of export to the West Indies to be used in the rum and molasses trade.

An extractive industry, no unit of which was likely operated in Petersburg but which thrived on most plantations up the Broad and Savannah River valleys, was the distillation of whiskey and apple and peach brandies. Before the end of the eighteenth century stills could be had in Augusta in sizes from thirty to seventy gallons. Later they could be had for larger capacities.[82] When Hillyer moved out of Petersburg to his Broad River plantation he secured an eighty gallon still,[83] which he operated to produce whiskey for the Petersburg and the Augusta market. He produced also peach brandy for markets as far away as Boston, sending there in 1813 by the first vessel possible (these being war times) "one quarter cask of Peach brandy of an excellent quality."[84] This was one of the few industries which the Georgia legislature neither inspected nor regulated because little or none was sent abroad, and its quality could be considered good. The planter and his family and neighbors relied upon it for conviviality and they would be satisfied with none but the best.

Although Petersburg for some years was one of the three or four most active trading centers in the state, it did not have a bank; but neither did any other town in Georgia until 1807, when the Planters' Bank of the State of Georgia was incorporated, to be set up in Savannah. As an indication of the financial standing of Petersburg, it was allotted 600 shares to be subscribed under the supervision of LeRoy Pope, Thomas Bibb, and John Watkins. All other towns were allotted fewer shares excepting Savannah, Augusta, and Washington.[85]

10

Society and Amusements

PETERSBURG sprang up as a sort of miracle town. Thus it attracted people who knowing what was going on in the world were ready and able to seek a high status in life and a fortune. They came not only out of previous migrations from Virginia, Maryland, and the Carolinas, but also a smattering of them heard the call of Petersburg from as far away as Massachusetts, Connecticut, New York, and New Jersey. One who was born in Petersburg and grew up on a Broad River plantation within the social shadow of the town wrote in his old age that Petersburg had "the very best society in the state."[1]

Traveling troups of theatrical players soon discovered Petersburg and made their periodic visits. A troup of eight actors appeared there in 1799 and spent a whole week giving different plays every night. John Williams Walker, now a schoolboy, wrote to his friend Larkin Newby, who had moved over into South Carolina at this time, "The play Actors have been in Town and went out on Sunday." He must have gone to every performance, for he gave their complete program. Every night they gave two plays, a comedy or a tragedy followed by a farce. The first night, it was the comedy *Provoked Husband* and the farce *Spoiled Child.* The second night, *Child of Nature* and *The Lawyer Nonsuited or no Song no Supper,* "which was peculiarly funny." The third night, *Tragedy of Jane Shore* and the farce *Virgin Unmasked.* The fourth night, the comedy *Country Girl* and the farce *The Poor Soldier,* "which was as funny a thing as I ever saw." The fifth night, the comedy *The Stranger* and the farce *The Sultan or a Peep into the Seraglio.* The sixth night, the comedy *The Mountaineers or Love and Madness* and the farce *Ramp.*[2] That Petersburgers were able to support twelve plays indicated their lively interest in intellectual excitement; the price of admission was fifty cents.[3]

Dancing and formal balls were a social diversion in Petersburg and up and down the long Broad River Valley. In Petersburg the "Senior Gentlemen" announced regularly their "High and Honorable Balls," from which the "younger set" were excluded. But the juniors were not to be denied their right to dance, for they organized their own club and were enjoying its activities by 1799. Sixteen-year-old John Williams Walker kept his friend Larkin Newby informed of what was going on.[4] By 1803 Newby had moved to Fayetteville, North Carolina, and Walker, now advanced in age and social status could tell him much more about the social whirl in Petersburg, where in early youth they had enjoyed life together—Walker having been born in 1783. Cupid always played an important part in these newsy letters, and Walker never failed to tell

> Who danced with whom and who are like to wed
> And who is gone and who is brought to bed.[5]

In 1803 Walker was twenty years old, and although he was thoroughly in tune with Petersburg society, he was not a giddy empty soul. Under the guidance of Moses Waddel he was preparing to enter Princeton and also much of his time was taken up with the management of the estate of his lately-deceased brother Memorable. He could well write near the end of 1803 that it had been some time "since I have shuffled a reel or hopped a congo."[6]

However, he was not one to give up balls, hops, and social visiting. The New Year's Ball ushering in the year 1805 was to be an outstanding event, "at which it is expected a great number of ladies will be present." Yet he looked forward to it with some trepidation, fearing that he would be "overpowered by the charms" of someone because he was holding his affections for another who was off at school in Bethlehem, Pennsylvania—none other than Matilda of the "royal family" of LeRoy Pope. Recently for the first time he had realized that he was in love with "a *little* creature scarce 12."[7] It turned out that he had to be in the Abbeville Courthouse on a little mission on the last day of the year and January 1 caught him there. However, he was determined to ride to Petersburg for the ball that night. It was a bad day, raining, sleeting, and snowing by succession, but he got there in time to "huddle on my *Sunday* clothes for the ball."

"Apollo played, the Graces danced, and I enjoyed the scene."

His Sunday clothes hardly fitted the occasion because they were too *"plain,* perhaps too unadorned, for such an assembly, where almost all the young bucks appeared in a new suit purchased for the set purpose." When he entered the hall, the manager "handed" him a seat. He was "surprised that many ladies were present 'who knew not Joseph' and whom Joseph knew not." That situation called for his presentation to the ladies, and when he was asked to "take the rounds in *a general* introduction to all the ladies in the room," he refused, "observing that the custom was hateful to me, because too formal." One of the ladies especially attracted him, and he finally got acquainted with her by casually taking a vacant seat next to her. "Conversation ensued—the badness of the weather—the rusticity of our up-country manners in comparison of those who dwell in the lower part of the state—the superiority of our climate—and fifty other things which I have forgot supplied me with a never failing theme, till the lady in whose place I sat came to resume her seat." He now took a fling with his newly-acquainted partner and could hardly prevent Cupid from taking over.

The weather was so bad the night of this ball that it prevented "many ladies in the vicinity" from coming; so it was decided to hold another ball the next evening. The weather moderated and fifty ladies showed up. The "young bucks" of Petersburg and the surrounding plantations, including Vienna and Lisbon, had another evening of enjoyment.[8] Before the month was out another ball was held which Walker attended only to be mildly infatuated with another beauty. However, at the beginning he was a little hesitant in awarding her this accolade, for "she had one *personal* fault—and that is the color of her hair—I never thought *red* handsome before—perhaps they should be dignified *golden locks.*"[9] Undoubtedly, these Petersburg grand balls made a lasting impression on the young ladies, for in 1888, a newspaper correspondent who was interested in Petersburg in all its glory reported that "one old gentleman told me that sixty years ago an old lady friend of his said she attended a grand ball in Petersburg."[10]

There were picnics, promenading the streets of Petersburg, celebrations, and visiting in Augusta, Athens, and other Georgia towns, and in the nearby towns across the river in South Carolina. An interesting place for holding picnics was a spot about three miles above Petersburg near the banks of the Savannah River. Here were some Indian mounds which had greatly attracted William Bartram when he came this way in 1776. He referred to them as "remarkable Indian monuments, which are worthy of every traveller's notice." There was a group of smaller conical mounds and square terraces, with a large mound having a spiral path leading to the top, about forty or fifty feet high and two hundred or three hundred yards around. The top was flat and on it was growing "a large, beautiful spreading Red Cedar."[11]

A picnic might well include a little fishing as a diversion, which would inevitably lead to a "fish fry," for the Savannah and the Broad and their tributaries were teeming with fish.[12] The fish wealth in these rivers was of special legislative concern. Had there been a method of preserving the catch, there might have developed here another extractive industry, but fishing never got beyond local consumption.

The Glorious Fourth was a day always to be celebrated with an oration followed by eating and drinking toasts to the heroes of the Revolution and to the political leaders of the day. It has already been stated that William Wyatt Bibb gave the oration in 1802. Also there were convivial gatherings with no day to be celebrated or no one to be honored except those who were present. There was such a day in June, 1799, when "a Large Company of Gentlemen met at the Spring to Drink Grog." The extra energy developed by the grog led to trials of strength, including a wrestling match between a Mr. McGrath and Littlebury Wilson, a merchant, in which the former won. McGrath bragged so much about it that Wilson replied with some mean remarks which McGrath resented and thereupon challenged Wilson to a duel. They selected their seconds "and went over the River and measured off the Ground took their Pistols and were almost ready to fire when Wilson asked *Pardon* and all was done with—for they are as good friends as ever."[13]

There was some promenading up and down the streets of Petersburg, but it is not known what kind of trees, if any, provided shade. It is possible that there might have been some Lombardy poplars, for the Petersburg newspaper editor published an article relating to the hazards of walking under this kind of tree, the incidents mentioned apparently not applying to Petersburg. It was reported that "the Lombardy poplar produced a worm whose bite was almost instant death." A cat bitten by one died soon afterwards, and a worm fell on the hand of a lady walking under a Lombardy poplar, and "though it did not bite, but only grazed her hand as it fell on the ground, yet the hand inflamed and became very sore." The author of this article was not opposed to having Lombardy poplars planted on the streets of towns, but they should be interspersed with other trees.[14]

There was much visiting back and forth between Petersburgers and families of planters in the neighborhood, especially if one had ever lived in Petersburg and then moved out into the country to a plantation, as was true of the Hillyers. There were longer trips both for social occasions and for pleasure otherwise, as in the latter instance when Petersburgers went down to Augusta in 1799 and paid a half dollar to see an elephant, a "stupendous animal, the only one in America."[15] Then there were visits to the North, wives accompanying merchant husbands on buying missions.

During the warm summer months some Petersburgers made tours into the mountains of the Carolinas. In 1803 Shaler Hillyer set out at two o'clock on June 7 and drove seventeen miles before putting up for the night. He was on his way to the warm springs of North Carolina, there to meet some other Petersburgers, the Freemans, whose daughter Rebecca was the special object of his journey.[16] Walker, who was keeping Newby informed on the social happenings and especially on "who are like to wed," reported this same month that Shaler and "Miss Rebecca Freeman have some idea of 'Joining issue,'" and that they and her parents and "some other relations" have been for sometime "at the warm springs in the upper part (I think) of South Carolina [really North Carolina]."[17] Walker was otherwise right; Shaler married Rebecca and they raised a family. Within a few years they built a summer home far up Broad River at a summer resort known as Madison Springs, for a hundred years a favorite with Georgians and South Carolinians.[18]

As Petersburg began to decline as a town, society there also began to fade out, so that those young ladies who were coming along at that time and hungering for social activities had to find them elsewhere. There was that sensitive soul Jane Kneeland of a cultured Petersburg family, who in the 1830's did much visiting around in Georgia and South Carolina. In 1831 she had been visiting in Augusta and Athens, and in a letter to a friend, comparing society in Athens and Petersburg, she wrote that "the contrast between Petersburg and Athens is I must warn you very great as we have no society here and no amusement of any kind," but for Athens "it has indeed many attractions more especially for the young and gay. I shall ever remember my visit there with delight."[19]

She had recently been visiting in Abbeville on a brief stay of only two weeks (social visits in those times might last a month or two), and she wrote, "I assure you that I enjoyed myself as much there as I ever did in my life." But with all her social inclinations, she had a streak of Puritanism which would not down. Oh why should the spirit of mortal be proud when life is short and one is so unworthy: "This is indeed a world of trial and disappointment and they that have the least feeling get along the best. I sometimes wonder that I should ever feel gay. . . . I must not devote all my time to amusement." She then remarked to her friend to tell an inquiring one (probably an interested young gentleman) that "there is nothing remarkable in Miss Kneeland, that she is superior to few and inferior to hundreds."[20]

Although Petersburg was by now taking on a melancholy look, which may have had its effect on Miss Kneeland's personality, yet there was still life and the amenities of the cultured few who were left. People traveling from upper South Carolina over into Georgia would likely be passing through Petersburg and stopping for a few social hours or more. Mary Morange, the cultured South Carolina girl, after a visit to Sparta was on her way to her home near Willington. She spent the night in Washington (Wilkes County) and reached Petersburg about one o'clock, "just as Mrs. Stokes was rising from a fine watermelon dessert." Mary sat for a piece, and after spending a few social hours, continued her journey to Willington. It was in July, 1839.[21]

This woman's world was not all inclusive of Petersburg's social activities and amusements; there was also a man's world into little of which women were supposed to enter. Every town large enough to claim the name should have one or more taverns. For stagecoaches and their passengers and for those traveling otherwise there were tavern stops in the country, but around town taverns there was a certain vigorous life which was for men only.

Regulating and licensing taverns was almost as old as the English common law itself. Coming out of the Revolution, Georgia passed its first tavern act in 1786 to put a stop to tippling houses "being erected by idle and disorderly persons, which are generally frequented by gambling and other profane persons—which tends to the corruption of youth, and the prejudice of virtue." Any proper person wishing to set up a tavern should secure a license from the Superior Court, which should extend only for one year. The court would fix the rates which must be posted "in some conspicuous part" of the tavern, for "liquors, diet, lodgings, provender, stablage and pasturage." Anyone running a tavern without a license should be subject to a heavy fine, but merchants might retail liquors in quantities of not less than one quart, which beverage, however, might not be drunk on the premises.[22]

As this act was not successful in suppressing tippling houses, the legislature two years later passed a more elaborate act. No person without a license should set up a tavern "or house of entertainment, or retail spirituous liquors by less measure than three gallons," or have a billiard table or shuffle-board. The act set up uniform rates for the whole state. A license for a tavern in a town or within four miles should pay a fee of ten pounds—but if at a greater distance the fee would be five pounds. Now a license would be required to retail liquors in less than three gallons but not less than one quart and would cost three pounds. A billiard table required a license of forty pounds and a shuffle-board, twenty pounds.[23]

To reduce the license fees and to make other changes, a new law was passed in 1791. Now the Inferior Courts were given the duty to issue licenses for taverns and the sale of liquors and also to fix tavern rates. Applicants for licenses must give bond "for their keeping an orderly and decent house, with good and sufficient accommodations for travellers, their horses and attendants." Any person without a license should be fined ten pounds for selling at retail "any wine, beer, cider, brandy, rum or other spirits, or any mixture of such liquors, in any house, booth, arbor, stall or other place whatsoever." But there was no prohibition against a merchant "retailing liquors [in] not less than one quart; nor to prevent any planter or other person from disposing of such brandy, rum or whisky, as they may make from their own grain, orchards, or distilleries, so that it be not sold in a less quantity than one quart, nor drank or intended to be drank at the house, store or plantation, where the same shall be sold." But in Chatham, Liberty, and Effingham counties merchants might not sell less than one gallon. Tavern licenses were now reduced to two pounds and a billiard table, to five pounds.[24] Shuffle-boards were to be free. Later it was made illegal for a tavern-keeper or any other person to sell spirituous liquors to a slave.[25]

In 1791 the Inferior Court of Elbert County fixed tavern rates for Petersburg and for all other licensed places in the county. With the passing of time, rates were changed, but in 1791 these were the rates: breakfast and supper, 1 shilling 2 pence, each; dinner, 1/6; lodging 6 pence; Jamaica rum, 16 shillings per gallon; brandy, 14/0; whiskey, 9/4; corn per bushel, 4/0; oats, 3/0; oats per dozen bundles, 1 shilling; "Stabalize [use of stable for one night]," 6 pence.[26] In 1801 a post boy and his horse were charged $1.00 per night.[27]

Soon Petersburg was doing a thriving tavern business, licenses having been granted by the early 1800's to James Coleman, George Cook, Thomas Oliver, John Ragland,[28] William Oliver, William Patterson, Henry Graves Walker, and others. In 1802 Henry Graves Walker announced that he had taken the dwelling house lately occupied by Memorable Walker "and the large red house nearly opposite thereto." The first was to be operated as a boarding house to accommodate travelers and town boarders and the "red house" was to be used as a public tavern. They were far enough apart to "entirely remedy the inconvenience, and disagreeableness too often experienced where a boarding house and a tavern are associated together."[29] In 1809 William Oliver announced that he had set up the home formerly occupied by Mrs. [John R.?] Ragland as a "House of Entertainment," and for all who come he "assures them they will at all times find the best accommodation and the utmost good order and regularity in his place."[30]

In 1811 William Patterson invited the public to "Stop at the Sign of the Farmer's Arms," which was his old home now turned into a boarding house. He would serve the best the country produced—"this with a good assortment of the best Liquors, and a Stable well supplied with good provinder."[31] For many years he was a merchant and tavern-keeper in Petersburg, and annually swore the following oath required after 1810: "I, William Patterson do solemnly swear that I will not during the next twelve months sell barter give or furnish to any slave or slaves or free persons of color any measure or quantity of distilled spirituous or intoxicating Liquors without the verbal or written consent of the owner overseer or employer of such slave or slaves or without the like consent of the Guardian of such free person of color and I do further swear that I will not suffer or allow any other person or persons to do so for me by my approbation knowledge or consent so help me God."[32]

Those Petersburgers who did not care to have a solitary drink of spirituous liquor could go to a tavern to play billiards, have a game of cards or, indeed, have a social drink with either activity. John Williams Walker greatly disliked to see any young men of Petersburg playing cards. He mentioned one of his acquaintances having been ruined by another having taught him to play cards. They were, he said, "pretty good customers at High, Low, Jack & the Game. Thus you see the Young and Giddy are Led to Destruction Like the Sheep to the Slaughter."[33] If a person liked to engage in chance not afforded by a game of cards, he could buy a lottery ticket, as some Petersburgers did, but he would have to send to Augusta to get it.[34]

A healthy bet could be laid at the Petersburg Race Track, where the Petersburg Jockey Club held three-day races beginning as early as the late 1790's. These races were open for "any horse, mare or gelding in the United States." The first day was a "three mile heat" for a purse of $250; the second day, a "two mile heat," for $150; and the third day, "the mile heats, for the entrance money of the two first days."[35] The breeding of fine horses was assured by at least two dozen stallions, which were stood in the vicinity of Petersburg and the outlying regions from Augusta to Washington (Wilkes County) and Greensboro. There were "Sterling Medly," which stood at Vienna; "Victorious," at the Robert L. Tait plantation; "Snap Dragon," at Elberton; and others at other places bearing such names as "Young Dare Devil," "Flag of Truce," "Janus," "Black Sultan," and "Democrat."[36]

Petersburg was, of course, not without its petty crimes and a few more serious ones. Horse-stealing was almost as major a crime as murder and was generally made a capital offense. There was no mistake as to how Georgia looked upon it. In 1793 the legislature enacted that if any person should "feloniously steal, lead, take or drive away, any horse, gelding, mare, colt, filly, ass or mule, or be accessory thereto, and being thereof duly convicted, shall be adjudged guilty of felony: Such person or persons convicted as aforesaid, shall suffer death, without the benefit of clergy, by being hanged by the neck, till he, she or they be dead."[37] Some years later (1809) the state mellowed its attitude toward the crime and decided that for the first offense thirty-nine lashes should be applied to the bare back of the criminal on "three several days," who should stand in the pillory one hour each day and be imprisoned at most one month and not less that twenty days. Any one guilty of a second offense should suffer death.[38]

There was not much horse-stealing in Petersburg or its vicinity, but in 1813 William H. Jones reported that his horse had been stolen. He described it as a large black one that "trots slow and somewhat sluggish" but was "remarkable for the best waggon horse in the state." He offered $20.00 reward for anyone arresting the thief and stopping the horse.[39] Earlier Henry G. Walker announced that his horse had been stolen at Memorable Walker's Mills. He was offering $15.00 reward "and reasonable charges for mileage; or fifty dollars for the horse and thief, if convicted to death."[40] This was at a time when the first offense was death.

With all of Petersburg's stores, it was not surprising that now and then one was broken into and something stolen. Robert S. Sayre reported that his store had been entered by a thief who stole some notes and a few articles of merchandise,[41] and John E. Stokes published the news that a thief had stolen from his store a silver watch, for which he was offering a reward.[42]

It was not recorded that Petersburg was ever the scene of a murder. Its crimes were few, and those who lived there could walks its streets in nighttime or day unterrified and unafraid.

11

Education and Religion

WITHIN A RADIUS of twenty-five miles from Petersburg for a quarter century and more no one in the fields of education and religion was better known than Moses Waddel. Born in North Carolina in 1770, he came to Georgia as a young man of eighteen and settled for a time in Greene County as a teacher. Being of a contemplative and religious nature he was soon drawn into the Presbyterian Church and a little later was licensed to preach.[1]

Combining teaching with preaching in the mid-1790's he moved into Columbia County, down the Savannah from Petersburg, and set up a school "on the Kiokas [Creek]," about two miles below Appling, the county seat. The school was known as Carmel Academy, but it seems that it was also designated as Columbia County Academy in order to receive a state endowment. In 1797 it was announced that Carmel Academy would hold its "exhibition," on October 19, at which two plays would be acted and "about twelve or fifteen speeches will be spoken."[2] Two years later Abraham Baldwin, who had written the charter of the University of Georgia in 1785, as one of the commissioners announced that Columbia Academy would open for its second year "under the care and instruction of the Revd. Moses Waddle [this spelling indicating how the name was at that time pronounced]."[3] In the meantime, on one of his preaching expeditions, Waddel had turned up in the "Calhoun Settlement," on the South Carolina side, some miles to the eastward of Petersburg, and had met Catherine Calhoun, the only sister of John C. Calhoun, and had married her. John C. Calhoun now attended Waddel's school in Columbia County, where he was prepared to enter the Junior Class at Yale. Another one of Waddel's students was William H. Crawford; it was here that Crawford received all the formal schooling he ever had.

154 Old Petersburg •

Catherine died only a year after her marriage, as announced in April, 1796: "Died. On Sunday the 10th instant, in the 22d year of her age, the lovely Kitty Waddel, wife of the Rev. Moses Waddel, of Columbia County. The fortitude with which she endured her tedious illness, and the resignation with which she met her dissolution, were such as excited the admiration of all who attended her at that time, and afforded a comfortable hope of her having made a happy exit."[4] While Waddel had been a student at Hampden-Sydney College from 1790 to 1793 he had met Miss Eliza Woodson Pleasants, who in 1800 became his second wife.[5]

Waddel never became an actual resident of Petersburg, however, in 1801 he moved from Columbia County and settled in Vienna, which was removed from Petersburg only by a ferry-ride across the Savannah. Here he set up his Vienna Academy, which served equally Petersburg and Vienna. LeRoy Pope acted as financial agent in making collections of tuition in Petersburg.[6] Waddel's school served not only as a highly efficient educational institution but it also became a center for social and intellectual activities for this "tri-city" area. Several times a year it held its "exhibitions," which consisted of plays, declamations, and orations; and it held its annual examinations, where the patrons could come and enjoy the festivities, later called "commencements," when they could see and hear the students perform their part in being examined for promotion. In 1803, when Petersburg neglected to appoint a Fourth of July orator, Waddel held a school exhibition, supplemented by a barbecue, which drew many of the Petersburgers across the river.[7]

One of the Petersburg boys, who had moved to Savannah, attended the exhibition in May (1803) and wrote to his friend Larkin Newby, now in Fayetteville, North Carolina, that "we had an exhibition in Waddles School which of course drew together all the Neighboring Girls & boys on either side [of the river]—we had a large party—& in the evening went over to Petersburg where we had a very social hop—early next morning I bid them a final adieu for I never more do expect to trouble the place again. I quitted them with great reluctance yet it was obliged to be so."[8]

John Williams Walker, one of Waddel's students who was preparing to enter Princeton, was now studying Latin and Greek and was entranced with Virgil. He prepared an oration on the "Death of Washington" for an exhibition to be held in May, 1804, when there were also to be given two plays, in one of which he was to have a part. The plays were Oliver Goldsmith's "She

Stoops to Conquer, or the Mistakes of a Night" and Joseph Addison's "The Haunted House."[9] Many other Petersburg youths were crossing the river to attend Waddel's school.

In 1804 Waddel moved his school to his plantation about five or six miles to the southeast near Willington, where it continued a record already established when it was at Vienna, adjudged as "equal to any institution of the kind in the United States."[10] There as David Ramsay, the South Carolinian historian, wrote in 1809, "The melody and majesty of Homer delight the ear and charm the understanding in the very spot, and under the identical trees, which sixty years ago resounded with the war-whoops and horrid yellings of savage indians."[11]

Thither young Walker followed Waddel, and he could report to his friend Newby: "I am now in the midst of a wood, leaning against a stately and venerable oak, with my ink stand by my side, and a sheet of paper on my knee."[12] The next year he entered the Junior Class at Princeton. Waddel's school was to be often praised, but not too often or too much, for among the hundreds of students who came under his tutelage, there were such outstanding leaders as John C. Calhoun, George McDuffie, George R. Gilmer, and Abraham Baldwin Longstreet.

Waddel was often in Petersburg to preach regularly every sixth Sunday in 1806[13] and thereafter for sometime, to deliver funeral sermons, to visit among the families (the Waddels and Hillyers being especially close friends), to perform marriage ceremonies,[14] and to trade at Petersburg stores.[15] He preached the funeral of Memorable Walker on May 29, 1803, using as his text Job, Chapter 14, verses 10, 11, and 12: "But man dieth, and wasteth away: yea, man giveth up the ghost, and where is *he? As* the waters fail from the sea, and the flood decayeth and drieth up: So man lieth down, and riseth not: till the heavens *be* no more, they shall not awake, nor be raised out of their sleep."[16] A little later in the year he gave an "eloquent and appropriate discourse" at the burial of John R. Ragland.[17] When Mary, the wife of Joseph Watkins, died, Waddel was called on for the funeral oration.[18] Waddel remained at his Willington school and made himself handy in Petersburg until 1819, when he was elected President of the University of Georgia and moved to Athens.

There were other schools in the neighborhood of Petersburg and in the town itself there were schoolmasters and schoolmistresses, however, no one approached Waddel in scholarship or in excellence of instruction. Not far from Willington and nearer to

Petersburg was a school which Charles Tew of Charleston announced he was establishing to teach reading, writing, arithmetic, grammer, and geography. He added that "Mrs. Tew will (if sufficiently patronized) instruct young Ladies in every branch of needle work."[19] This school was a far cry from Waddel's Willington academy.

In an attempt to emulate Waddel, James Armor under the heading of "Education & Health" announced in 1809 that he had commenced a private academy in the neighborhood of "Col. Benjamin Taliaferro, in Wilkes county, on Broad River, about seven or eight miles above Petersburg, in a high, healthy and moral neighborhood—in which Academy students will be taught the Latin, Greek and English languages correctly, and likewise, all those different branches of science, which are necessary to prepare them for entering a College or University." "Good and decent board" could be had for $5.00 or $6.00 a month or $72.00 for the year.[20]

In Petersburg itself there were schools run by a Mr. Reid and Nathan Warner,[21] and there was Mrs. Solomon Roundtree's school catering especially to "young ladies." Mrs. Roundtree being the wife of a Petersburg merchant who had come down from New York, advertised herself as having had great success in teaching in that Northern city, and thought that she should "merit the patronage of a generous public." The purpose of her school was for "Educating young Ladies, in the useful and ornamental arts of Tambor Embroidery, Lacework, Plain Work, also Reading, Writing and Drawing."[22] Many of the young Petersburg girls attended this school, including Rebecca Freeman (Mrs. Shaler Hillyer), her cousin Polly Freeman (Mrs. William Wyatt Bibb), and Sarah Herndon Watkins (Mrs. Stephen Willis Harris).[23]

Just as some of the Petersburg boys attended the University of Georgia and even went as far away as Princeton and Yale, so some of the Petersburg girls continued their education at Salem College in North Carolina and especially at the Moravian College in Bethlehem, Pennsylvania. In 1803 Matilda Pope "together with some of her acquaintances" was off to Bethlehem. With her were Prudence and Sally Oliver, daughters of John Oliver (son of old Dionysus). Matilda's going North to school was not pleasing to John Williams Walker, her sweetheart, for he was afraid "that this Northern College will make 'old things become entirely new,' will render the disposition of Matty quite the contrary of what it was. Or will put such highflying notions into her head that she may become short sighted toward her former acquaintances, and to your humble servant among them."[24] Only three years later Walker himself entered Princeton, but in neither case did their Northern education wean them from each other, for in due time they were married and on their way to Alabama, where Walker became one of the outstanding leaders of that state.

School books were for sale by the Petersburg merchants, who as the forerunners of department stores sold anything a person might want and be able to buy. Noah Webster's "Blue-Back Spellers" was a stand-by for the elementary schools, and for the academies the ancient classics were always in good supply. In 1806 Oliver & Watkins announced in the Petersburg newspaper that they had "a choice collection of Latin & Greek Books, of nearly every description taught in the schools of this country."[25]

School children read books because they were made to do so by their teachers, but the intellectual atmosphere in Petersburg was so well developed as to lead grown-ups to buy books and read them for pleasure and profit. John Marshall's *Life of George Washington*, which was being published during the years 1804 to 1807, was a favorite in Petersburg; LeRoy Pope, the sales agent for Petersburg, was helping to make it so.[26] Robert Thompson ("Old Blue"), the merchant, was promoting the sale of a religious work, *Solemn Truths, Stated and Urged in a Lecture & Sermon: By the Late Rev. John Springer, A. M. To which is Prefaced a Short Sketch of the Author's Life.*[27]

A Petersburger signing himself "Observer" called attention in 1806 to the heritage recorded in books, awaiting all who would bestir themselves to read them. "The living world," he wrote, "is but a small part of the scope of human intellect. No man can be wise, who is contented with passing events, and he only, who combines the past with the present; he alone is able to predict the future." He proposed a library to serve Petersburg and the surrounding country, to be financed by the issuance of one hundred shares at $6.00 a share, with no one allowed to own more than three shares. Three volumes could be borrowed for each share and be kept for one month. He estimated that with the $600 which would be secured by the sale of the one hundred shares the co-operative library would be able to buy 300 volumes, since he believed that books could be bought at an average of $2.00 a volume. There should be histories, biographies, travels, voyages, ethics, sermons, novels, and "well selected" poetry. He noted, "Newspapers are excellent means of scattering information, but a man must be a miserable ignoramus, who has no other source of information."[28]

There is no record indicating that this proposed library association ever came into existence; however, there was going at this time the Petersburg Union Society, which had been incorporated in 1802. The purpose of the Society was stated in the preamble of the act: "Whereas it is a matter of the highest importance in a free government, to increase and diffuse knowledge, and the height of benevolence to alleviate the wants of distress," the people composing the Society "have formed themselves together for the above laudable purpose." This statement of purpose was in such general terms that it left a question as to what the Society intended to do. Other records indicate that it resolved itself into a debating society, which certainly could result in diffusing knowledge among its members. In the act of incorporation the membership was listed, with Shaler Hillyer as president and John Williams Walker as secretary. There were eighteen members, including such important Petersburgers as Robert Watkins, William Wyatt Bibb, and his brother Thomas.[29]

There was no more perfect combination of teacher and preacher than was to be found in Moses Waddel. As was understood in those days, education without religion was hardly worthwhile. Petersburg was not imbued with a religious complex equal to some communities in Puritanical Massachusetts, but there was a wholesome respect for preachers and an attempt to follow their teachings—and certainly some of the Petersburgers had as tender a regard for the welfare of their souls as did anyone in New England have for the welfare of his soul or the souls of others.

Anyone coming down east of the mountains and wanting to enter Georgia north of Augusta would likely find it most convenient to cross the Savannah at Petersburg—or in the reverse direction anyone leaving Georgia to go through central or upper South Carolina would likewise cross at Petersburg. This strategic location led William Bartram there in 1776, just as it led John Lyon, another botanist and plant-hunter less well know, there in 1803 and 1808.[30] So it was, then, that Bishop Francis Asbury in spreading Methodism in Georgia entered and left Georgia through Petersburg at least a dozen times. He first came to Georgia in 1788[31] and noted in his journal for April 1, "We crossed the Savannah at the Forks, and came where I much wanted to be, in Georgia." Although Petersburg was now about two years old, he referred to the place as "the Forks." The next day he rested, and on the fifth he noted that he began preaching at the quarterly meeting, and on "Sunday 6. There was a moving on the souls of the people." On the ninth he wrote in his journal, "Our conference began at the Forks of Broad-River, where six members, and four probationers attended." And during the next two days, "I felt free, and preached with light and liberty each day. Many that had no religion in Virginia, have found it after their removal into Georgia and South Carolina: here at least the seed sprung up, wherever else it may have been sown."[32]

Since this was the first Methodist Conference to have been held in Georgia, there has long been confusion and dispute as to the exact spot. There is reason to believe that it might have been in Petersburg, for Asbury first referred to Petersburg as "the Forks," and when he named "the Forks of Broad-River" as the location of the Conference, it would seem logical to think that he meant the same "Forks." At that time the only other place the term "Forks of Broad River" came to be used was where the South Fork entered Broad River more than thirty miles above Petersburg, in a region wild and uninhabited. Whether or not the Conference was held in Petersburg, it was somewhere in the vicinity of that town,[33] and the Bishop might have used the term to refer to any place in that extensive triangle between the Broad and Savannah rivers.

In 1792 Bishop Asbury passed through Petersburg on his way out of Georgia,[34] and after another visit in 1796 he noted "I must needs go through Petersburg."[35] Three years later he came back, crossing the Savannah at the Cherokee Ford, some miles above Petersburg, and went on to the home of William Tait, who lived up the Broad river some distance. He wrote in his journal for November 18, "We attended at Tait's chapel, in the Forks [a term which undoubtedly meant the region above Petersburg, but in the forks of the Broad and Savannah rivers]": and continuing, "it was a cold day. I gave a short exhortation on Rev. XXI, 7. I passed a night with Charles Tait, formerly of Cokesbury [College in Maryland], and was made exceedingly welcome and comfortable."[36] The next year he was in Georgia again and after wandering around in the upper Broad River Valley, "then had we to cross Broad-River, and pierce through the woods, *scratch and go in* the by-paths—wind round the plantations—creep across the newly cleared ground by clambering over trees, boughs, and fence-rails: thus we made our way fifteen miles to Charles Tait's, in Elbert County." Pushing on down the river to Petersburg he crossed the Savannah on Robert Martin's ferry, a few miles above the town.[37]

For two years in succession the Bishop had been making visits to Georgia, and now in November, 1801, after a ride "in the rain and evening damps we arrived at Richard Easter's in Petersburg, at the junction of the rivers, on which are the towns of Lisbon and Vienna in South-Carolina." After describing Petersburg as previously quoted in this narrative,[38] Asbury continued, "At noon we held a meeting; the day was cold, and the house open. At night I preached in Richard Easter's house on Isai. XL, 31; the people were very attentive." He journeyed on up the Broad River Valley, where he ran into Baptists and Presbyterians, and noted that "I was often interrupted by singing and shouting"—not making it clear whether these manifestations were by his own people or as hostile gestures by the other denominations.[39]

Asbury must have been especially attracted to Petersburg, for some of the Petersburgers were his fast friends. Skipping a year, "On Saturday [December 10, 1803] I came to Petersburg. The text for today was Thess. V. 8, 9." The next day "It rained. I spoke in a very open house on Ephes. VI. 18, 19. I lodged at Mr. [John] Oliver's. The face of affairs here is greatly altered for the better; but I expect greater things yet: We have a society, it is true; but we want a house of our own to preach in." He went on up Broad River and lodged at the home of his friend "Judge Tait [Charles Tait, it was, who was now judge of the Superior Court of the Western Circuit]."[40]

Two years later, Asbury was back in Petersburg, where there was a going Methodist congregation or "society." On October 30, 1805, he had ridden twenty miles through South Carolina and had crossed the Savannah into Petersburg before he had breakfast. He lodged at the home of John Oliver. The next day he preached at 11 o'clock. He had hoped that he would find a commodious Methodist Church building: "Instead of building a small convenient house, they have bought an old house, and fitted up a room for every body: this did not please me." Here he ran across a volume of John Marshall's *Life of George Washington,* and could hardly put the book down before reading 400 pages. He judged it to be a wonderful book. He was soon visiting Richard Easter and Judge Charles Tait, two families in addition to John Oliver's, whom he especially admired.[41]

Back in Georgia again in 1806, the Bishop rode into Petersburg from (Wilkes County), a distance of thirty-two miles; after that long ride he preached in the evening at 7 o'clock. "Reverend—Cummins [Francis Cummins] and Reverend—Doke [Samuel Doak?], our Presbyterian brethren, were present."[42] Apparently the Presbyterians were paying some attention to Petersburg. Whenever Asbury came near Petersburg he was impelled to ride to the home of "Charles Tait, a judge," and to preach in "Tait's meeting-house."[43] He came again into Petersburg the next year with his companion Daniel Hitt. The latter "preached at John Oliver's: our host has a son-in-law converted at camp meeting. Our preachers have passed by this town, but the Lord will not pass by Petersburg, but will visit precious souls here." The next day they rode on to Judge Tait's.[44] Asbury inferred that the Methodists were sowing the seeds of repentance through the fervor of their camp meetings, but many of these seeds of repentance were sprouting up Baptists.[45]

For the next half dozen years Bishop Asbury was neglecting Petersburg and Georgia; however, in 1813 he arrived again in Petersburg, went on and "lodged at senator Tait's [being now a United States Senator], and I retired to bed with a fever." There was a drought and much sickness in the Valley. On the 14th of November he "preached at Peter Oliver's: my host and wife are both sick."[46] During the months of December, 1814, and January, 1815, Asbury made his last visit to Georgia, passing over the Savannah at Petersburg into South Carolina.[47] The next year he was dead. He had undergone amazing hardships in his travels over the eastern United States, moving mostly on horseback but sometimes in a gig. He had devoted more time to Petersburg than had any other Methodist preacher of that period, and Methodism there was largely his handiwork.

A little of the religious awakening that had come to Petersburg grew out of several visits by Lorenzo Dow, one of the most eccentric and yet most powerful preachers who operated on the early American frontiers. "Crazy Dow," as he was often called, was born in Connecticut in 1777 and lived until 1834. He first appeared in Petersburg in February, 1802, with an introduction to Solomon Roundtree, who opened his house for a meeting, and, as Dow wrote, "showed me the greatest kindness of any man since I came to the south." To drum up a crowd Dow had walked the streets of Petersburg passing out handbills; so great an impression did he make on the people, that they offered him $10.00 and a horse to ride to Augusta. He accepted the money but true to his method of traveling, he set out walking. Before leaving Petersburg he visited Vienna and Lisbon.[48]

The same month, a year later, he made his way into Petersburg, having passed down through South Carolina, where the Methodists treated him very cool—although claiming to be a Methodist he was not very orthodox. He had a better reception in Petersburg, for "as soon as I entered Petersburg," he said, "a lad knew me, and soon word flew over the town that the *walking preacher* had got back, and I spoke to an assembly of magnitude that night." He added, "A society of Methodists was raised here when I was walking this country last year, though religion was cold. Now it seemed to flourish, my way was opened, and I sent appointments, and visited the country extensively as Providence enabled me to succeed."[49] John Williams Walker wrote to his friend Newby a few weeks later, "Lorenzo Dow has been here sometime ago—the same eccentric genius—the same logical reasoner—the same insignificance in his appearance."[50]

Dow had a habit of announcing months ahead just when he would be at a given place to preach. When he had left Petersburg in February he promised to be back about eight months later, and true to his word he turned up at the appointed time. Traveling without purse or profit, he depended on the people he met to take care of his wants. "Here [in Petersburg]," he wrote, "my wants were relieved, mostly by Major John Oliver, who came and called me his spiritual father, and so did several others, and I saw a great alteration in the inhabitants." The Major told him that "when you preached in Petersburg last, your text was constantly ringing in my ears, for days together, whether I would deal kindly and truly with the master, &c. So I had no peace until I set out to seek the Lord; and since, my wife and I have been brought to rejoice in the Almighty."

Dow continued, "He gave me a vest, pantaloons, umbrella, stockings, handkerchief, and a *watch,* &c. Another gave me a pair of shoes and a coat; and a third a cloak; and a few shillings for spending money from a few others." Satisfied with what he had accomplished in Petersburg, he set out to the westward.[51]

John Williams Walker, a son of old Jere Walker, was duly religious, but was often called a Deist because he stated his rule of conduct thus: "Be a good man—Be religious if you choose but do not be a fanatical bigot."[52] Walker had this comment on Dow's latest visit to Petersburg: "That eccentric preacher, Lorenzo Dow, has made an appointment to preach in Petersburg this evening, and I have no doubt but what the house will be very much crowded." Furthermore, "this man Dow, altho of the most contemptible appearance, impeded in his utterance and of the most inharmonious voice, is yet heard with a great deal of pleasure, and is admired as a great preacher. Tho I am convinced that the oddity of his manner is the principal foundation of his fame, yet I will not do him so much injustice as to insinuate that this is his only talent, for to speak truth, he has one of the soundest and most cogent reasons I ever heard: and with this one advantage I think the mean appearance of his person and the badness of his enunciation do but serve to set him off."[53]

Dow was no orator nor was Bishop Asbury a spellbinder. No one who passed up and down the Broad River Valley was the equal of James Russell in winning converts both by his personality and his powerful language. He was of lowly and obscure ancestry and was said to have been born in Mecklenburg County, North Carolina, about 1786. Being left an orphan early in life he did not learn to read and write until he was grown—according to general agreement, "while not the greatest, certainly the most remarkable man in Georgia Methodism."[54] Bishop James O. Andrew, around whom the Methodist Church split into Northern and Southern branches, in his youth heard Russell with "feelings of awe and veneration." Russell's great oratorical power and an unparalleled ability at pathos and exhortation brought conversion to thousands of his hearers.[55]

In 1812 he moved down to Savannah to establish Methodism, where in Colonial times, John Wesley as a minister of the Church of England had preached. To build a meeting house Russell cut the timber and did the construction with little help from anyone. To support himself he cut and sold marsh grass; however, by the time Bishop Asbury visited Savannah in 1813, Russell had awakened the people and gained their support sufficiently for him to present to the Bishop a gig, costing $45.00.[56] His acumen extended beyond employing the methods of saving souls, for about the end of the War of 1812 he deserted the ministry and entered into speculations which gained him a small fortune. He moved back into the Petersburg region, where he engaged in some business ventures and settled in Vienna; here it seems he had visions of building the town into a great metropolis largely to be his own. This grand scheme soon failed and left him with nothing. Hereafter he led a pathetic life; it was said that he tried to make a living in Augusta by delivering packages in a wheelbarrow. He died in Abbeville, South Carolina, in 1825.[57]

Preachers came and went through Petersburg and the Broad River Valley, seeking to gather their hearers into the church. Most of these men who had heard the call to preach the Gospel were Methodists and Baptists, but some like Moses Waddel were Presbyterians, less colorful and more stationary. Now and then an impostor would turn up, as did a person calling himself John Malona and asserting that he represented the Baptists. Charged with immorality he demanded a trial, but not appearing, he "was proved by incontrovertable evidence to be a Drunkard, a Lyar, a Boaster, in fine a common Rake, to the discredit of the Christian name."[58]

Religion became entrenched as much in Petersburg as probably in any other town in the state. John Williams Walker in his correspondence with his friend Newby was a faithful reporter of most happenings in Petersburg during the first decade of the nineteenth century. He wrote in 1804 that "the people of Petersburg are getting very religious," and noted that wives were fast converting their husbands.[59] It is not known how many church buildings there were in Petersburg; but certainly there was one,[60] which might have served different congregations—this in addition to the meeting house which had displeased Bishop Asbury.

12

The Decline of Petersburg
and the Broad River Valley

THE FIRST INDICATION that all was not well with Petersburg came with the decline in real estate. Near the end of 1809 John Williams Walker, contemplating a move to the westward, wrote, "I could hardly give away my lands now—they are in so little request."[1] This stagnation was not entirely the result of any fundamental decay in Petersburg; the embargo on trade with Europe had caused a similar situation in many other places as the prices of cotton and tobacco reached almost the vanishing point. The war which broke out in 1812 made the situation worse, for this very year the sheriff of Elbert County sold for taxes a one-acre lot adjoining Petersburg, which Archibald Stokes bid in for $36.00.[2]

The spurt of prosperity following the end of the war in 1815 gave new life to Petersburg, when in 1818 Lot 81 with improvements sold for $2,500; but the recession which set in the next year and continued for some years led to the resale of this lot in 1826 for $275.[3] It would seem that there must have been other considerations or that disaster had in the meantime hit some of the improvements since in 1821 a half-acre lot with a house on it was sold for $1,200;[4] in 1824 three acres of land adjoining Petersburg was sold for $1,000,[5] and as late as 1832 Henry Kneeland bought for $1,400 a two-acre lot containing a dwelling house large enough to have a part of it devoted to a store.[6]

By the late 1830's Petersburg was fast falling into decay. In December, 1834, this transaction took place: Henry Kneeland sold to Zinny (Zimri?) Tate and Drury B. Cade for $8,500, 2,322 acres extending all the way from the Savannah River across the Broad into Lincoln County, including nine Petersburg lots, eight slaves, and all ferry privileges from Petersburg to Lisbon and across the Savannah to the site of Vienna.[7]

The Cades were gradually buying up the remnants of Petersburg during the next thirty years. In 1837 Drury B. and Guilford Cade, Sr., bought a lot with a dwelling on it for $800; in 1863 the latter Cade bought the Archibald Stokes' storehouse lot for $200; and in 1876 this lot was bought by Drury B. Cade, Jr., for $100.[8] The previous year Cade had bought for $100 two lots in the "old town of Petersburg" and fifty acres lying on the road to Elberton.[9] What had previously been Petersburg was now becoming a cotton plantation.

The town government having been abandoned some years before 1831, the citizens who were left appealed this year to the legislature for relief against "sundry persons" who had "obstructed and closed up some of the public streets . . . to the inconvenience and injury of the owners of property and others residing in said town." The legislature complied by passing a law giving the road commissioners the right to order all obstructions removed and to fine any offender two dollars a day for refusal to act.[10] The encroachment of the countryside in extending its fields and pastures into the very streets of Petersburg was not long stayed; the town had disintegrated so far by 1850 that an attempt was made in the legislature to repeal the law of 1831. The dying town supporters were able to hold out a while longer by killing the bill in the House of Representatives by the close vote of 56 to 51.[11]

A recognition of Petersburg's growing insignificance in the financial world appeared in 1815 when the legislature in apportioning stock in the act incorporating the Bank of the State of Georgia awarded none at all to this town.[12] The same omission was made three years later when it incorporated the Bank of Darien.[13] Postal receipts gave a valid index to a town's business prosperity, and in this respect Petersburg was fast falling by the wayside. The Petersburg postal receipts for the year ending March 31, 1827, were only $105.17, as compared with $10,493.26 for Augusta. Some of Petersburg's rivals for oblivion were at this time not much ahead: Frederica, in Glynn County, $145.49; Hartford, in Pulaski County, $143.09; Jacksonboro, in Screven County, $150.06; Powelton, in Hancock County, $172.78; and Sunbury, in McIntosh County, $127.36. Only the following towns, destined to die, had smaller postal receipts: Salem, in Clarke County; Shoals of Ogeechee, in Warren County; Mount Zion, in Hancock County; Scull Shoals, in Greene County; Standing Peachtree, in

Gwinnett County (with $4.34); and Wrightsboro, in Columbia County.[14]

Some of the principal leaders in Petersburg and the hinterland began leaving as early as 1810. They believed the town had reached its zenith, as far as their opportunities were concerned, when they heard the beckoning cry of the West, which at that time meant the United States public domain beyond the Chattahoochee River, organized as the Mississippi Territory and extending to the Mississippi River. LeRoy Pope's interest in land and land speculation was well known, and as early as 1804 he could not resist making a trip to inspect these public lands. John Freeman, the father-in-law of Shaler Hillyer, wrote to "Dear Children" on July 9 saying, "Capt. L. Pope has returned from the westward, has stirred up the citizens of Petersburg. They are all offering their property for sale."[15] From this time on, Pope could hardly keep his mind from wandering "westward," and in 1808 he made another trip. This time he went on horseback with Thomas Bibb all the way across the Mississippi Territory to New Orleans. On the way back he was joined by his prospective son-in-law, John Williams Walker.[16]

Back in 1803 when the United States purchased Louisiana, Walker had been much impressed with the possibilities there and thought of going to embrace some of them, but he observed, "an immediate departure from *this* country to dwell in *that* would be quite imprudent."[17] After graduating at Princeton and returning to Petersburg, to remain only a short time, he took passage by ship to New Orleans in search of health and fortune. After two months there he pushed on up the river and over to Washington, in the Mississippi Territory. He was much impressed with the country, finding the land "exceedingly fertile & productive, beyond all comparison superior to that of Georgia."[18]

In 1809 a land office was opened in Nashville, Tennessee, for the sale of Mississippi Territory lands in the Big Bend of the Tennessee River country (later to be northern Alabama), and a group of Petersburgers, including LeRoy Pope, John Williams Walker, William Wyatt Bibb, and his brother Thomas immediately made purchases.[19] The next year Walker married his Matilda, and in company with his father-in-law he set out for their new lands. Writing on May 20, 1810, to Dr. Samuel Brown, a former professor in Transylvania University in Kentucky, whom Walker had met in his 1808 travels, he said, "In less than a fortnight we shall take up the line of march toward your own blessed territory." At this time Brown was living at Fort Adams, on the Mississippi River.[20] Pope was the principal commissioner appointed to choose the county seat of Madison County, and having selected the site of Huntsville he was often called thereafter the "Father of Huntsville." He became a judge, a banker, and otherwise a man of outstanding importance in Alabama history.[21]

From this time on, Petersburgers and other Georgians began moving to the Mississippi Territory, the eastern part being cut off in 1817 to become the Territory of Alabama and two years later the State of Alabama. The "Westward Movement" in America was now in full swing, to take uplands at $2.00 an acre with some variations in price in the course of time. Advertisements of fertile lands and the promotion of towns in Alabama began appearing in the Georgia newspapers as well as in letters from some of those settlers who had gone there. Praising the opportunities to be had in Huntsville and Madison County and generally throughout Alabama, a Huntsville resident wrote in 1817, "The planters in the county have become wealthy by their own industry in a few years, in the worst of times." Concluding his panegyric, he asked, "I say, with all these privileges and luxurious bounties of nature, which are not mere creatures of fance, but substantial realities, who is not ready to exclaim that the Alabama is an American Canaan."[22]

Yet to prevent a headlong migration to Alabama and Mississippi, the Georgia newspapers were always glad to publish any news of a discouraging nature. There were Indian troubles, floods, and disease. In the summer of 1811 a great flood on the Mississippi River had covered up several hundred cotton plantations; 5,000 head of stock had drowned; and the river was still rising.[23] A few years later it was reported that crops were a failure, that there was hardly any corn to be had, and that "many families, almost in a state of starvation, are retracing their steps, and endeavoring to get back to this state."[24]

Yet the tide could not be stemmed; the Western fever was spreading among the high and the low. George Weissinger, down below Petersburg in Columbia County, "contemplating a removal to the Western country" was offering his plantation for sale,[25] and many other Georgians were doing likewise. John Williams Walker, now no longer a Petersburger but a full-blown Alabaman, was in correspondence with Senator Charles Tait in 1816-1817 relative to the division of the Mississippi Territory into the two states of Mississippi and Alabama. He urged the Senator to come to Alabama.[26] In 1817 Mississippi became a state and Alabama a territory. The next year Tait announced that he would not run for the Senate again, as he was contemplating moving to Alabama.[27] The next year he moved there. The following year Secretary of the Treasury William H. Crawford, representing a friendship extending back to the duelling days around Petersburg, saw to it that President Monroe appointed Tait a district judge for Alabama.

In 1816 Congress voted to change the method of Congressmen's pay from $6.00 a day for every day in attendance to a salary of $1,500 for the year. Although this system might well have actually reduced the amount paid Congressmen, depending on the length of the sessions, there was a furious outcry all over the country against this "pay grab." William Wyatt Bibb, now a Senator, voted for the new system and was pilloried all over the state of Georgia for having done so—as, indeed, were all the other Georgia Congressmen who had voted for it. The Grand Jury of Wilkes County (into whose dominion Bibb had moved up the Broad from Petersburg) made a stinging presentment, calling for universal detestation of those who had voted for the "grab" and recommending their defeat in any subsequent attempt to re-enter Congress. Bibb was hurt by this attack and in a long communication he made an excellent defense, high-toned and convincing: "Deplorable indeed is the state of man, if against such foul aspersions a life of unimpeached and unimpeachable integrity affords him no protection. . . . From my public labours I never have derived pecuniary profit; nor in that respect is there any thing in the present compensation to render a continuance in congress desirable. But to lose your good opinion would be to lose the richest, the only reward for years of toil in the country's service. Such an event I should most deeply deplore; but still there would be a source of consolation, which we owe to the bounty of Providence, and which cannot be taken away—the consolation of 'a conscience void of offense.' "[28] A few months later (November 9, 1816) he resigned from the United States Senate and moved to Alabama.

It was not for nothing that Bibb had from early days in politics been alligned with the Jackson-Crawford-Troup faction. When Alabama became a territory Crawford recommended Bibb to President Monroe for appointment to the governorship, which he received.[29] Georgia was proud of her self-exiled son, who never lost his love for his native state, and the legislature in 1822 named a county for him. On the occasion of Bibb's message to the Alabama legislature in 1818, the *Augusta Chronicle* remarked, "He was highly esteemed by the good and learned as a distinguished statesman, and an amiable and honest citizen. A public ebullition of intemperate feeling, however, *drove him from our state.* His loss was poignantly felt by all who properly estimated talent and virtue." But his appointment as governor could not "palliate the ingratitude of his native state."[30]

When Alabama became a state in 1819 Bibb was elected governor by the people, and when he died the next year as a result of being thrown from a horse,[31] his brother Thomas, who also had moved from Petersburg to Alabama, succeeded to the governorship. With two Petersburgers as governors in succession, another as Federal judge, and others from Petersburg and the Broad River Valley in responsible positions, it became almost a matter of Petersburgers running the State of Alabama during its infant years—indeed, with the help of other Georgians who had moved to Alabama, this group came to be called the "Georgia Party."[32] No one of these Petersburgers became more distinguished than John Williams Walker, in succession a member of the Territorial House of Representatives and its speaker, president of the State Constitutional Convention in 1819, and Alabama's first United States Senator. He and his wife Matilda Pope Walker were the parents of another United States Senator, Percy Walker, and also of the first Secretary of War of the Confederate States of America, LeRoy Pope Walker.

Thus had Alabama absorbed much of Petersburg. Other Petersburgers drifting away levied further on the life of the town. One moving away in 1831 "regretted leaving very much but his interest compelled him to go," and a young lady of Petersburg, reporting this fact, added, "Petersburg is duller of course now than ever, since Mr. Turnbull and Dr. Johnson have left."[33]

The biggest news to reach the town since Lee's surrender at Appomattox in April, 1865, came the following May 3. On the verge of death itself, Petersburg now saw the last dying grasp of the Southern Confederacy, as Jefferson Davis and those accompanying him fleeing southward crossed the Savannah River on a pontoon bridge a short distance below town.[34] Judah P. Benjamin, a member of Davis' Cabinet, left the party here, after throwing the Great Seal of the Confederacy into the river and thereafter traveling in a hack disguised as a French gentleman.[35] To add to the drama after Davis had left, a detachment of Federal troops intercepted at the pontoon bridge some Confederate cavalrymen under Col. George G. Dibrell, who had been accompanying the fleeing President, and forced their surrender—but not before they had received a distribution of some of the Confederate treasure which they had been guarding on the retreat.[36] As Col. Basil W. Duke remembered the occasion about twenty years later, "At Savannah river all of the silver coin, amounting, to the best of my recollection, to some $105,000, was paid out to the troops composing the escort and to paroled Confederate soldiers who were present." The remainder of the treasure, amounting to about $300,000 in gold, was seized a few miles west of Petersburg by a motley band, never certainly identified but thought to have been made up principally of former Confederate soldiers.[37] Years later a few old cannon were still lying around in the vicinity of Petersburg as a reminder of the war that nearly reached that place;[38] children who knew not their significance played marbles around them.

Long before the Civil War, gazetteers and geography books began singing dirges over Petersburg. In 1827 Adiel Sherwood referred to it as "once a large and flourishing village and the great depot for the Tobacco raised in the country North, and thence floated to Augusta." And mentioning its two rivals, Lisbon and Vienna, he said further, "these little towns have dwindled almost to nothing."[39] George White, a Georgia historian, visited Petersburg in 1849, or perhaps a year or two earlier, and wrote, "This was once among the most prosperous towns in Georgia; but it is now in a state of dilapidation. A feeling of melancholy and loneliness is experienced by the visitor when he remembers what the town was in former days."[40] A national gazetteer called it in 1854 "a decayed post-town . . . once an important place. It now has only 3 families."[41] The post office was discontinued in 1855.

The melancholy note which White struck was echoed in accounts by almost every other person who visited the place or who wrote about it without the added pathos instilled by a sight of the spot. It was especially a poignant experience for those whose ancestors had once helped to add to the brilliance of the community. A son of Moses Waddel wrote, "A visit to the spot once occupied by these towns [Petersburg, Lisbon, and Vienna] at a later period of his life filled him with melancholy emotions, as all that once made them so flourishing and pleasant is obliterated by the restless sweep of time and change, and buried by desolation and ruin."[42] An Alabaman thinking of a visit by some descendant of a former Petersburg family, who by leaving had helped to hasten the town's decay, remarked that in "seeking to find 'where the home of his forefathers stood,' would have to employ a guide to show him the site of the ruined town."[43]

Charles C. Jones, Jr., a historian who lived in Augusta, always attracted by the sad fate of dead towns, must have visited the place about 1878, when he wrote that "now sunken wells and the mounds of fallen chimneys are all that attest the former existence of the town. Its corporate limits are wholly included within the confines of one well-ordered plantation; and extensive fields of corn and cotton have obliterated traces of warehouse, shop, town-hall, church, and dwelling."[44] Seven years later it seemed that the plantation was not so "well-ordered," to a person who described the spot as "a wilderness of cotton-wood, broomsedge, and blackberry bushes, with not even a solitary chimney to mark the spot where once it stood."[45]

A newspaper correspondent visiting there in 1888 "found it a very difficult matter to glean authentic information in regard to the early history of the town, for the oldest citizens can only remember the place after its desertion, and when only a few scattered families inhabited it. . . . What was once the flourishing city of Petersburg is now occupied by Captain Cade as a cotton field and stock farm. Lands that once sold by the foot, and streets that were thronged by busy tradesmen, are now given over to the more peaceful and quiet pursuits of agriculture. Had the curse of God fallen upon this town, its obliteration from the face of the earth could not have been more complete." Also he visited the old town graveyard whose atmosphere cast even a greater spell upon him. "There is not a sadder sight on earth than a discarded graveyard," he continued; "The vaults fallen in, the stately marble shafts toppling over, and the monuments and tombstones wrenched as if by some convulsion of nature." It was now "a dense and almost inpenetrable thicket of vines and all manner of shrubbery, that have been allowed to run wild."[46]

A cause of Petersburg's decline first mentioned by Sherwood in 1827 and restated by almost every writer thereafter was the coming of cotton, which supplanted tobacco as a principal crop. Petersburg had grown up as an inspection point for tobacco; cotton needed no inspection in any given place—wherever it was sold a sample was ripped out of each bale. Cotton was "thrown upon Boats all along the river without being inspected," Sherwood wrote.[47] Another cause was disease brought on by the damp location and stagnant water allowed to stand in cellars. This sickness was most likely malaria, as has been diagnosed by some writers[48]—but certainly not yellow fever, which some traditions have pronounced it to have been, and not one grand pestilence of it which drove the survivors away all at once. The yellow fever theory was that Petersburg had no machinery to pump water from cellars and therefore it remained to stagnate, causing "an epidemic of yellow fever. Some died, many fled from the town, the stores and houses fell into decay, and today [1902] broad fields of cotton and corn mark the place where the Savannah and Broad rivers flow together."[49]

Another theory, as stated by a visitor in 1888, held that "Fulton's invention of the steam boat sounded its death knell."[50] By 1816 steamboats were plying up the Savannah to Augusta, but beyond that point they were not practicable, being stopped by the rapids there and by shoals and other obstructions on up the river to Petersburg. Augusta thus supplanted Petersburg as the center of trade for upper Georgia and South Carolina. Steam applied to land transportation was a most potent cause of Petersburg's final extinction. Augusta's advantage over Petersburg was further enhanced when the Charleston and Hamburg Railroad reached the opposite side of the Savannah in 1833. The river strategy of Petersburg's location in 1786 was its undoing by this time. Rivers were now hazards to railroad construction and never before Petersburg's death did a railroad come within seventy-five miles of the place.

And finally, both as cause and effect, there was the departure of Petersburg's most enterprising citizens, beginning in 1810, when the Popes and the Walkers went to Alabama, followed by the Taits, the Bibbs, the Watkinses, the Thompsons, the Olivers, and many others—many to Mississippi, to Tennessee, and to beckoning lands of promise in Georgia. For the most part, they had caught the "Western Fever" that powerful urge among the inhabitants of the Eastern seaboard states, which led them not only to the Mississippi River but finally all the way across the continent to the Pacific Ocean.

Petersburg and its environs represented only the lower part of the Broad River Valley. Those Virginians who had appropriated the Valley farther up, and especially the Goose Pond region, discovered also that the course of empire led westward and they were caught in the movement as early as were the Petersburgers. They left behind a region soon to be overgrown with broomsedge and blackberry briars, as pathetic reminders of past glory. A traveler passing through the Goose Pond section declared that it was "the most perfect picture of desolation I have ever seen. For miles not a sign of improvement is to be seen, while a silence as profound as that which reigns over the great desert suggests that the Curse of God must rest over the land."[51]

A pathetic and more detailed picture of this region came from the pen of a newspaper editor who visited it in 1878: "the desolate wilds of Lower Goose-Pond—a section of country that was once the Eden of Georgia, but since the late war has been given over to decay and Bermuda grass. The wealthy land-owners have moved to a more congenial clime, and their places are filled by vagrant blacks or a thriftless class of whites. Occasionally you see an antiquated old nabob, who in years gone by owned and worked a large number of slaves and was then a leading spirit of his homestead, who still, through affection for his old homestead, or dire poverty, clings to the old farm, and gleans a meagre subsistence by renting patches of land here and there on his place to tenants. It is a sad thing to think that in a few years, at most, even these, the last sad relict of Goose-Pond's ancient grandeur, will have passed away. The former stately mansions, whose hospitable doors were ever open, have either succumbed to the torch of the incendiary, or, like their owners, are fast crumbling to decay. But even in this dilapidation they present a sad, but interesting study, and it is an easy matter for the stranger to read in them the grand past of this fine old section."

There was a fine barn on one of the vacant plantations, and at the end of the war "a party of thieves went for it and actually tore down and carried off the building—a portion of its timbers being utilized in building a negro church and the remainder going into an illicit still-house." In addition to "moonshine" whiskey the chief products of the region were "bench-legged fice, blue collards and tow-headed children, with a sprinkling of sorghum and pumpkins," the latter piled up in yards for sale at two and a half cents each. In the fall, persimmon beer was "the strongest beverage used by the Gooseponders. They have its manufacture down to a science and use it in inordinate quantities."[52] Another visitor found that "that section of country seems to have sunk at one time into a sort of half barbaric condition, which rendered it almost obnoxious to its more civilized neighbors."[53]

One other product which this deserted region produced was spooks and haunts, which both Negroes and whites felt sure they saw. As a person might be riding on horseback or in a buggy down one of the roads, the "thing" would be seen darting and dodging ahead until suddenly it disappeared into one of those plantation burial grounds, which the departing grandees had to leave behind.[54]

Not being grouped together as were the Petersburgers, who had their own central graveyard, these Virginia planters developed their separate burial grounds, erected imposing monuments or placed impressive marble slabs over graves, and enclosed the whole with attractive metal fences or brick or stone walls. In the course of time, nature crept in upon these plots and scattered over them bramble briars and pine saplings which grew into trees to push over some imposing monument, and at the same time allowing to run riot those mourning tokens of periwinkle, English ivy, and Virginia creeper, interspersed with untrimmed cedars. The Micajah McGehee cemetery was surmounted by a monument eight feet high, enclosed by a metal fence, which by the twentieth century had been broken down by a fallen tree. The Gilmer graveyard had suffered a sadder fate. A stone's throw from the old 1800-built homestead, this plot, unprotected by any enclosure, was included in a cow pasture to be trampled upon by grazing bovines and rooting swine, desecrating, overturning, and breaking the gravestones. In the midst of a cultivated field stood a little wilderness of cedars and chinaberries, shading several marble slabs overgrown with brambles. Under one rested a wife of General George Mathews; under another, the wife of the General's son, Charles L. Mathews. In the Huff graveyard were the remains of Richard Huff without benefit of a marker, though at one time he had owned many acres of land and enough slaves to tend them. Nearby were buried many of those slaves who did not choose to accept his offer of freedom and transportation to Liberia.[55] These and others were precious possessions which the Virginians could not take with them to Alabama, Mississippi, and even beyond.

The fundamental reason for the migration of the Gilmers, the Mathewses, the Lewises, the McGehees, and others was the opening of the fertile cotton lands to the westward and the soil exhaustion of the tobacco lands of Georgia. Of the five principal towns in the Broad River Valley, only Petersburg disappeared completely. Lexington, being the chief center of the Goose Pond Virginians and deserted by them, continued to live an arrested existence, whose growth was further stunted by the removal from Oglethorpe County of the Barrows, the Cobbs, the Crawfords, the Lumpkins, the Phinizys, the Upsons, and other prominent families, who went to other parts of Georgia. Furthermore, Francis

Meson, an early Lexington merchant, endowed the local academy with much of the land on which Lexington would have grown greater, thereby removed it from fee simple sale.

The other towns—Washington, Elberton, and Lincolnton—had not depended for their growth on those two special groups of Broad River Valley people, the Petersburgers and the Goose Pond Virginians; therefore, their departure was not a devastation to these towns and to the rest of the Valley.

After these migrations there was still life left in the old land, and by the twentieth century it was coming back as resplendent as it had ever been a century previously, but in a changed form. Well-kept plantations and cattle pastures and attractive residences were replacing the desolation which followed the migration of the Virginians. A son of Wilkes County, James Monroe Smith, of Maryland extraction, moved across Broad River into Oglethorpe County, and by the time of his death in 1915 he had become a millionaire by farming and stock-raising and processing the products therefrom.

For Petersburg there was no return, inasmuch as by the mid-twentieth century the waters of the Savannah and Broad rivers had been merged by the Clark Hill Dam into a vast lake which put the site of the old town under fifty feet of water. The living Petersburgers had long since moved away; the remains of those who slept in the old graveyard were taken to the old cemetery of Bethlehem Methodist Church, up on high ground a few miles away, where Bishop Asbury had once preached—there to await the sound of Gabriel's horn.

Notes

Numbers in brackets at the top of the following pages indicate
the pages in the text to which these notes refer.

CHAPTER 1

1. Charles C. Jones, Jr., *The History of Georgia* (2 vols. Boston, 1883) , II, 127;
"Letters from Sir James Wright," in *Collections of the Georgia Historical Society*
(12 vols. Savannah, 1840-) , III (1873) , 160. Governor Wright stated the acreage
to be 2,116,298.

2. William Bartram, *Travels through North and South Carolina, Georgia, East
and West Florida, the Cherokee Country, the Extensive Territories of the Muscogulges or Creek Confederacy, and the Country of the Chactaws* . . . (Dublin, Ire-
land, 1793) , 322. For Wright's Proclamation, see Jones, *History of Georgia*, II,
130-31. An original handbill is in the De Renne Collection in the General Library
of the University of Georgia. Adding to Wright's description of the New Purchase,
Bartram said that it was "a body of excellent and fertile land, well watered by
innumerable rivers, creeks and brooks." *Travels*, 322.

3. Alex M. Hitz, "The Earliest Settlements in Wilkes County," in *Georgia His-
torical Quarterly* (49 vols. Savannah, 1917-) , XL (1956) , 269-70; Jones, *History of
Georgia*, II, 131-32; Grace Gillam Davidson, comp., *Early Records of Georgia, Wilkes
County* (2 vols. Macon, 1932) , I, 4-5.

4. Robert L. Meriwether, *The Expansion of South Carolina, 1729-1765* (Kingsport, Tenn., 1940) , 116, 246-47; Bartram, *Travels*, 322.

5. Bartram, *Travels*, 321-22.

6. Hitz, "Earliest Settlements in Wilkes County," 262, 274-80; Louise Frederick
Hays, *Hero of Hornet's Nest. A Biography of Elijah Clark [e], 1733-1799* (New York,
1946) , 12-14; Elbert County Deed Record G, 124 (Elberton, Ga.) . There had been
hesitation by some of the Indians at the Augusta Treaty Conference in giving up
their lands; and they left with some feeling of bitterness. Before the end of the
year Indian hostilities began against the settlers, in which murdering and pillaging
took place. After about a year of scattered hostilities, a conference was held in
Savannah and a peace agreement was signed on October 20, 1774. Jones, *History
of Georgia*, II, 132-35. Dart River was a name that never came into common use,
hardly getting off the official papers on which it was written. Even the surveyors
appointed by Sir James Wright to run the boundary lines on the New Purchase
never used the name on their official map—they used Broad River. This latter name
was given to the stream by the early settlers as a compliment in view of the
smaller stream to the southward which was called Little River. An early undated
map "par les Freres Lotter à Ausburg" listed the Broad as "Cherakeehaw." On a
map published in 1794 in London by Laurie & Whittle, entitled "A New and

General Map of the Southern Dominions belonging to the United States of America...," the river is called "Salwegee or Broad River." For a full description of this map, see *Catalogue of the Wymberley Jones De Renne Georgia Library*... (3 vols. Wormsloe [Savannah], 1931), III, 1225.

7. George R. Gilmer, *Sketches of Some of the First Settlers of Upper Georgia, of the Cherokees, and of the Author* (New York, 1855), 237-38; George White, *Statistics of the State of Georgia: Including an Account of its Natural, Civil, and Ecclesiastical History, Together with a Particular Description of Each County* . . . (Savannah, 1849), 234; Hitz "Earliest Settlements in Wilkes County," 276; Eliza A. Bowen, *The Story of Wilkes County, Georgia* (reprint. Marietta, Ga., 1950), 3-4; Davidson, comp., *Early Records of Georgia*, I, 15; John H. McIntosh, *The Official History of Elbert County, 1790-1935* (Elberton, Ga., 1940), 12.

CHAPTER II

1. The governors of Georgia were, George Mathews, George R. Gilmer, Matthew Talbot, and Wilson Lumpkin. The two governors of Alabama were William W. Bibb and Thomas Bibb. The counties named for residents of Broad River Valley (Virginians and others) were Clarke, Cobb, Crawford, Dooly, Gilmer, Hart, Heard, Lamar, Lumpkin, Meriwether, Talbot, Taliaferro, Toombs, Upson, and Walker.

2. Gilmer, *Georgians*, 175, 176.

3. *Ibid.*, 175. A Georgian writing in 1855 said, "We have met the Broad River people in scattered groups, talked with them, and shared their hospitality, without knowing the distinction which attached to their original locality." *Southern Recorder*, July 3, 1855, quoted in Stephen F. Miller, *The Bench and Bar of Georgia: Memoirs and Sketches* . . . (2 vols. Philadelphia, 1858), II, 439.

4. Gilmer, *Georgians*, 228.   5. *Ibid.*, 6.   6. *Ibid.*, 9-13.

7. *Ibid.*, 14, 17, 232. Oglethorpe County Deed Book, B, 341-42; G, 224-25; I, 13-14, 15, 201-204, 345-46; Oglethorpe County Tax Digest, 1800-1805, pp. 13, 30. These county records are in the Office of the Clerk of Court, in Lexington. For Thomas Meriwether Gilmer's will, see Oglethorpe County Will Book, B, 138-40, in the Office of the Ordinary.

8. Oglethorpe County Annual Returns on Estates, 1815-1830, pp. 285-87. This record is in the Office of the Ordinary. Gilmer owned a "lot of land at the Chalebate Springs in Madison County."

9. Miller, *Bench and Bar of Georgia*, II, 439.

10. Gilmer, *Georgian*, 29.

11. Letters from Mrs. Grace Lewis Miller to the present writer, St. Louis, August 4, 19, 1958; Charlottesville, Va., April 15, 1960. Mrs. Miller has spent many years gathering information on Lewis for a biography of him. See also Gilmer, *Georgians*, 104-105.

12. *Georgia Express* (Athens), January 14 (1, 1), 1809; *Oglethorpe Echo* (Lexington, Ga.), January 15 (1, 2), 1909; White, *Statistics of Georgia*, 456-60; James Edmonds Saunders, *Early Settlers of Alabama. With Notes and Genealogies, by his Granddaughter, Elizabeth Saunders Blair Stubbs* (New Orleans, 1899), 216; Gilmer, *Georgians*, 82-88, 115-23.

13. Gilmer, *Georgians*, 89.   14. *Ibid.*, 95.   15. *Ibid.*, 88-107, *passim*.

16. *Ibid.*, 91-92; *Biographical Director of the American Congress, 1774-1927* (Washington, 1928), 1306.

17. Gilmer, *Georgians*, 139-56   18. *Ibid.*, 161.

19. Saunders, *Early Settlers of Alabama*, 513; Adiel Sherwood, *A Gazetteer of the State of Georgia* (2nd edition, Philadelphia, 1829), 227; Gilmer, *Georgians*, 156-63; *Augusta Chronicle*, November 14 (3, 1), 1807.

20. Gilmer, *Georgians*, 115-23, 482.

21. *Ibid.*, 130-39; *Biographical Director of the American Congress*, 672.

22. Saunders, *Early Settlers of Alabama,* 448-54, 519-20; Gilmer, *Georgians,* 163-73. In 1800 Micajah McGehee gave in for taxes 3,165 acres on Broad River and Long Creek, and 28 slaves. Oglethorpe County Tax Digest, 1800-1805.

23. For instance (out of many which could be cited) there was Ralph Banks who with his family of a wife and thirteen children moved from North Carolina to the Broad River Valley. Intermarrying with some of the Petersburg families, several of these children moved on into Alabama. Saunders, *Early Settlers of Alabama,* 446. Many of these settlers were, of course, veterans of the Revolution. Edward Lloyd Wailes died there in 1809. "He served as an officer [in] three or four campaigns in our revolutionary war." *Georgia Express,* February 11 (3, 4), 1809.

24. Ferdinand Phinizy Calhoun, *The Phinizy Family in America* (Atlanta, 1925?), 43.

25. George W. Paschal, *Ninety-Four Years. Agnes Paschal* (Washington, 1871), 15, 32 ff. In 1805 George Paschal owned in Lexington a lot given in for taxes at $400 and merchandise at $1,000. The next year his stock in trade was valued at $600. Oglethorpe County Tax Digest, 1800-1805, p. 1; *ibid.,* 1806-1811, p. 2. See also E. Merton Coulter, *Auraria: The Story of a Georgia Gold-Mining Town* (Athens, 1956), 130-31, n. 10; *Weekly Atlanta Intelligencer,* September 15 (1 6), 1869.

26. For further information on Meson, see E. Merton Coulter, "Francis Meson, An Early Georgia Merchant and Philanthropist," in *Georgia Historical Quarterly,* XLII (1958), 27-43. At the time of his death, Meson owned 232 acres, six town lots in Lexington (valued at $5,000), merchandise listed at $7,000, and various personal effects. Oglethorpe County Tax Digest, 1811-1816, p. 4.

27. Bowen, *Wilkes County,* 56; Lucian Lamar Knight, *Georgia's Landmarks, Memorials and Legends* (2 vols. Atlanta, 1913, 1914), I, 540; White, *Historical Collections,* 447.

CHAPTER III

1. Oglethorpe County Inventories and Appraisements, Books, A, G, L, *passim* (all in the Office of the Ordinary, Lexington); George G. Smith, *The Life and Letters of James Osgood Andrew . . .* (Nashville, Tenn., 1883), 23.

2. Oglethorpe County Inventories and Appraisements, Books, A. G. *passim;* Oglethorpe County Inventories and Annual Returns on Estates, 1811-1826, 1815-1831, *passim;* Oglethorpe County Annual Returns on Estates, 1798-1814, *passim* (all in the Office of the Ordinary, Lexington); Gilmer, *Georgians,* 121.

3. Oglethorpe County Annual Returns on Estates, 1815-1830, pp. 238-39; Oglethorpe County Will Book, A, 105-106 (all in Office of the Ordinary, Lexington, Ga.).

4. Oglethorpe County Tax Digest, 1800-1805, p. 46 (In Office of Clerk of Court).

5. Oglethorpe County Will Book, A, 105-106. As an indication of the patriarchal nature of slavery, when George R. Gilmer returned to his father's home with his Virginia bride the slaves went wild with joy, shouting "Massa George is married and come home." They then grabbed the bride and carried her into the house. Gilmer, *Georgians,* 291. Bishop Francis Asbury on a trip through Oglethorpe County in 1803 visited James Marks and noted in his journal that "he is a kind master to his slaves, and hints the probability of liberating them by will; but he may change his mind before he dies." Elmer T. Clark, J. Manning Potts, and Jacob S. Payton, eds., *The Journal and Letters of Francis Asbury* (3 vols. London and Nashville, 1958), II, 416.

6. Oglethorpe County Will Book, A, 61-62.   7. *Ibid.,* C, 42; Gilmer, *Georgians* 146.

8. "1850 Census Population Schedules, Georgia, Microcopy, T-6, Roll, 71, Macon through Pike," 95; *ibid.,* Roll, 63, p. 274; *ibid.,* 1860, T-7, Roll, 33, pp. 79-80. For the tradition, see *Oglethorpe Echo,* November 15 (3, 3), 1878; August 28 (1, 3), 1908; August 21 (8, 2), 1925. Of course he might have sent some of his slaves to Africa before 1850. Census records before that time were unavailable.

9. Oglethorpe County Inventories and Appraisements, Book, H, 57; I, 57, 125,170.
10. Gilmer, *Georgians,* 166.   11. *Ibid.,* 111.
12. *Augusta Weekly Constitutionalist,* July 16 (7, 6) , 1856.
13. Gilmer, *Georgians,* 85-86. As late as the 1950's part of the old log residence was still standing.
14. *Ibid.,* 116, 160-61, 165; Lodowick Johnson Hill, Sr., *The Hills of Wilkes County, Georgia and Allied Families* (Atlanta, 1922?) , 57: Smith, *Andrew,* 23; *Oglethorpe Echo,* May 26 (8, 3) , 1899.
15. *Oglethorpe Echo,* May 26 (8, 3) , 1899.
16. Jedidiah Morse, *The American Geography or, A View of the Present Situation of the United States of America* (Elizabethtown, 1789) , 451; Gilmer, *Georgians,* 83-84, 165.
17. Oglethorpe County Inventories and Appraisements, Book G, H, I, *passim;* Inventories Annual Returns on Estates, 1815-1831, *passim.*
18. Bowen, *Wilkes County,* 47; *Oglethorpe Echo,* May 26 (1, 4) , 1899. For some school expenses charged to an estate, see Oglethorpe County Inventory Book, H, 17, 18.
19. George White, *Historical Collections of Georgia: Containing the Most Interesting Facts, Traditions, Biographical Sketches, Anecdotes, Etc.* . . . (New York, 1854) , 581; Smith, *Andrew,* 26; Gilmer, *Georgians,* 91, 92, 170-171, 232-34.
20. Gilmer, *Georgians,* 152-56; Smith, *Andrew, passim.*
21. Gilmer, *Georgians,* 142, 146.
22. *Oglethorpe Echo,* September 18 (1, 4) , 1896; *ibid.,* May 30 (5, 2) , 1913; Oglethorpe County Inventory, C, 47-48.
23. Gilmer, *Georgians,* 85-86. In drumming up a crowd for a political speaking, such an invitation as this might be heard: "O yes! O yes! all you who want to hear a speech, come here." *Ibid.,* 259-60.
24. *Ibid.,* 146.
25. Elbert County Superior Court Records (fragment) , October term, 1805 (in the Office of Clerk of Court, Elberton, Ga.) .
26. Elbert County Minutes of Inferior Court, May, 1791 to May, 1801, p. 124 (in the Office of Clerk of Court) .
27. See Oglethorpe County Minutes of Superior Court, A (1794-1799) , *passim.*

CHAPTER IV

1. Saunders, *Early Settlers of Alabama,* 419; Grace Gillam Davidson, "Dionysius Oliver, Georgia's Pioneer Realtor," in *Atlanta Journal,* October 2 (8, 4-5) , 1934; McIntosh, *Elbert County,* 36, 516. Oliver was buried in the Stenchcomb Churchyard, near Elberton. His tombstone has this inscription: "Dionysius Oliver, Capt. of a Privateer. Rev. War."
2. Allen D. Candler, comp., *The Revolutionary Records of the State of Georgia* (3 vols. Atlanta, 1908) , II, 140; Bowen, *Wilkes County,* 23; *Historical Collections of the Joseph Habersham Chapter, Daughters American Revolution* (5 vols. Places vary, 1902-1929) , I (1902) , 61.
3. Candler, comp., *Revolutionary Records of Georgia,* II, 667, 672, 674, 714; Grace Gillam Davidson, comp., *Historical Collections of the Georgia Chapters Daughters of the American Revolution.* Volume III. *Records of Elbert County, Georgia* (Atlanta, 1930) , 210.
4. Hitz, "Earliest Settlements in Wilkes County," 277.
5. Candler, comp., *Revolutionary Records of Georgia,* II, 701.
6. Robert & George Watkins, comps., *A Digest of the Laws of the State of Georgia. From its First Establishment as a British Province down to the Year 1798, Inclusive, and the Principal Acts of 1799:* . . . (Philadelphia, 1800) , 325-26. The date of the law is given here as February 3. A separate contemporary publication of this law

gives the date February 8. An original of the separate law may be found in the De Renne Collection in the University of Georgia Library.

7. Included in many of the deed records is this expression: "plan laid of [off] by Dionysius Oliver . . . and exhibited to the first purchasers." For example see Elbert County Deed Record, D, 73-74. A plan ordered to be drawn in 1804 and to be deposited in the Elbert County Courthouse with the Clerk of Court has been lost; but the original Oliver plan has been preserved and is now in the Dionysius Oliver Manuscripts, in the University of Georgia Library, with this legend: "A Plan of the Town of Petersburg in the fork of Savannah and Brd. Rivers." It bears the date, April 27, 1786.

8. Wilkes County Deed Record, DD, 85.

9. Elbert County Deed Record, L, 101.

10. Watkins, comp., *Digest of the Laws of Georgia, 1755-1799*, p. 658.

11. *Georgia & Carolina Gazette* (Petersburg), August 15 (3, 4), 1805. This firm was known as Jones, Walton & Company, and was made up of these men: William Jones, Thomas Walton, Jr., John H. Walton, and Henry Jones. Thomas Walton, without any indication as to junior or senior, died in 1806, in Lincoln County, and a sale of his effects was held, including 100 barrels of corn, 1,000 pounds of bacon, "a quantity of spirits consisting of rum, brandy and whiskey, all of the best quality," and many other items "too tedious to mention." *Ibid.*, June 5 (4, 3), 1806. The other Thomas Walton died in 1809 in Lisbon. *Mirror of the Times* (August), March 6 (3, 3), 1809.

12. Adiel Sherwood, *A Gazetteer of the State of Georgia* (Charleston, 1827), 69, 87.

13. John Drayton, *A View of South-Carolina, as Respects her Natural and Civil Concerns* (Charleston, 1802), 213.

14. Robert Mills, *Statistics of South Carolina, Including a View of its Natural, Civil and Military History, General and Political* (Charleston, 1829), 349, 350; Sherwood, *Gazetteer of Georgia* (1827 edition), 87; *Oglethorpe Echo*, September 14 (1, 5), 1888.

15. Elbert County Deed Record, A, 2; B, 2; K, 9; L, 31; Saunders, *Early Settlers of Alabama*, 422.

16. *Augusta Chronicle*, August 6 (1, 2), 1796; January 27 (4, 3), 1819; Saunders, *Early Settlers of Alabama*, 430; Francis Butler Simkins, *Pitchfork Ben Tillman, South Carolinian* (Baton Rouge, 1944), 24-25.

17. For instance, Elbert County Deed Record, H, 26. Thomas Evans, a free man of color, bought and sold a few lots. In 1803 he sold Lot 20 to Philip King of the Abbeville District in South Carolina. *Ibid.*, H, 169.

18. Wilkes County Deed Record, GG, 74-75.

19. Elbert County Deed Record, G, 66, 67; H, 17; K, 39, 108; McIntosh, *Elbert County*, 39-40; *Augusta Chronicle*, April 21 (3, 1), 1804; Pope was a member of the Elbert County Land Court in 1801. Davidson, comp., *Historical Collections*, III, 226.

20. S. G. McLendon, *History of the Public Domain of Georgia* (Atlanta, 1924), 46.

21. Wilkes County Deed Record, CC, 14; Elbert County Deed Record, F, 49.

22. Elbert County Deed Record, D, 73-74.

23. *Ibid.*, L, 42.   24. *Ibid.*, O, 84.   25. *Ibid.*, H, 2.

26. "Letters 1798-1819," in John Williams Walker Papers in Alabama Department of Archives and History, Montgomery.

27. *Ibid.*   28. Elbert County Deed Record, L, 70.

29. *Ibid.*, M, 69.   30. *Ibid.*, N, 33.   31. *Ibid.*, W, 40.

32. Archibald Stokes, Petersburg, Ga., February 27, 1825 to William S. Stokes, near Madison, Morgan County, Ga. Courtesy of Mrs. Daniel Hickey, Madison, Georgia, owner of the letter.

33. A. Y. Stokes, New York, July 7, 1821, to William S. Stokes, Madison, Morgan County, Ga. *Ibid.*

34. Elbert County Writs Superior Court, 1799-1803, pp. 416-18; Elbert County Deed Record, D, 31; G, 24; H, 27, 52; K, 43, 84.

35. For information on the Watkins families, see Saunders, *Early Settlers of Alabama*, 10, 215, 238-57, 476-80, 492-503, 506, 509-11; *Augusta Chronicle*, March 11 (3, 2), 1797; August 16 (supplement, 2, 1), 1800; December 14 (3, 2), 1805; Elbert County Deed Record, E, 76; G, 129. For the will of James Watkins, II, see Elbert County Will Book, M, 334. This will was published in *Habersham Historical Collections*, II, 297-98. The will of John Watkins may be found, *ibid.*, 299-301.

36. Gilmer, *Georgians*, 137-38.

37. *Augusta Chronicle*, July 31 (3, 1), 1802.

38. W. H. Sparks, *The Memories of Fifty Years: Containing Brief Biographical Notices of Distinguished Americans, and Anecdotes of Remarkable Men; Interspersed with Scenes and Incidents Occurring during a Long Life of Observation, Chiefly Spent in the Southwest* (Philadelphia, 1872), 118; Saunders, *Early Settlers of Alabama*, 255.

39. Letter dated February 25, 1803 in Larkin Newby Collection in Duke University Library. For a life of Walker, see Hugh C. Bailey, *John Williams Walker . . .* (University, Ala., 1964).

40. Elbert County Deed Record, J, 170.

41. Petersburg *Georgia & Carolina Gazette*, June 15 (1, 1), 1805.

42. Athens *Foreign Correspondent & Georgia Express*, September 29 (3, 2); October 6 (3, 1), 1810.

43. Sherwood, *Gazetteer of Georgia* (1837 edition), 258; *ibid.* (1829 edition), 183; Saunders, *Early Settlers of Alabama*, 434-43; Gilmer, *Georgians*, 107-11, 252; Davidson, comp., *Historical Collections*, III, 214; *Augusta Chronicle*, February 19 (3, 2), 1803; Albert James Pickett, *History of Alabama, and Incidentally of Georgia and Mississippi, from the Earliest Period* (2 vols. Third edition. Charleston, 1851), II, 374-75, 444; White, *Statistics of Georgia*, 266; Elbert County Deed Record, J, 170-71; "Letters 1798-1819," in John Williams Walker Papers.

44. *Augusta Chronicle*, December 2 (2, 4), 1818; Alma Cole Tompkins, *Charles Tait* (Alabama Polytechnic Institute Historical Papers, 4th Series, 1910), 1-3, 27; Charles and James A. Tait Collection, in Alabama Department of Archives and History, Montgomery; Davidson, comp., *Historical Collections*, III, 10.

45. Saunders, *Early Settlers of Alabama*, 298, 493; *Augusta Chronicle*, September 12 (4, 2), 1789; Elbert County Deed Record, C, 30; Davidson, comp., *Historical Collections*, III, 5, 153.

46. Elbert County Will Book, 1803-1806, pp. 56, 117-33; *Augusta Chronicle*, August 20 (3, 4), 1803.

47. *Augusta Chronicle*, May 7 (3, 3), 1803.

48. Pickett, *Alabama*, II, 402-406.

49. Hitz "Earliest Settlements in Wilkes County," 276; "Memoirs of the Early Life and Times of Judge Junius Hillyer [1807-1886]" (being a typescript in the University of Georgia Library), 1.

50. "Hillyer Memoir," 34-35. For an obituary of John Freeman, see Petersburg *Georgia & Carolina Gazette*, May 20, 1806. This citation is from the "Hillyer Memoir," which gives the text of the obituary.

51. Candler, comp., *Revolutionary Records of Georgia*, II, 702, 712, 722.

52. She was the daughter "of the late venerable and patriotic Gen. Elijah Clark." *Augusta Chronicle*, December 31 (3, 4), 1813.

53. Augusta *Mirror of the Times*, April 24 (4, 4), 1813.

CHAPTER V

1. David Ramsay, *The History of South-Carolina, from its First Settlement in 1670 to the Year 1808* (2 vols. Charleston, 1809), II, 579; Sherwood, *Gazetteer of Georgia* (1827 edition), 125-26.

2. *Augusta Chronicle,* January 12 (2, 3) , 1793.

3. Allen D. Candler, comp., *The Colonial Records of the State of Georgia* (26 vols. with XX never published. Atlanta, 1904-1916) , XIX, Pt. II (1911) , 534-40; Watkins, comps., *Digest of the Laws of Georgia, 1755-1799,* p. 334.

4. Watkins, comps., *Digest of the Laws of Georgia, 1755-1799,* p. 347.

5. *Augusta Chronicle,* August 7 (3, 2) , 1790.

6. Thomas Cooper, comp., *The Statutes at Large of South Carolina* (Columbia, 1839) , 179.

7. *Ibid.,* 264.

8. Watkins, comps., *Digest of the Laws of Georgia, 1755-1799,* pp. 597-98.

9. Horatio Marbury and William H. Crawford, comps., *Digest of the Laws of the State of Georgia . . . 1755 to 1800, Inclusive. . . .* (Savannah, 1802) , 371-74; Charles C. Jones, Jr. and Salem Dutcher, *Memorial History of Augusta, Georgia. . . .* (Syracuse, 1890) , 446; Savannah *Georgia Gazette,* February 28 (3, 3) , 1799.

10. Augustin Smith Clayton, comp., *A Compilation of the Laws of the State of Georgia . . . 1800 to the Year 1810, Inclusive . . .* (Augusta, 1812) , 80-81.

11. *Ibid.,* 80, 564-65.

12. Lucius Q. C. Lamar, comp., *A Compilation of the Laws of the State of Georgia, . . . since . . . 1810 to . . . 1819, Inclusive . . .* (Augusta, 1821) , 488-90.

13. *Ibid.,* 506.   14. *Ibid.,* 490-92.

15. *Augusta Chronicle,* April 26 (3, 3) , 1816. Praising the speed of the *Enterprise,* an editorial in the *Augusta Herald,* April 4 (3, 2) , 1817 said that it left Savannah on Monday at 8 a. m., with two fully laden freight boats in tow, "rested, as is their practice on the Lord's day, and arrived here on Tuesday, about noon; no instance is recalled of a loaded boat having made a passage in so short a time." By these calculations it took seven and a half days for this up-river trip.

16. Oliver H. Prince, comp., *A Digest of the Laws of the State of Georgia . . . to Dec. 1837* (2nd edition. Athens, 1837) , 297; Lamar, comp., *Compilation of the Laws of Georgia, 1811-1819,* pp. 510-12.

17. Lamar, comp., *Compilation of the Laws of Georgia, 1811-1819,* p. 498. This law carried also an appropriation of $10,000 for the Oconee River.

18. *Augusta Chronicle,* June 28 (3, 1-2) , 1816.

19. Lamar, comp., *Compilation of the Laws of Georgia, 1811-1819,* pp. 513-15. This law did not specifically state that the northern point was Panther Creek, but this intent was brought out in the act of December 18, 1818. *Ibid.,* 515-16.

20. *Augusta Chronicle,* May 23 (3, 2) , May 30 (2, 3) , 1818.

21. Lamar, comp., *Compilation of the Laws of Georgia, 1811-1819,* pp. 515-16.

22. *Ibid.,* 521-23.   23. *Ibid.,* 1232-33.

24. Jones and Dutcher, *Memorial History of Augusta,* 449; H. Niles, ed., *Niles' Weekly Register . . .* (Baltimore) , XIX (1820-1821) , 215.

25. Thomas Cooper, comp., *The Statutes at Large of South Carolina* (Columbia, 1836), I, 422-24; David McCord, comp., *ibid.,* VI, 269; Jones and Dutcher, *Memorial History of Augusta,* 449-51, 52.

26. Jones and Dutcher, *Memorial History of Augusta,* 452.

27. Ulrich Bonnell Phillips, *A History of Transportation in the Eastern Cotton Belt to 1860* (New York, 1908) , 103; Fletcher M. Green, "Georgia's Board of Public Works, 1817-1826," in *Georgia Historical Quarterly,* XXI (1938) , 117-37.

28. *Acts of the State of Georgia, 1845* (Columbus, 1846) , 203.

29. *Acts of the General Assembly of the State of Georgia, . . . Annual Session in November and December, 1859* (Milledgeville, 1860) , 333-35.

30. Watkins, comps., *Digest of the Laws of Georgia, 1755-1799,* p. 609.

31. *Ibid.,* 679.

32. Clayton, comp., *Compilation of the Laws of Georgia, 1800-1810,* pp. 461-62.

33. *Ibid.,* 547-48.

34. Marbury and Crawford, comps., *Compilation of the Laws of Georgia, 1755-1800*, p. 376.

35. Clayton, comp., *Compilation of the Laws of Georgia, 1800-1810*, pp. 648-50.

36. Lamar, comp., *Compilation of the Laws of Georgia, 1811-1819*, p. 485.

37. *Ibid.*, 501-503.   38. *Ibid.*, 494-98.   39. *Ibid.*, 513-15.

40. William C. Dawson, comp., *A Compilation of the Laws of the State of Georgia, . . . Since the Year 1819 to the Year 1829, Inclusive . . .* (Milledgeville, 1831), 45 (Resolutions).

41. *Ibid.*, 359.   42. *Ibid.*, 354.

43. *Ibid.*, 353, 355; *Acts of the General Assembly of the State of Georgia . . . November and December, 1834* (Milledgeville, 1835), 190-91; *ibid., 1837* (Milledgeville, 1838), 233-34; *ibid 1842* (Milledgeville, 1843), 143; *ibid., 1847* (Milledgeville, 1848), 274-75. In 1891 the Superior Court of Oglethorpe County granted a charter to Emory Cason to set up a line of boats on Broad River, but it seems that his company never acted on it. *Oglethorpe Echo,* May 15 (5, 4), December 4 (5, 6), 1891; March 11 (1, 2), 1892.

44. *Augusta Chronicle,* December 11 (2, 3), 1790; December 29 (3, 2), 1792; February 9 (1, 4), 1799; January 17 (3, 3), 1801.

45. *Ibid.*, December 26 (1, 3), 1801.   46. *Ibid.*, July 29 (3, 2), 1797.

47. George Sibbald, *Notes and Observations on the Pine Lands of Georgia, Shewing the Advantages they Possess, Particularly in the Culture of Cotton . . .* (Augusta, 1801), 53; J. Hillyer, "Memoirs," 147; White, *Statistics of Georgia,* 228; Jones and Dutcher, *Memorial History of Augusta,* 145, 465.

48. *Augusta Herald,* January 14 (3, 1), 1817.

49. Letter Book of Shaler Hillyer, 1805-1820 (MS in University of Georgia Library), February 19, 1813.

50. *Ibid.*, 1808.   51. *Ibid.*, November 27, 1806, also *passim.*

52. Lamar, comp., *Compilation of the Laws of Georgia, 1811-1819,* pp. 112-13, 114-15.

53. J. Hillyer, "Memoirs," 148.

54. *Augusta Chronicle,* July 19 (2, 2 in supplementary sheet), 1794.

55. *Ibid.*, December 31 (4, 1), 1808. See also *Acts of the General Assembly of the State of Georgia . . . Annual Session in November and December, 1840* (Milledgeville, 1841), 219.

56. Clayton, comp., *Compilation of the Laws of Georgia, 1800-1810,* pp. 200-202.

57. Sherwood, *Gazetteer of Georgia* (1837 edition), 60.

58. Watkins, comps., *Digest of the Laws of Georgia, 1755-1799,* p. 499.

59. *Ibid.*, 505-11.

60. Copy in Keith-Jones Collection (in possession of present writer).

61. Milledgeville *Georgia Journal,* September 30 (2, 3), 1823.   62. *Ibid.*

63. Jeannette Mirsky and Allan Nevins, *The World of Eli Whitney* (New York, 1952), 155.

64. William Few, "Autobiography of Col. William Few of Georgia," in John Austin Stevens, ed., *The Magazine of American History with Notes and Queries* (New York and Chicago), VII (November, 1881), 343.

65. Elsa G. Allen, "John Abbot, Pioneer Naturalist of Georgia," in *Georgia Historical Quarterly,* XLI (March, 1957), 153-54.

66. Augusta *Mirror of the Times,* May 20 (4, 5), 1811.

67. Milledgeville *Georgia Journal,* May 17 (3, 2), 1815.

68. F. A. Michaux, *Travels to the Westward of the Alleghany Mountains in the States of the Ohio, Kentucky, and Tennessee, and Return to Charlestown, through the Upper Carolinas . . .* (London, 1805), 338.

69. Milledgeville *Georgia Journal,* January 14, 1823.

70. Garnett Andrews, *Reminiscences of an Old Georgia Lawyer* (Atlanta, 1870), 14.

71. S. Hillyer, Letter Book, December 9, 1812.

72. J. W. Walker, Augusta, December 30, 1813 to Larkin Newby, Fayetteville, N. C., in Larkin Newby Collection, Duke University.

73. *Augusta Herald,* December 19 (3, 1), 1817.

74. Drayton, *View of South-Carolina,* 141.

75. J. Hillyer, "Memoirs," 202.

76. Paschal, *Agnes Paschal,* 113.

77. John Lambert, *Travels throug Canada and the United States of North America, in the Years 1806, 1807, & 1808* . . . (2 vols. 2nd edition. London, 1814), II, 289.

78. McCord, comp., *Statutes at Large of South Carolina,* IX, 284-85.

79. Wilkes County Deed Record, DD, 1783. See also Davidson, comp., *Historical Records,* III, 197.

80. McCord, comp., *Statutes at Large of South Carolina,* IX, 351.

81. *Ibid.,* 490, 492, 496. See also Lamar, comp., *Compilation of the Laws of Georgia, 1811-1819,* pp. 307, 313-14.

82. Clayton, comp., *Compilation of the Laws of Georgia, 1800-1810,* p. 527.

83. Watkins, comps., *Digest of the Laws of Georgia, 1755-1799,* p. 500.

84. *Ibid.,* 603.   85. *Ibid.,* 666.

86. Clayton, comp., *Compilation of the Laws of Georgia, 1800-1810,* p. 460.

CHAPTER VI

1. Drayton, *View of South-Carolina,* 33.

2. Clark et al., eds., *Asbury Journal,* II, 80. An earlier edition of Asbury's journal is *Journal of the Rev. Francis Asbury, Bishop of the Methodist Episcopal Church, from Augusta 7, 1771, to December 7, 1815* (3 vols. New York, 1821), II, 246.

3. *Augusta Chronicle,* January 23 (3, 2), 1796. For comments on the flood of 1793, see *ibid.,* March 16 (3, 1), 1793.

4. *Atlanta Constitution* ("The Great Southern Weekly"), August 21 (1, 1), 1888. The same news story by "T. L. G." (T. Larry Gantt) appeared in *Oglethorpe Echo,* September 17 (1, 4), 1888.

5. John W. Walker, May 20, 1803 to Larkin Newby, in Larkin Newby Collection; *Habersham Historical Collections,* II, 231.

6. Clark et al., eds., *Asbury Journal,* II, 312; *ibid.* (old edition), III, 41-42.

7. Sibbald, *Pine Lands of Georgia,* 62-63.

8. McIntosh, *Elbert County,* 37, 39.

9. Charles C. Jones, Jr., *The Dead Towns of Georgia* (in Collections of the Georgia Historical Society, Savannah, 1878), IV, 237.

10. *Aggregate Amount of Each Description of Persons within the United States of America, and Territories thereof, Agreeable to Actual Enumeration Made According to Law in the Year 1810* (Book I of the Third Census), 80a; *Augusta Chronicle,* January 12 (3, 1), March 15 (3, 2), 1811.

11. *Augusta Chronicle,* March 15, 1811; *The Statistics of the Population of the United States . . . From the Original Returns of the Ninth Census (June 1, 1870)* . . . (Washington, 1872), I, 20.

12. Elbert County Minutes of the Inferior Court, 1791-1801, p. 42.

13. *Ibid.,* 78.

14. Elbert County Superior Court Records, 1790-1800, p. 141.

15. Clayton, comp., *Compilation of the Laws of Georgia, 1800-1810,* p. 92.

16. John W. Walker, "Hebron" (Petersburg), June 23, 1803, to Larkin Newby, Fayetteville, N. C., in Larkin Newby Collection.

17. *Augusta Chronicle,* June 11 (3, 4), 1803.

18. John W. Walker, "Hebron" (Petersburg), June 23, 1803, to Larkin Newby, Fayetteville, N. C., in Larkin Newby Collection.

19. Clayton, comp., *Compilation of the Laws of Georgia, 1800-1810,* pp. 42-46, 86-87.

20. *Ibid.*, 182.   21. Elbert County Deed Record, L, 76.

22. *Ibid.*, W, 39; X, 228.

23. Dawson, comp., *Compilation of the Laws of Georgia, 1820-1829,* pp. 478-79.

24. McIntosh, *Elbert County,* 39-40.

25. Petersburg *Georgia & Carolina Gazette,* December 14 (2, 4), 1805.

26. *Ibid.*, June 15 (3, 2), 1805.   27. *Ibid.*, December 7 (3, 2), 1805.

28. *Ibid.*, June 5 (3, 1-2), 1806.   29. *Ibid.*, July 31 (2, 4), 1806.

30. *Augusta Chronicle,* October 31 (2, 3), 1807.

31. John W. Walker, Petersburg, February 25, 1803, to Larkin Newby, Fayette-ville, N. C., in Larkin Newby Collection.

32. S. Hillyer, Letter Book, December 3, 1808 to Oliver Whyte.

33. Archibald Stokes, Petersburg, June 17, 1818, to Wm. S. Stokes, Oglethorpe County, in Mrs. Daniel Hickey Collection.

34. White, *Statistics of Georgia,* 229.

35. John W. Walker, "Hebron" (Petersburg), June 20, 1803, to Larkin Newby, Fayetteville, N. C., in Larkin Newby Collection.

36. *Augusta Chronicle,* April 10 (3, 5), 1812.

37. S. Hillyer, Letter Book, July 4, 1807 to Lawrence Vansenderere & Co.; *ibid.,* July 2, 1807.

38. *Ibid.*, July 15, 1807.

39. *Augusta Chronicle,* March 26 (3, 1), 1803.

40. *Ibid.*, September 26 (3, 4), 1801.

41. *Ibid.*, June 6 (3, 4), 1801.

42. *Ibid.*, July 23 (3, 4), 1803.

43. Petersburg *Georgia & Carolina Gazette,* November 23 (3, 3), 1805.

44. *Augusta Chronicle,* August (4, 5), 1818.

45. *Ibid.*, September 12 (4, 2), 1789.

46. Petersburg *Georgia & Carolina Gazette,* November 30 (3, 1), 1805.

47. *Ibid.*, January 2 (3, 1), 1806.

48. This notice appeared in the *Augusta Chronicle,* January 7 (3, 3), 1809: "DIED, at Petersburg, on the 4th Dec. Mr. William Pope, in two days after his arrival from the Western Country."

49. *Ibid.*, October 15 (3, 3), 1813. See also *ibid.,* January 10 (3, 3), 1807; December 18 (3, 3), 1812.

50. John W. Walker, "Hebron" (Petersburg), July 22, 1803, to Larkin Newby, Fayetteville, N. C., in Larkin Newby Collection. See also *Augusta Chronicle,* July 23 (3, 3), 1803.

CHAPTER VII

1. Niles wrote of the Troup and Clark parties in 1831, "We know not what they differ about—but they do *violently* differ." *Niles' Register,* XLI (1831-1832), 150.

2. John W. Walker, "Hebron" (Petersburg), August 12, 1803 to Larkin Newby, Fayetteville, N. C., in Larkin Newby Collection.

3. Same to same, July 28, 1803.

4. There has been some dispute as to how Elijah spelled his family name, whether *Clarke* or *Clark;* but the generally accepted way is the former. John, his son, who gave his name to the party, spelled it *Clark.*

5. Miller, *Bench and Bar of Georgia,* I, 34.

6. *Augusta Chronicle,* June 26 (2, 1-3); July 3 (2, 1-2), 1802; Thomas Gamble, *Savannah Duels and Duellists, 1733-1877* (Savannah, 1923), 45-49.

7. Cook himself was a lawyer and loved the profession. Garnett Andrews, writing in 1870 said of Cook: "When I first visited Elbert court—some 45 years since—I saw an old gentleman, hardly decently clad, come to the court-house door in his carriage. A servant carried his split-bottomed chair and pillow inside the bar, then helped his master in, who—by permission of the Judge—with cotton night-cap and broad-brimmed hat on and papers in hand, took his seat. This was 'old George

Cook,' a lawyer who clung to the profession with such tenacity that he continued to practice under such difficulties. Not able to stand, or hardly speak intelligently, he would get some of the young lawyers to do it for him, after giving them the points." *Reminiscences*, 60.

8. *Augusta Chronicle*, May 29 (3, 2), 1802.

9. *Ibid.*, June 12 (4, 2-4), 1802.   10. *Ibid.*

11. *Ibid.*, July 3, (4, 1), 1802.

12. *Ibid.*, July 31 (4, 2-4), 1802; *Savannah Georgian*, December 3 (2, 2), 1822.

13. *Ibid.*   14. *Augusta Chronicle*, August 7, (3, 3), 1802.

15. Andrews, *Reminiscences*, 59.

16. *Savannah Georgian*, December 3 (2, 2), 1822. For several accounts of the duel see Gilmer, *Georgians*, 125-26; George R. Gilmer, *The Literary Progress of Georgia* . . . (Athens, 1851), 20; J. E. D. Shipp, *Giant Days or the Life and Times of William H. Crawford* (Americus, Ga., 1909), 48-49; Knight, *Landmarks*, II, 16; Sparks, *Memories of Fifty Years*, 40; Jones and Dutcher, *Memorial History of Augusta*, 226-27.

17. Lollie Bell Wylie, ed., *Memoirs of Judge Richard H. Clark* (Atlanta, 1898), 219.

18. Wilkes County Records of Wills, 1806-1808, pp. 66-67; Wilkes County Appraisments, Sales, LL (1806-1807), pp. 27-28. See also Davidson, comp., *Historical Records*, I, 71, 307, 333.

19. Sparks, *Memories of Fifty Years*, 76.

20. *Augusta Chronicle*, June 12 (4, 2), 1802.   21. *Ibid.*

22. Sparks, *Memories of Fifty Years*, 76.

23. *Augusta Chronicle*, September 18 (1, 2-4), 1802.   24. *Ibid.*

25. Miller, *Bench and Bar of Georgia*, I, 336; Moffat, Tait (Ph. D. Dissertation), 13. For an extended account of this affair, see E. Merton Coulter, "A Famous Duel that was Never Fought," in *Georgia Historical Quarterly*, XLIII (1959), 365-77.

26. John Clark, *Considerations on the Purity of the Principles of William H. Crawford, Esq.* . . . (Augusta, 1819), 42-49; Shipp, *Giant Days*, 49-65; Knight, *Landmarks*, II, 18.

27. Clark, *Considerations on Crawford*, 100, 101; Shipp, *Giant Days*, 69-75.

28. *Augusta Herald*, August 20 (3, 1), 1800.

29. *Augusta Chronicle*, August 28 (1, 3), 1802.

30. Clayton, comp., *Compilation of the Laws of Georgia, 1800-1810*, p. 529.

31. *Augusta Chronicle*, August 1 (3, 2), 1807.

32. S. Hillyer, Letter Book, July 15, 1807.

33. *Augusta Chronicle*, July 31 (2, 1), 1812.

34. S. Hillyer, Letter Book, August 8, 1813.

35. S. Hillyer, July 21, 1813, to Potts & McKinnie, in Letter Book.

CHAPTER VIII

1. Morse, *American Geography*, 447.

2. Drayton, *View of South-Carolina*, 135-36.

3. Candler, comp., *Colonial Records of Georgia*, XIX, Pt. I, 204-208.

4. *Ibid.*, Pt. II, 380-94.

5. *Act for the Inspection of Tobacco, February 10, 1787* (separate leaflet).

6. Watkins, comps., *Digest of the Laws of Georgia, 1755-1799*, pp. 444-53.

7 Lewis Cecil Gray, *History of Agriculture in the Southern United States to 1860* (2 vols. Washington, 1933), I, 218.

8. Prince, comp., *Digest of the Laws of Georgia to 1837*, p. 825.

9. Watkins, comps., *Digest of the Laws of Georgia, 1755-1799*, pp. 340, 683.

10. *Acts of the General Assembly of the State of Georgia, . . . 1841* (Milledgeville, 1842), 199; *ibid., 1842* (Milledgeville, 1843), 176-77; Watkins, comps., *Digest of the Laws of Georgia, 1755-1799*, pp. 531, 683; *Acts of the General Assembly of the State*

of Georgia . . . 1799 (Augusta, 1800), 6-7; Clayton, comp., *Compilation of the Laws of Georgia, 1800-1810*, pp. 121, 216. As late as 1860 small patches of tobacco were being cultivated in upper Georgia. Adiel Sherwood, *A Gazetteer of Georgia . . .* (4th edition. Macon, 1860), 19.

11. Thomas Cooper, comp., *Statutes at Large of South Carolina* (Columbia, 1838), IV, 327-31, 604-607, 681-87, 749-50.

12. Clayton, comp., *Compilation of the Laws of Georgia, 1800-1810*, pp. 240-42; Lamar, comp., *Compilation of the Laws of Georgia, 1811-1819*, pp. 334-35.

13. Elbert County Minutes of the Inferior Court, 1791-1801, pp. 9, 34, 57; Gilmer, *Georgians*, 129.

14. Elbert County Deed Records, A, 76; F, 50; H, 6, 22; J, 64; Elbert County Writs of the Superior Court, 1799-1803, p. 369; Watkins, comps., *Digest of the Laws of Georgia, 1755-1799*, p. 658.

15. Elbert County Superior Court Records, 1790-1800, p. 142.

16. Elbert County Records of the Inferior Court, 1804-1806, pp. 47-49.

17. *Augusta Chronicle*, May 11 (1, 1), 1799.

18. *Ibid.*, November 21 (3, 2), 1801.

19. *Ibid.*, February 9 (3, 2), 1816.

20. Gray, *Agriculture in the Southern United States*, II, 606.

21. *Augusta Chronicle*, December 26 (3, 2), 1789.

22. *Ibid.*, November 18 (3, 4), 1797.

23. Petersburg Store Account Book, 1799, p. 127.

24. E. White, Savannah, June 6, 1786 to Dionysius Oliver, Petersburg, in Oliver MSS Collection.

25. Augusta *Georgia State Gazette or Independent Register*, November 25 (3, 2), 1786; February 10 (4, 1), November 24 (3, 3), 1787.

26. Elbert County Writs of Superior Court, 1799-1803, p. 369; *Augusta Chronicle*, February 5 (1, 2), 1791.

27. Davidson, comp., *Historical Collections*, III, 193; Elbert County Deed Record, C, 137.

28. Candler, comp., *Colonial Records of Georgia*, XIX, Pt. II, 500.

29. S. Hillyer, Letter Book, May 10, 1808.

30. Petersburg *Georgia & Carolina Gazette*, January 2 (3, 3), 1806.

31. *Augusta Chronicle*, November 9 (1, 3), 1805.

32. *Ibid.*, June 20 (3, 3), 1801; February 7 (1, 3), 1807.

33. Elbert County Writs of the Superior Court, 1799-1803, p. 212.

34. Quotations were given regularly in the *Augusta Chronicle*.

35. Quotations may be found in both the *Augusta Herald* and the *Augusta Chronicle*.

36. Augusta *Georgia State Gazette*, May 31 (1, 1), 1788.

37. Whitemarsh B. Seabrook, "Memoir on the Cotton Plant," in *Proceedings of the State Agricultural Society of South Carolina from 1839 to 1846*, pp. 140, 141.

38. Mirsky and Nevins, *Eli Whitney*, 57, 59.

39. *Ibid.*, 67.

40. Constance McL. Green, *Eli Whitney and the Birth of American Technology* (Boston, 1956), 91; Mirsky and Nevins, *Eli Whitney*, 67, 68, 76, 93, 124.

41. *Augusta Chronicle*, March 15 (3, 3), 1794.

42. Green, *Eli Whitney*, 68, 69.

43. Mirsky and Nevins, *Eli Whitney*, 89-101.

44. Hugh N. Starnes, "The Cotton-Gin; its invention and Effects," in *The Southern Bivouac: A Monthly Literary and Historical Magazine* (edited by Basil W. Duke and R. W. Knott), New Series, Vol. I (1885-1886), 390, 392; Saunders, *Early Settlers of Alabama*, 253-54, 390, 510; *Habersham Historical Collections*, II, 634-37.

45. *Augusta Chronicle*, July 30 (1, 3), 1796.

46. *Ibid.*, October 1 (2, 3), 1796.   47. *Ibid.*, December 24 (3, 4), 1796.

48. *Ibid.*, December 31 (3, 1), 1796.   49. *Ibid.*, February 11 (3, 1), 1797.

50. *Ibid.*, July 22 (2, 4), 1797.

51. *Ibid.*, February 25 (4, 2), June 10 (2, 4), 1797.

52. D. A. Tompkins, *Cotton and Cotton Oil* . . . (Charlotte, N. C., 1901), 9, 28; Mirsky and Nevins, *Eli Whitney*, 113.

53. Tomkins, *Cotton*, 26; Mirsky and Nevins, *Eli Whitney*, 113.

54. *Augusta Chronicle*, December 10 (1, 3), 1796.

55. Mirsky and Nevins, *Eli Whitney*, 161 n.

56. Seabrook, "Memoir," 127; John Donald Wade, *Augustus Baldwin Longstreet* (New York, 1924), 10; Jones and Dutcher, *Memorial History of Augusta*, 163, 388; Green, *Eli Whitney*, 75; Mirsky and Nevins, *Eli Whitney*, 111.

57. Tomkins, *Cotton*, 24.

58. Green, *Eli Whitney*, 73; Mirsky and Nevins, *Eli Whitney*, 107.

59. Denison Olmsted, *Memoir of Eli Whitney, Esq.* (New Haven, 1846), 32.

60. *Ibid.*, 20, 27, 41, 42, 44; Green, *Eli Whitney*, 89; Mirsky and Nevins, *Eli Whitney*, 115.

61. *Augusta Chronicle*, February 19 (2, 4), 1803.

62. Miller and Whitney vs. Jesse Bull, United States District Court, 1800; Miller and Whitney vs. Daniel W. Easly, 1801, United States Fifth Circuit Court. The records of these suits and others are in Court Records in the United States District Court and also in the Circuit Court, of Suits Brought by Miller and Whitney, in the Federal Records Center in East Point, Georgia.

63. Tomkins, *Cotton*, 475.

64. Mirsky and Nevins, *Eli Whitney*, 174.

65. *Augusta Chronicle*, February 16 (3, 2), 1793.

66. *Ibid.*, February 16 (3, 3), 1793.

67. *Ibid.*, December 13 (3, 2), 1806.

68. Augusta *Georgia State Gazette*, September 13 (3, 3), 1788.

69. *Ibid.*, May 31 (1, 1), 1788.

70. *Augusta Chronicle*, August 20 (3, 1), 1803; October 4 (3, 2), 1806.

71. Olmsted, *Eli Whitney*, 40-41.

72. *Pendleton Farmers' Society* (Atlanta, 1908), 96.

73. Starnes, "Cotton-Gin," 392.

74. *An Act for the Inspection of Cotton, February 21, 1796* (a separate leaflet in the De Renne Collection).

75. Watkins, comps., *Digest of the Laws of Georgia, 1755-1799*, p. 616.

76. Clayton, comp., *Compilation of the Laws of Georgia, 1800-1810*, pp. 346-47.

77. *Ibid.*, 135-36.

78. Jones and Dutcher, *Memorial History of Augusta*, 388.

79. *Augusta Herald*, July 16 (3, 2), 1800.

80. *Georgia and South Carolina Almanac . . . 1808 . . .* (Augusta, no date), no page numbers.

81. Seabrook, "Memoir," 155.

82. Mirsky and Nevins, *Eli Whitney*, 100.

83. J. Hillyer, "Memoirs," 147; S. Hillyer, Letter Book, December 1, 1806.

84. John W. Walker Papers, Folder, "Letters 1798-1819," February 5, 1803.

85. S. Hillyer, Letter Book, 1807-1808, *passim*.

86. *Ibid.*, March, 1809.   87. *Ibid.*, May, June, 1809.

88. *Ibid.*, May 24, 1812.   89. *Augusta Chronicle*, June 30 (3, 1), 1815.

90. *Ibid.*, September 22 (3, 3), 1815.

91. S. Hillyer Letter Book, July 27, 1816.

92. *Ibid.*, October 28, 1819.

93. Seabrook, "Memoir," 155.

94. Z. B. Rogers, "First Tobacco Warehouse, First Cotton Mill. Petersburg's Claim to Past Glory Uncovered; Once had 2 Senators," in *Atlanta Constitution*, March 31 (section 2-B), 1946.

95. White, *Statistics of Georgia*, 228. The legislature in 1810 incorporated the Wilkes Manufacturing Company "for the purpose of manufacturing cotton and woolen goods." Clayton, comp., *Compilation of the Laws of Georgia, 1800-1810*, pp. 667-68.

96. Augusta *Georgia State Gazette*, January 20 (3, 1) , 1787.

97. *Ibid.*, May 10 (1, 1-3) , 1788.

98. J. Hillyer, "Memoir," 92; Moffat, Tait (Ph. D. Dissertation) , 26.

99. *Augusta Chronicle*, December 10 (Supplement, 1, 2) , 1791; December 5 (3, 1) , 1789.

100. *Ibid.*, July 25 (3, 2) , 1807.

101. The *Augusta Chronicle* regularly listed the price of corn.

102. *Ibid.*, April 4, 1807.

103. Elbert County Deed Records, D, 118.

104. Petersburg *Georgia & Carolina Gazette*, July 18 (3, 4) , 1805.

105. *Ibid.*, October 5 (3, 3) , 1805.

106. *Ibid.*, January 23 (3, 3), January 30 (3, 4) , 1806.

107. S. Hillyer, Letter Book, May 22, 1819.

108. *Columbian Museum and Savannah Advertiser*, June 22 (2, 1) , 1803; *Augusta Chronicle*, June 11 (3, 3) , 1803.

109. Petersburg *Georgia & Carolina Gazette*, January 23 (3, 3) , 1806.

110. *Augusta Chronicle*, May 24 (3, 6), 1816.

111. Petersburg *Georgia & Carolina Gazette*, July 24 (4, 4) , 1806; *Augusta Chronicle*, May 11 (3, 4) , 1799; October 25 (3, 3) , 1800.

112. Elbert County Deed Record, G, 91.

113. Davidson, comp., *Historical Collections*, III, 25.

CHAPTER IX

1. Elbert County Deed Record, E, 91; G, 48; *Augusta Herald*, February 19 (2, 2) , 1800; *Oglethorpe Echo*, December 11 (3, 3) , 1925; Oliver Whyte, New York, November 29, 1798, to "Dr. Larkin [Newby?]," Petersburg, in Larkin Newby Collection.

2. Elbert County Deed Record, H, 22.   3. *Ibid.*, G, 49, 89.

4. *Augusta Herald*, May 14 (1, 4), 1800.

5. *Augusta Chronicle*, October 8 (1, 1) , 1803.

6. Elbert County Deed Record, G, 89.

7. *Augusta Chronicle*, May 2 (3, 4) , 1801.

8. Petersburg *Georgia & Carolina Gazette*, July 24 (3, 3) , 1806.

9. *Ibid.*, August 15 (3, 4) , 1805.

10. *Augusta Chronicle*, February 27 (3, 4) , 1808.

11. *Ibid.*, May 28 (3, 2) , 1813.

12. Elbert County Deed Record, A, 10, 60; F, 30; H, 34, 63, 153; K, 126.

13. Clark *et al.*, eds., *Asbury Journal*, I, 367; II, 458.

14. *Ibid.*, I, 367 n.   15. *Ibid.*, I, 669 n.

16. *Augusta Chronicle*, January 18 (3, 2), 1794. Forsyth was highly respected in Augusta, and his death called forth two long poems of mourning and appreciation.

> "Low in the dust the SON of LIGHT now lies,
> He's left our Lodge to join one in the skies;
> May angels with their silver wings o'ershade,
> The ground now sacred by the relics made."
> *Ibid.*, February 8 (3, 3) , 1794.

> "High rear memorial, in honor of his name
> Let marble cupids round his urn still weep,
> Let sculptor's hand his character define
> And troops of angels his hallow'd ashes keep."
> *Ibid.*, July 5 (4, 1) , 1794.

He was buried in St. Pauls Churchyard in Augusta, where a great marble slab covered a well-kept grave, even into the twentieth century.

17. Clark *et al.*, eds., *Asbury Journal*, II, 4-5.

18. *Augusta Chronicle*, March 1 (3, 2) , 1794.

19. *Ibid.*, June 21 (3, 2) , 1794.

20. White, *Statistics of Georgia*, 231-33; George G. Smith, *History of Georgia Methodism from 1786 to 1866* (Atlanta, 1913) , 31; William Bailey Williford, *Williford and Allied Families* (Atlanta, 1961) , 27-28; Bowen, *Wilkes County*, 118-19.

21. Oliver Whyte, Petersburg, Georgia, November 27, 1804, to Larkin Newby, Fayetteville, North Carolina, in Larkin Newby Collection.

22. Elbert County Deed Record, U, 117. In the course of time there was no end to the glamour that was heaped on Petersburg. In 1888 an old lady remembered the time when the town had 33 stores, evidently an extreme exaggeration. *Oglethorpe Echo,* September 14 (1, 5) , 1888.

23. Watkins, comps., *Digest of the Laws of Georgia, 1775-1799*, p. 660.

24. *Ibid.*, 539.

25. J. Hillyer, "Memoirs," 70-71, 259.

26. *Ibid.*, 73; S. Hillyer, Letter Book, December 16, 1806.

27. Petersburg *Georgia & Carolina Gazette,* June 15 (1, 1), 1805.

28. *Ibid.*, November 23 (3, 2) , 1805.

29. J. Hillyer, "Memoir," 73.

30. S. Hillyer, Letter Book, September 24, November 27, 1806, March 16, 1816.

31. For instance, *ibid.*, June 11, 1811. In 1812 Whyte married Mrs. Elizabeth Grafton near Boston. *Augusta Chronicle*, February 14 (3, 3) , 1812.

32. S. Hillyer, Letter Book, November (first page of letter torn away) , 1806.

33. *Ibid.*, February 10, 1807. Hillyer never forgot his kindred back in Connecticut. He and his wife Rebecca visited there at least once, and in 1807 he sent his father a draft for $300, merely "a mite in Conn." but "my mite to soften the Pillow of an aged Parent." Letter Book, May (no number) , 1807; Shaler Hillyer Collection (Microfilm Box 21, Reel 17, Department of Archives and History, Atlanta) .

34. S. Hillyer, Letter Book, July 15, 1807.

35. J. Hillyer, "Memoirs," 79.

36. S. Hillyer, Letter Book, March (no number) , 1808.

37. *Ibid.*, June 19, 1807; May 10, 1808; February 9, 1809; Petersburg *Georgia & Carolina Gazette,* January 30 (3, 2) , 1806.

38. S. Hillyer, Letter Book, August 23, 1809.

39. Augusta *Mirror of Times,* May 7 (2, 2-3); 3, 1) , 1810.

40. S. Hillyer, Letter Book, February 14, 1810.

41. *Ibid.*, June 19, 1807; April 12, 1812; June 6, 1813.

42. *Ibid.*, February 8, 1813.   43. *Ibid.*, April 12, August 15, 1813.

44. *Ibid.*, April 12, July 21, 1813; Shaler Hillyer Collection (Microfilm Box 21, Reel 17) .

45. Clayton, comp., *Compilation of the Laws of Georgia, 1800-1810*, p. 458. See text in this book relative to note 33, Chapter V.

46. See text in this book relative to note 36, Chapter V.

47. Lamar, comp., *Compilation of the Laws of Georgia, 1811-1819*, p. 501. See text in this book relative to note 37, Chapter V.

48. Shaler Hillyer Collection (Microfilm Box 21, Reel 17) .

49. S. Hillyer, Letter Book, September 24, 1806.

50. A. Y. Stokes, New York, July 7, 1821 to W. S. Stokes, Madison, Georgia, in Mrs. Daniel Hickey Collection.

51. These items were obtained from Petersburg Store Account Book, 1799, and from newspaper advertisements in the *Augusta Chronicle.*

52. Items obtained from Day Book B, William S. Stokes Store, 1818 (in University of Georgia Library) .

53. William Calhoun bought a set of "Elegant Ivory Knives and Forks" for $22.00, an "Elegant Dining Sett" for $50.00, and an "Elegant Sett Tea China" for $35.00. Patrick Calhoun bought an "Elegant Gold Watch & Appendage" for $121. Stokes Day Book B, 265.

54. A. Stokes to W. S. Stokes, June 17, 1818, in Mrs. Daniel Hickey Collection. In 1799 James Oliver, Jr., received $250.00 for clerking in a Petersburg store. Petersburg Store Account Book, 1799, p. 120.

55. See text in this chapter relative to note 9.

56. Elbert County Superior Court Minutes, fragment.

57. Clayton, comp., *Compilation of the Laws of Georgia, 1800-1810*, p. 426.

58. *Ibid.*, 447-48.   59. *Ibid.*, 533.

60. Lamar, comp., *Compilation of the Laws of Georgia, 1811-1819*, pp. 33-36.

61. *Ibid.*, 36-38.   62. *Ibid.*, 39-41. See also *ibid.*, 41-42.

63. S. Hillyer, Letter Book, January 19, 1808 [1809].

64. *Ibid.*, August 23, 1809.   65. *Ibid.*, July 12, 1810.

66. Petersburg *Georgia & Carolina Gazette*, June 5 (3, 4), 1806.

67. *Ibid.*, June 2 (3, 3), 1806.   68. *Ibid.*, July 31 (3, 4), 1806.

69. Act Relating to Tolls for Grist Mills, June 26, 1786 (separate leaflet in De Renne Collection). For a reference without text, see Watkins, comps., *Digest of the Laws of Georgia, 1755-1799*, p. 321.

70. Petersburg *Georgia & Carolina Gazette*, June 15 (1, 1), 1805.

71. *Augusta Chronicle*, August 26 (4, 4), 1814. Another establishment known as "The Millford Merchant-Mills" began operations on the Broad River about a mile and a half above Petersburg, in July of 1813. It was set up by Benajah Smith, who promised to manufacture "at least 60 barrels of superfine flour per day . . . [and he felt] warranted in saying, that his mills will not be inferior to any in the southern, or even in the middle states." His mill house was fifty feet square and four stories high, but it contained five floors. When in full operation he would run "three pairs of five feet Georgia-Burr Mill-stones," with all necessary equipment such as reels, screens, elevators, and so on. There was excellent navigation from his mill race to Augusta, which would save at least a half of the cost by wagons. "All boats coming by or to Petersburg," said Smith, "from the upper country or elsewhere, will not have more than two and a half miles out of their way, both in going to, and returning from the mills; and a good river to navigate." *Ibid.*, July 9 (3, 2), 1813.

72. Clayton, comp., *Compilation of the Laws of Georgia, 1800-1810*, pp. 27-28.

73. Lamar, comp., *Compilation of the Laws of Georgia, 1811-1819*, pp. 326-28.

74. *Ibid.*, 329.

75. *Ibid.*, 329-32.   76. *Ibid.*, 332-33.

77. S. Hillyer, Letter Book, June 6, July 21, 1813.

78. See text relative to note 38 in Chapter V.

79. S. Hillyer, Letter Book, June 12, 1816.

80. *Ibid.*, June 22, 1816; November 30, 1817; May 27, 1818.

81. Watkins, comps., *Digest of the Laws of Georgia, 1755-1799*, pp. 429, 541.

82. *Augusta Chronicle*, June 24 (1, 3), 1797. See also *ibid.*, March 19 (1, 2), 1808.

83. S. Hillyer, Letter Book June 11, 1807.   84. *Ibid.*, February 5, 1813.

85. Clayton, comp., *Compilation of the Laws of Georgia, 1800-1810*, p. 374.

CHAPTER X

1. S. Hillyer, "Memoirs," 64.

2. John Williams Walker, Petersburg, August 20, 1799, to Larkin Newby, Newark, S. C., in Larkin Newby Collection.

3. Petersburg Store Account Book, 1799, p. 157.

4. John Williams Walker, Petersburg, April 10, 1799 to Larkin Newby, Vienna,

S. C., in Larkin Newby Collection. See also Hugh C. Bailey, "The Petersburg Youth of John Williams Walker," in *Georgia Historical Quarterly*, XLIII (1959), 123-37.

5. Walker to Newby, August 12, 1803, in Larkin Newby Collection.

6. Walker to Newby, November 10, 1803, in Larkin Newby Collection.

7. Walker to Newby, December 28, 1804, in Larkin Newby Collection.

8. Walker to Newby, January 4, 1805, in Larkin Newby Collection.

9. Walker to Newby, January 31, 1805, in Larkin Newby Collection.

10. *Oglethorpe Echo*, September 14 (1, 5), 1888.

11. Bartram, *Travels*, 322-23. See also White, *Statistics of Georgia*, 229-30; *Oglethorpe Echo*, August 3 (2, 2), 1888.

12. Ramsay, *History of South-Carolina*, II, 581.

13. Walker, Petersburg, August 20, 1799, to Newby, Newark, S. C., in Larkin Newby Collection.

14. Petersburg *Georgia & Carolina Gazette*, July 31 (3, 1), 1806.

15. *Augusta Chronicle*, May 11 (1, 3), 1799.

16. Shaler Hillyer Collection (Microfilm Box 21, Reel 17).

17. Walker, "Hebron" (Petersburg), June 20, 1803, to Newby, Fayetteville, in Larkin Newby Collection.

18. See E. Merton Coulter, "Madison Springs, Georgia Watering Place," in *Georgia Historical Quarterly*, XLVII (1963).

19. Jane Kneeland, Petersburg, Ga., October 13 (1831?), to Eliza M. A. Carter, Washington, Ga., in Mrs. Mercer Sherman Collection, Albany, Georgia.

20. Kneeland to Carter, January (no day), (1831?), in Mrs. Mercer Sherman Collection.

21. Mary E. Moragne, *The Neglected Thread. A Journal from the Calhoun Community, 1836-1842*, edited by Delle Mullen Craven (Columbia, S. C., 1951), 151.

22. Georgia Tavern Act, August 14, 1786 (leaflet in the De Renne Collection). See also, Watkins, comps., *Digest of the Laws of Georgia, 1755-1799*, p. 345.

23. Georgia Tavern Act, February 1, 1788 (leaflet in De Renne Collection).

24. Watkins, comps., *Digest of the Laws of Georgia, 1755-1799*, pp. 453-54.

25. Clayton, comp., *Compilation of the Laws of Georgia, 1800-1810*, p. 653.

26. Elbert County Minutes of the Inferior Court, 1791-1801, p. 16.

27. Memorandum bill in John Williams Walker Papers, "Letters, 1798-1819."

28. Elbert County Minutes of the Inferior Court, 1791-1801, pp. 19, 63, 126.

29. *Augusta Chronicle*, January 20 (3, 2), 1802.

30. Athens *Georgia Express*, July 15 (4, 4), 1809.

31. Augusta *Mirror of the Times*, June 17 (1, 2), 1811.

32. Elbert County Retailers Oaths, 5. The date of this oath was January 20, 1840.

33. John Williams Walker, Petersburg, Ga., August 20, to Larkin Newby, Newark, S. C., in Larkin Newby Collection.

34. S. Hillyer, Letter Book, November, 1806.

35. *Augusta Chronicle*, September 28 (1, 3), 1799. See also *ibid.*, September 24 (3, 4), 1800; October 17 (1, 4), 1801.

36. Petersburg *Georgia & Carolina Gazette*, August 7 (4, 4), 1806; *Augusta Herald* January 28 (2, 1), 1801; *Augusta Chronicle, passim*, 1803.

37. Watkins, comps., *Digest of the Laws of Georgia, 1755-1799*, pp. 531-32. See also *ibid.*, 430, 455.

38. Clayton, comp., *Compilation of the Laws of Georgia, 1800-1810*, p. 536.

39. *Augusta Chronicle*, May 28 (3, 2), 1813.   40. *Ibid.*, February 6 (3, 3), 1802.

41. *Ibid.*, December 10 (3, 5), 1813.   42. *Ibid.*, August 11 (3, 3), 1815.

CHAPTER XI

1. John N. Waddel, *Memorials of Academic Life: Being an Historical Sketch of the Waddel Family* . . . (Richmond, 1891), 25-48.

2. *Augusta Chronicle*, October 14 (3, 1), 1797; White, *Statistics of Georgia*, 193.

3. *Augusta Chronicle,* September 28 (3, 4) , 1799.

4. *Ibid.,* April 23 (3, 1), 1796.

5. Waddel, *Memorials of Academic Life,* 48.

6. *Ibid.,* 46; *Augusta Chronicle,* November 13 (1, 2) , 1802; John A. Chapman, *History of Edgefield County from the Earliest Settlement to 1897* (Newberry, S. C., 1897) , 189.

7. John Williams Walker, "Hebron" (Petersburg) , June 20, 1803 to Larkin Newby, Fayetteville, N. C., in Larkin Newby Collection.

8. C. S. Cosby, Savannah, May 5, 1803, to Larkin Newby, Fayetteville, N. C., in Larkin Newby Collection.

9. John Williams Walker, Vienna Academy, April 1, 1804, to Larkin Newby, Fayetteville, N. C., in Larkin Newby Collection.

10. Mills, *Statistics of South Carolina,* 350; Waddel, *Memorials of Academic Life,* 46-47; Gilmer, *Georgians,* 239.

11. Petersburg *Georgia & Carolina Gazette,* July 25 (3, 3) , 1805; July 24 (4, 4) , 1806. For quotation see Ramsay, *History of South-Carolina,* II, 370-71.

12. John Williams Walker, "Rural Retirement," June 29, 1804, to Larkin Newby, Fayetteville, N. C., in Larkin Newby Collection.

13. Petersburg *Georgia & Carolina Gazette,* June 5 (1, 1) , 1806.

14. *Habersham Historical Collections,* II, 358-63.

15. For instance, Stokes Petersburg Store Account Book, 1818, pp. 24, 30, 52, 60, 83, 95, 114, 272, 294, 337.

16. John Williams Walker, "Hebron" (Petersburg), June 20, 1803, to Larkin Newby, Fayetteville, N. C., in Larkin Newby Collection.

17. *Augusta Chronicle,* July 23 (3, 3) , 1803.

18. Petersburg *Georgia & Carolina Gazette,* November 30 (3, 1) , 1805.

19. *Ibid.,* July 31 (3, 4) , 1806.

20. Washington (Georgia) *Monitor,* February 4 (4, 2) , 1809; *Augusta Chronicle,* January 21 (3, 3) , 1809.

21. Saunders, *Early Settlers of Alabama,* 495.

22. *Augusta Herald,* March 19 (3, 1) , 1800.   23. J. Hillyer, "Memoirs," 63, 72.

24. John Williams Walker, "Hebron" (Petersburg), December 2, 1803, to Larkin Newby, Fayetteville, N. C., in Larkin Newby Collection. See also Bailey, "Petersburg Youth of John Williams Walker," 126; John Williams Walker, Petersburg, May 20, 1803, to Larkin Newby, Fayetteville, N. C. in Larkin Newby Collection; Gilmer, *Georgians,* 229; Saunders, *Early Settlers of Alabama,* 422, 459.

25. Petersburg *Georgia & Carolina Gazette,* July 24 (4, 4) , 1806. See also *Augusta Chronicle,* October 19 (4, 3) , 1805.

26. Petersburg *Georgia & Carolina Gazette,* November 23 (3, 2) , 1805.

27. *Augusta Herald,* June 6 (4, 4) , 1805.

28. Petersburg *Georgia & Carolina Gazette,* August 7 (4, 1-4) , 1806.

29. Clayton, comp., *Compilation of the Laws of Georgia, 1800-1810,* pp. 58-59; J. Hillyer, "Memoirs," 72. The other members of the Society, named in the act, were Memorable Walker, Oliver White (Whyte) , James Sanders Walker, John A. Casey, Thomas Casey, Robert Watkins, William Jones, Albert Brux, Robert H. Watkins, Reginal N. Groves, Nicholas Pope, Andrew Green Semmes, James Coulter, and Garland T. Watkins. An example to exaggerate and romanticise the history of Petersburg is seen in the statement that "it was always believed by the people of Petersburg that Smithson got the idea of his bequest from this society organized in Petersburg." James Smithson died in 1829, and the Smithsonian Institution was not established until 1846. See Rogers, "Petersburg's Claims to Past Glory Uncovered," in *Atlanta Constitution,* March 31 (Section 2-B) , 1946.

30. Joseph and Nesta Ewan, eds., *John Lyon, Nurseryman and Plant Hunter, and his Journal, 1799-1814* (Philadelphia, 1963), 25, 42.

31. Asbury said that he was first in Georgia in 1785, but his recorded journal does not substantiate this assertion. Asbury's *Journal* (1815 edition, III, 361).

32. Clark *et al.*, eds., *Asbury Journal*, I, 565, 567 (1815 edition, II, 29-30).

33. *Ibid.*, I, 567.   34. *Ibid.*, 709, fn. 22.

35. *Ibid.*, II, 80 (1815 edition, II, 247).

36. *Ibid.*, II, 213 (1815 edition, II, 361).

37. *Ibid.*, II, 270-71 (1815 edition, III, 8).

38. See the paragraph in Chapter VI, of this narrative, supported by note 6.

39. *Ibid.*, II, 312 ff. (1815 edition, III, 41-145).

40. *Ibid.*, II, 416 (1815 edition, III, 123).

41. *Ibid.*, II, 484 (1815 edition, III, 181).

42. *Ibid.*, II, 523 (1815 edition, III, 211).

43. Asbury's *Journal* (1815 edition), III, 212.

44. Clark *et al.*, eds., *Asbury Journal*, II, 558 (1815 edition, III, 236).

45. *Ibid.*, II, 620 (1815 edition, III, 279).

46. *Ibid.*, II, 745 (1815 edition, III, 358).

47. *Ibid.*, II, 765.

48. Lorenzo Dow, *The Dealings of God, Man, and the Devil; as Exemplified in the Life, Experience and Travels of Lorenzo Dow* . . . (2 vols. in one. Middletown, Ohio, 1849), I, 62.

49. Dow, *Dealings of God*, I, 74-75.

50. John Williams Walker, Petersburg, February 25, 1803, to Larkin Newby, Fayetteville, N. C., in Larkin Newby Collection.

51. Dow, *Dealings of God*, 80, 81.

52. Bailey, "Petersburg Youth of John Williams Walker," 128.

53. John Williams Walker, "Hebron" (Petersburg), October 27, 1803, to Larkin Newby, Fayetteville, N. C., in Larkin Newby Collection.

54. W. B. Sprague, *Annals of the American Methodist Pulpit* . . . (New York, 1861), 408-14.

55. Smith, *Life and Letters of Andrew*, 132-37.

56. Clark *et al.*, eds., *Asbury Journal*, II, 746 (1815 edition, III, 359).

57. George G. Smith, Jr., *The History of Methodism in Georgia and Florida, from 1785 to 1865* (Macon, 1877), 114, 117; Sprague, *Annals of American Methodist Pulpit*, 408-14; Elbert County Deed Record, R, 142.

58. Petersburg *Georgia & Carolina Gazette*, July 25 (3, 4), 1805.

59. John Williams Walker, "Hebron" (Petersburg), January 6, 1804, to Larkin Newby, Fayetteville, N. C., in Larkin Newby Collection.

60. *Augusta Chronicle*, November 11 (3, 4), 1809. The *Augusta Herald*, March 6 (4, 4), 1806 announced that it had in its possession the manuscripts of the Rev. James H. Ray sermons "together with Poems Sacred to Christianity," which would be published if enough subscriptions could be secured. Shaler Hillyer and Moses Waddel were to act as agents in the Petersburg and Vienna region.

As another claim of Petersburg to past glory, Rogers in "Petersburg's Claims to Past Glory Uncovered," in *Atlanta Constitution*, March 31 (Section 2-B), 1946 wrote that a preacher happening through Petersburg saw a square dance going on. He scolded the dancers and made them get down on their knees and ask for forgiveness. Rogers asserted that this incident was "the only such where a dance was turned into a prayer meeting."

CHAPTER XII

1. John Williams Walker, Petersburg, October 25, 1809, to Larkin Newby, Fayetteville, N. C., in Larkin Newby Collection.

2. Elbert County Deed Record, P, 199. This sale need not be taken as representing the actual value of the property; for it could be reclaimed within a certain period by recompensing the purchaser.

3. Elbert County Deed Record, R, 186; W, 39.

4. *Ibid.*, S, 84.   5. *Ibid.*, U, 69.   6. *Ibid.*, W, 41.   7. *Ibid.*, X, 95.

8. *Ibid.*, X, 129; DD, 121; EE, 531, 532.   9. *Ibid.*, EE, 504.

10. *Acts of . . . Georgia . . . 1831* (Milledgeville, 1832) , 231-32.

11. *Journal of the House of Representatives of . . . Georgia . . . 1849 & '50* (Milledgeville, 1849) , 394-95.

12. Lamar, comp., *Compilation of the Laws of Georgia, 1811-1819,* pp. 85-92.

13. *Ibid.*, 94-102.

14. "Letter from the Postmaster General Transmitting a Statement of the Nett Amount of Postage accruing at each Office, in each State and Territory of the U. States, for the Year Ending 31st March, 1827," in *Reports and Communications Made by the Executive Departments of the Government, and Memorials, &c. to the House of Representatives during the First Session of the 20th Congress,* H. R. Document 60, p. 58 (Binder's title, *State Papers*) , Serial Number 170.

15. John Freeman, "Poplar Grove," July 9, 1804, to "Dear Children," in Shaler Hillyer Collection.

16. Saunders, *Early Settlers of Alabama,* 493.

17. John Williams Walker, "Hebron" (Petersburg) , July 28, 1803, to Larkin Newby, Fayetteville, N. C., in Larkin Newby Collection.

18. Bailey, "Petersburg Youth of John Williams Walker," 135-36.

19. Albert Burton Moore, *History of Alabama and her People* (3 vols. Chicago, 1927) , I, 105; Hugh C. Bailey, "John W. Walker and the 'Georgia Machine' in Early Alabama Politics," in *Alabama Review,* July, 1955, pp. 181-82.

20. John Williams Walker, Petersburg, May 20, 1810, to Dr. Samual Brown, Fort Adams, Miss., in John Williams Walker Papers (folder marked "Letters, Family").

21. William H. Brantley, *Banking in Alabama, 1816-1860* (1 vol. so far published. Birmingham, Privately Printed, 1961) , I, 3-36, 426.

22. Quoted from *New York Herald* by *Augusta Chronicle,* September 6 (2, 4) , 1817. See also Daniel Watkins (?), February 20, 1838, to William Dearing, Petersburg, in Mrs. William Ray Collection; *Augusta Chronicle,* September 3 (3, 5) , 1817. The Petersburgers going to the Mississippi Territory (later Alabama) passed up the Federal Road through Athens, Georgia, crossing the Tennessee River where Chattanooga was later to be built and onto the road from Knoxville to the southwestward. Thomas Perkins Abernethy, *The Formative Period in Alabama, 1815-1828* (Historical and Patriotic Series No. 6 of the Publications of the Alabama State Department of Archives and History. Montgomery, 1922) , 17, 30.

23. *Augusta Chronicle,* July 19 (3, 1) , 1811.

24. Quoted from the Milledgeville *Georgia Journal* by the *Augusta Herald,* February 25 (3, 1) , 1817.

25. *Augusta Chronicle,* August 5 (3, 2) , 1818.

26. Malcolm C. McMillan, *Constitutional Development in Alabama, 1789-1901 . . .* (Volume 37 in the James Sprunt Studies in History and Political Science. Chapel Hill, 1955) , 19, 23.

27. *Augusta Chronicle,* May 6 (2, 1), 1818.

28. *Ibid.*, July 26 (3, 1) , 1816.

29. *Ibid.*, October 29 (3, 2) , 1817.

30. *Ibid.*, February 25 (2, 1) , 1818.   31. *Ibid.*, September 5 (2, 3) , 1820.

32. Bailey, "Petersburg Youth of John Williams Walker," 137; Abernethy, *Formative Period in Alabama,* 38; Moore, *History of Alabama,* I, 156; McMillan, *Constitutional Development in Alabama,* 34; Edward Chambers Betts, *Early History of Huntsville, Alabama, 1804 to 1870* (Revised edition. Montgomery, 1916) , 22-23.

33. Jane Kneeland, Petersburg, January (no day, year 1831 [?]) to Eliza M. A. Carter, Washington, Ga., in Mrs. Mercer Sherman Collection.

34. A. J. Hanna, *Flight into Oblivion* (Richmond, 1938), 85; Weekly *Atlanta Constitution,* August 21 (1, 1) , 1888.

35. W. H. Swallon, "Retreat of the Confederate Government from Richmond to the Gulf," in *Magazine of American History with Notes and Queries* (New York), XV (January-June, 1886), 605; (George Morley Vickers, ed.,) *Under Both Flags* . . . (Philadelphia, 1896), 234; Pierce Butler, *Judah P. Benjamin* (Philadelphia, 1906), 362-63; Rembert T. Patrick, *Jefferson Davis and his Cabinet* (Baton Rouge, 1944).

36. *War of the Rebellion: A Compilation of the Official Records of the Union and Confederate Armies* (127 books and index. Washington, 1880-1901), Ser. I, Vol. XLIX, Pt. II, 634-35.

37. Quoted from the Louisville (Ky.) *Courier-Journal* by the Daily *Athens Banner*, January 1 (1, 1), 1882. See also Weekly *Atlanta Constitution*, August 21 (1, 1), 1888; *Habersham Historical Collections*, I, 9 ff.; Otis Ashmore, "The Story of the Confederate Treasure," in *Georgia Historical Quarterly*, II (September, 1918), 119-38; Otis Ashmore, "The Story of the Virginia Banks Funds," *ibid*, II (December, 1918), 171-97.

38. *Oglethorpe Echo*, September 14 (1, 5-6), 1888.

39. Sherwood, *Gazetteer of Georgia* (1927 edition), 86.

40. White, *Statistics of Georgia*, 227.

41. Thomas Baldwin and J. Thomas, *A New and Complete Gazetteer of the United States* . . . (Philadelphia, 1854), 906. An amazing misstatement of fact appeared in Richard Swainson Fisher, *A New and Complete Statistical Gazetteer of the United States of America* . . . (New York, 1853), 668: "A thriving v. with a valuable trade, growing manufactures, and a population of 400."

42. Waddel, *Memorials of Academic Life*, 47.

43. Saunders, *Early Settlers of Alabama*, 238.

44. Jones, Jr., *Dead Towns of Georgia*, 237.

45. Starnes, "The Cotton-Gin; its Invention and Effects," 300.

46. Weekly *Atlanta Constitution*, August 21 (1, 1), 1888.

47. Sherwood, *Gazetteer of Georgia* (1827 edition), 87.

48. Weekly *Atlanta Constitution*, August 21 (1, 1), 1888.

49. Jones and Dutcher, *Memorial History of Augusta*, 255; *Habersham Historical Collections*, II, 231; McIntosh, *Elbert County*, 39.

50. *Oglethorpe Echo*, August 3 (2, 3), 1888. See also J. Hillyer, "Memoirs," 63.

51. *Oglethorpe Echo*, June 18 (3, 6), 1875.   52. *Ibid.*, November 15 (3, 3), 1878.

53. *Ibid.*, May 31 (3, 5), 1878.   54. *Ibid.*, April 26 (2, 4), 1889.

55. *Ibid.*, June 1 (1, 1-2), 1906. The present writer visited the site of old Petersburg on July 21, 1957, before the waters had covered up the place.

Bibliography

I. BOOKS

Abernethy, Thomas Perkins, *The Formative Period in Alabama, 1815-1828.* Publication of the Alabama State Department of Archives and History. Historical and Patriotic Series, No. 6. Montgomery: The Brown Printing Co., 1922.

Andrews, Garnett, *Reminiscences of an Old Georgia Lawyer.* Atlanta: Franklin Steam Printing House, 1870.

Asbury, Francis, *Journal of the Rev. Francis Asbury, Bishop of the Methodist Episcopal Church, from August 7, 1771, to December 7, 1815.* 3 vols. New York: N. Bangs and T. Mason, 1821. For a new edition see Elmer T. Clark, below.

Bailey, Hugh C., *John Williams Walker* . . . University, Ala.: University of Alabama Press, 1964.

Bartram, William, *Travels through North and South Carolina, Georgia, East and West Florida, the Cherokee Country, the Extensive Territories of the Muscogulges or Creek Confederacy, and the Country of the Chactaws.* . . . Dublin: J. Moore, W. Jones, R. M'Allister, and J. Rice, 1793.

Betts, Edward Chambers, *Early History of Huntsville, Alabama, 1804 to 1870.* Revised edition. Montgomery: The Brown Printing Co., 1916.

Bowen, Eliza A., *The Story of Wilkes County Georgia.* Reprint edition. Marietta, Ga.: Continental Book Company, 1950.

Boykin, Samuel, *History of the Baptist Denomination in Georgia.* . . . Atlanta: Jas. P. Harrison & Co., 1881.

Brantley, William H., *Banking in Alabama, 1816-1860.* Vol. I, more in prospect. Birmingham: Privately printed, 1961.

Butler, John C., *Historical Record of Macon and Central Georgia.* . . . Macon: J. W. Burke & Co., 1879.

Butler, Pierce, *Judah P. Benjamin.* American Crisis Biographies, edited by Ellis Paxon Oberholtzer. Philadelphia: George W. Jones & Company, 1906.

Calhoun, Ferdinand Phinizy, *The Phinizy Family in America.* Atlanta: Johnson-Dallis, Printers, 1925?

Chapman, John A., *History of Edgefield County from the Earliest Settlements to 1897.* Newberry, S. C.: Elbert H. Aull, 1897.

Clark, Elmer T., J. Manning Potts, and Jacob S. Payton, eds., *The Journal and Letters of Francis Asbury.* 3 vols. Published jointly: London: Epworth Press and Nashville: Abingdon Press, 1958.

Clark, John, *Considerations on the Purity of the Principles of William H. Crawford, Esq.* . . . Augusta: Printed at the Georgia Advertiser Office, 1819.

Coulter, E. Merton, *Auraria: The Story of a Georgia Gold-Mining Town.* Athens: University of Georgia Press, 1956.

Craven, Delle Mullen, ed., *The Neglected Thread. A Journal from the Calhoun Community, 1836-1842, by Mary E. Moragne.* Columbia: University of South Carolina Press, 1951.

Dow, Lorenzo, *The Dealings of God, Man, and the Devil; as Exemplified in the Life Experience and Travels of Lorenzo Dow.* . . . 2 vols. in one. Middletown, Ohio: Glasner & Marshall, 1849.

Drayton, John, *A View of South-Carolina, as Respects her Natural and Civil Concerns.* Charleston: W. P. Young, 1802.

Ewan, Joseph and Nesta, eds., *John Lyon, Nurseryman and Plant Hunter, and his Journal, 1799-1814.* Transactions of the American Philosophical Society. . . . New Series, Vol. 53, Pt. 2. Philadelphia: The American Philosophical Society, 1963.

Gamble, Thomas, *Savannah Duels and Duellists, 1733-1877.* Savannah: Review Publishing and Printing Company, 1923.

[Gilmer, George R.,] *Sketches of Some of the First Settlers of Upper Georgia, of the Cherokees, and of the Author.* New York: D. Appleton and Company, 1855.

Gray, Lewis Cecil, *History of Agriculture in the Southern United States to 1860.* 2 vols. Washington: Carnegie Institution of Washington, 1933.

Green, Constance McL., *Eli Whitney and the Birth of American Technology.* Library of American Biography, edited by Oscar Handlin. Boston: Little, Brown and Company, 1956.

Hanna, A. J., *Flight into Oblivion.* Richmond: Johnson Publishing Company, 1938.

Hays, Louise Frederick, *Hero of Hornet's Nest. A Biography of Elijah Clark[e], 1733 to 1799.* New York: The Hobson Book Press, 1946.

Hill, Lodowick Johnson, Sr., *The Hills of Wilkes County, Georgia and Allied Families.* Atlanta: Johnson-Dallis Company, 1922?

Hillyer, S. G., *Reminiscences of Georgia Baptists.* Atlanta: Foote & Davies Company, 1902.

Historical Collections of the Joseph Habersham Chapter, Daughters American Revolution. 5 vols. Places and printers vary, 1902-1929.

Jones, Charles C., Jr., *The Dead Towns of Georgia.* Vol. IV of Collections of the Georgia Historical Society. Savannah: Morning News Steam Printing House, 1878.

Jones, Charles C., Jr., *The History of Georgia.* 2 vols. Boston: Houghton, Mifflin Company, 1883.

Jones, Charles C., Jr. and Salem Dutcher, *Memorial History of Augusta, Georgia.* . . . Syracuse, N. Y.: D. Mason & Co., 1890.

Knight, Lucian Lamar, *Georgia's Landmarks, Memorials and Legends.* 2 vols. Atlanta: The Byrd Printing Company, 1913, 1914.

Lambert, John, *Travels through Canada and the United States of North America, in the Years 1806, 1807, & 1808.* . . . 2 vols. 2nd edition. London: C. Craddock and W. Joy, 1814.

McIntosh, John H., *The Official History of Elbert County, 1790-1935.* Elberton, Ga.: Stephen Heard Chapter, Daughters of the American Revolution, 1940.

McLendon, S. G., *History of the Public Domain of Georgia.* Atlanta: Published by the author, 1924.

McMillan, Malcolm C., *Constitutional Development in Alabama, 1789-1901.* . . . Volume 37, The James Sprunt Studies in History and Political Science. Chapel Hill: The University of North Carolina Press, 1955.

Meriwether, Robert L., *The Expansion of South Carolina, 1729-1765.* Kingsport, Tenn.: Southern Publishers, Inc., 1940.

Michaux, F. A., *Travels to the Westward of the Allegheny Mountains in the States of Ohio, Kentucky, and Tennessee, and Return to Charlestown, through the Upper Carolinas.* . . . "Faithfully translated from the original French by B. Lambert." London: J. Mawman, 1805.

Miller, Stephen F., *The Bench and Bar of Georgia: Memoirs and Sketches.* . . . 2 vols. Philadelphia: J. B. Lippincott & Co., 1858.

Mills, Robert, *Statistics of South Carolina, Including a View of its Natural, Civil, and Military History, General and Political.* Charleston: Hurlbut and Lloyd, 1829.

Mirsky, Jeannette and Allan Nevins, *The World of Eli Whitney.* New York: The Macmillan Co., 1952.

Moffat, Charles Hill, The Life of Charles Tait. Ph. D. dissertation in manuscript at Vanderbilt University, 1946.

Moore, Albert Burton, *History of Alabama and her People.* 3 vols. Chicago: American Historical Society, 1927.

Morange, Mary E. (See Craven, above).

Morse, Jedidiah, *The American Geography, or, A View of the Present Situation of the United States of America.* Elizabethtown: Shepard Kollock, MDCCLXXXIX.

Olmsted, Denison, *Memoir of Eli Whitney, Esq.* First published in the *American Journal of Science,* 1832. New Haven: Durrie & Peck, 1846.

Paschal, George W., *Ninety-Four Years. Agnes Paschal.* Washington: M'Gill & Withrow, 1871.

Patrick, Rembert T., *Jefferson Davis and his Cabinet.* Baton Rouge: Louisiana State University Press, 1944.

Pendleton Farmers' Society. Atlanta: Foote & Davies Company, 1908.

Phillips, Ulrich Bonnell, *A History of Transportation in the Eastern Cotton Belt to 1860.* New York: The Columbia University Press, 1908.

Pickett, Albert James, *History of Alabama, and Incidentally of Georgia and Mississippi, from the Earliest Period.* 2 vols. Third edition. Charleston: Walker and James, 1851.

Ramsay, David, *The History of South-Carolina, from its First Settlement in 1670 to the Year 1808.* 2 vols. Charleston: David Longworth, 1809.

Saunders, James Edmonds, *Early Settlers of Alabama. With Notes and Genealogies by his Granddaughter, Elizabeth Saunders Blair Stubbs.* New Orleans: L. Graham & Son, Ltd., 1899.

Seabrook, Whitemarsh B., "Memoir on the Cotton Plant. . . . Read Before the State Agricultural Society, on the 6th December, 1843." Pages 113-168 in *Proceedings* of the State Agricultural Society of South Carolina, 1839-1846.

Shipp, J. E. D., *Giant Days or the Life and Times of William H. Crawford.* Americus, Ga.: Southern Printers, 1909.

Sibbald, George of Augusta, *Notes and Observations, on the Pine Lands of Georgia, Shewing the Advantages they Possess, Particularly in the Culture of Cotton. . . .* Augusta: William J. Bunce, 1801.

Simkins, Francis Butler, *Pitchfork Ben Tillman, South Carolinian.* Baton Rouge: Louisiana State University Press, 1944.

Smith, George G., *The History of Georgia Methodism from 1786 to 1866.* Atlanta: A. B. Caldwell, 1913.

Smith, George G., *The Life and Letters of James Osgood Andrew. . . .* Nashville: Southern Methodist Publishing House, 1883.

Sparks, W. H., *The Memories of Fifty Years. . . .* Philadelphia: Claxton, Remsen & Haffelfinger, 1872.

Sprague, W. B., *Annals of the American Methodist Pulpit. . . .* Volume 7 in "Annals of the American Pulpit." New York: Robert Carter & Brothers, 1861.

Tompkins, D. A., *Cotton and Cotton Oil. . . .* Charlotte: Published by the author, 1901.

[Vickers, Geo. Morley,] *Under Both Flags. . . .* Philadelphia: People's Publishing Company, [1896].

Waddel, John N., *Memorials of Academic Life: Being an Historical*

Sketch of the Waddel Family. . . . Richmond: Presbyterian Committee of Publication, 1891.

Wade, John Donald, *Augustus Baldwin Longstreet. A Study of the Development of Culture in the South.* New York: The Macmillan Company, 1924.

White, George, *Historical Collections of Georgia: Containing the Most Interesting Facts, Traditions, Biographical Sketches, Anecdotes. Etc.* . . . New York: Pudney & Russell, 1854.

White, George, *Statistics of the State of Georgia: Including an Account of its Natural, Civil, and Ecclesiastical History, together with a Particular Description of Each County.* . . . Savannah: W. Thorne Williams, 1849.

Williford, William Bailey, *Williford and Allied Families.* Atlanta: Published privately, 1961.

Wylie, Lollie Belle, ed., *Memoirs of Judge Richard H. Clark.* Atlanta: Franklin Printing and Publishing Company, 1898.

II. GOVERNMENT DOCUMENTS, PRINTED AND MANUSCRIPT

A. *United States*

Aggregate Amount of Each Description of Persons within the United States of America, and Territories thereof, Agreeable to Actual Enumeration Made According to Law in the Year 1810. Book I of the Third Census.

Carter, Clarence Edwin, ed., *Territory of Mississippi, 1798-1817.* Volume V of Territorial Papers of the United States. Washington: Government Printing Office, 1937.

"Letter from the Postmaster General Transmitting a Statement of the Nett Amount of Postage Accruing at Each Office, in Each State and Territory of the U. States, for the Year Ending 31st March, 1827," being *House Document* No. 60 of the 20 Cong., 1 sess. Washington: Gales & Seaton, 1828. Serial number 170.

Return of the Whole Number of Persons within the Several Districts of the United States, According to [Act of Congress] . . . *Passed February the twenty eighth, One Thousand Eight Hundred.* Printed by Order of the House of Representatives. (No other information given).

Statistics of the Population of the United States . . . *From the Original Returns of the Ninth Census, (June 1, 1870,).* . . . Volume I. Washington: Government Printing Office, 1872.

United States Manuscript Censuses: 1850 Census Population Schedules, Georgia, Microcopy T-6, Roll 63, Roll 71; *ibid.,* 1860, Microcopy T-7, Roll 33. (These microfilms are in the University of Georgia Library.)

War of the Rebellion: A Compilation of the Official Records of the Union and Confederate Armies. 127 books, listed by volumes and parts in four series. Washington: Government Printing Office, 1880-1901.

All of the items listed above are printed except as indicated.

B. *Georgia, State*

Act for the Inspection of Cotton, February 21, 1796. Separate leaflet in the De Renne Collection, University of Georgia Library.

Act to Amend an Act for Regulating the Inspection of Tobacco, and for Other Purposes therein Mentioned, February 10, 1787. Separate leaflet in the De Renne Collection, University of Georgia Library.

Act to Establish and Regulate the Inspection of Tobacco, February 21, 1785. Separate leaflet in the De Renne Collection, University of Georgia Library.

Act to Regulate the Toll to be Taken at Mills, January 26, 1786. Separate leaflet in the De Renne Collection, University of Georgia Library.

Acts of the General Assembly of the State of Georgia . . . November and December, 1799; ibid., 1831; *ibid.,* 1834; *ibid.,* 1837; *ibid.,* 1840; *ibid.,* 1841; *ibid.,* 1842; *ibid.,* 1845; *ibid.,* 1847; *ibid.,* 1859. The places, publishers, and dates of the above items vary.

Candler, Allen D., comp., *The Colonial Records of the State of Georgia.* 26 volumes, Vol. XX never having been published. Atlanta: Printers vary, 1904-1916.

Candler, Allen D., comp., *The Revolutionary Records of the State of Georgia.* 3 vols. Atlanta: The Franklin-Turner Company, 1908.

Clayton, Augustin Smith, *A Compilation of the Laws of the State of Georgia . . . 1800 to the Year 1810, Inclusive. . . .* Augusta: Adams & Duyckinck, 1812.

Davidson, Grace Gillam, comp. and abstracter, *Early Records of Georgia, Wilkes County.* 2 vols. Macon: The J. W. Burke Company, 1932.

Davidson, Grace Gillam, comp., *Historical Collections of the Georgia Chapters Daughters of the American Revolution. Volume III. Records of Elbert County, Georgia.* Atlanta: Stein Printing Company, 1930.

Dawson, William C., *A Compilation of the Laws of the State of Georgia, . . . since the Year 1819 to the Year 1829, Inclusive. . . .* Milledgeville: Grantland and Orne, 1831.

Journal of the House of Representatives of the State of Georgia, at the Biennial Session of the General Assembly of 1849 & '50. Milledgeville: Richard M. Orme, 1849.

Lamar, Lucius Q. C., *A Compilation of the Laws of the State of Georgia, . . . since 1810 to . . . 1818, Inclusive. . . .* Augusta: T. S. Hannon, 1821.

Marbury, Horatio & William H. Crawford, *Digest of the Laws of the State of Georgia . . . 1785 to 1800. Inclusive.* . . . Savannah: Seymour, Woolhopter & Stebbins, 1802.

Prince, Oliver H., *A Digest of the Laws of the State of Georgia . . . to Dec. 1837.* . . . Athens: Published by the author, 1837.

Watkins, Robert & George, *A Digest of the Laws of the State of Georgia. From its Establishment as a British Province down to the Year 1798, Inclusive, and the Principal Acts of 1799.* . . . Philadelphia: R. Aitken, 1800.

C. *Georgia Counties*

Elbert County (courthouse in Elberton) Deed Record, A, B, C, D, E, F, G, H, J, K, L, M, N, O, P, R, S, U, W, X, EE; Minutes of the Inferior Court, 1791-1801, 1804-1806, 1807-1815; Minutes of the Superior Court, 1790-1800; Retailers' not to Sell or Give Whiskey to Slaves or Free Men of Color; Will Book, M; Writs of the Superior Court, 1799-1803.

Oglethorpe County (courthouse in Lexington) Annual Returns on Estates, 1798-1814, 1815-1830; Deed Record, B, C, D, E, G, I, M, N, EE; Docket, 1800-1805, 1806-1811, 1811-1816; Inventories and Annual Returns on Estates, 1811-1826, 1815-1831; Inventories and Appraisements, A (1794-1799), B (1796), C (1796-1802), G (1802-1805), H (1802-1803), I (1803-1804), J (1804-1805), L (1806-1809); Minutes of the Superior Court, A (1794-1799), B (1800-1807); Tax Digest, 1800-1805, 1806-1811, 1811-1816; Will Book, A, A-B, B, C.

Wilkes County (courthouse in Washington) Appraisements and Sales, 1806-1807; Deed Record, CC, DD, GG, LL; Will Book, 1806-1808.

D. *South Carolina*

Statutes at Large of South Carolina, I. Columbia: A. S. Johnston, 1836). IV. Columbia: A. S. Johnston, 1838. V. Columbia: A. S. Johnston, 1839. IX. Columbia: A. S. Johnston, 1841.

III. MANUSCRIPTS, OFFICIAL AND UNOFFICAL

A. In Alabama Department of Archives and History (Montgomery): William Wyatt Bibb Papers; Charles and James A. Tait Papers; John W. Walker Papers.

B. In Duke University Library (Durham, N. C.): Larkin Newby Collection.

C. In Federal Records Center (East Point, Ga.): Records of the United States District Court and of the Circuit Court relating to suits brought by Miller and Whitney.

D. In Georgia Department of Archives and History (Atlanta): Shaler Hillyer Collection (on microfilm, Box 21, Reel 17).

E. In Medical College of Georgia Library (Augusta): Store Account

Book of 178 pages, without identification of firm or location; but internal evidence makes it unmistakably Petersburg.

F. In private possession of

    E. M. Coulter: Keith-Jones Collection (plantation documents relating to a plantation in Columbia County, Ga.) ; Letters from Mrs. Grace Lewis Miller of St. Louis, 1958-1960.

    Mrs. Daniel Hicky (Madison, Ga.) : Collection, containing four letters relating to Petersburg.

    Mrs. William Ray (Athens, Ga.) : Collection, containing one letter relating to Petersburg.

    Mrs. D. Mercer Sherman (Albany, Ga.) : Collection, containing two letters relating to Petersburg.

G. In the University of Georgia Library: "Memoirs of the Early Life and Times of Junius Hillyer [1807-1886]" (a typed copy of the original manuscript) ; Letter Book of Shaler Hillyer for the period 1805-1820; Dionysius Oliver Collection; Store Book of William S. Stokes, 1818; Telamon Cuyler Collection (folder, "Letters, 1819") .

IV. MAPS

"Map of the Former Territorial Limits of the Cherokee 'Nation of' Indians Exhibiting the Boundaries of the Various Cessions of Land Made by them to the Colonies and to the United States . . . ," Plate VIII in *Fifth Annual Report of the Bureau of Ethnology.* . . . Washington: Government Printing Office, 1887. This is the C. C. Royce map of 1884.

"Map of the Lands Ceded to His Majesty by the Creek and Cherokee Indians at a Congress held in Augusta the 1st June 1773. . . ." This is a manuscript map in the Department of Archives and History, in Atlanta.

Mills, Robert, "Atlas of the State of South Carolina." A New Facsimile Edition of the Original Published in 1825. With an Introduction by Francis Marion Hutson. Columbia, 1938.

"A New and General Map of the Southern Dominions Belonging to the United States. . . ." London: Published by Lowrie & Whittle, 12th May, 1794.

V. NEWSPAPERS

Athens Daily Banner, 1882.

Athens *Georgia Express,* 1809-1810. Title changed in 1810 to *Foreign Correspondent & Georgia Express.*

Atlanta Constitution, 1888 (weekly) , 1946 (daily) .

Atlanta Journal, 1934.

Atlanta Weekly Intelligencer, 1869.

Augusta Chronicle, 1786-1822. Title changes variously. Was originally called *The Georgia State Gazette or Independent Register,* the name

changing April 11, 1789 to *Augusta Chronicle and Gazette of the State.*
Augusta Constitutionalist, 1856 (weekly).
Augusta Herald, 1800-1821 (with gaps).
Augusta *Mirror of the Times,* 1809-1814.
Lexington *Oglethorpe Echo,* 1874-1925.
Milledgeville *Georgia Journal,* 1815-1823.
Milledgeville *Southern Recorder,* 1832.
Petersburg *Georgia & Carolina Gazette,* 1805-1806.
Savannah *Georgia Gazette,* 1798-1802.
Savannah *Columbian Museum & Savannah Advertiser,* 1803.
Washington *Monitor,* 1809.
Washington *News,* 1822-1825.
(All of these newspapers were published in Georgia.)

VI. Pamphlets

Gilmer, George R., *The Literary Progress of Georgia.* . . . Athens: Wm. N. White & Brother, 1851. Much of this work was included in his later *Georgians.*

Tompkins, Alma Cole, *Charles Tait.* Alabama Polytechnic Institute Historical Papers, 4th Series, 1910.

VII. Periodicals

Allen, Elsa G., "John Abbot, Pioneer Naturalist of Georgia," in *Georgia Historical Quarterly,* XLI (June, 1957), 143-57.

Ashmore, Otis, "The Story of the Confederate Treasure," *ibid.,* II (September, 1918), 120-38.

Ashmore, Otis, "The Story of the Viriginia Banks Fund," *ibid.,* II (December, 1918), 171-97.

Bailey, Hugh C., "John W. Walker and the 'Georgia Machine' in Early Alabama Politics," in *Alabama Review,* July, 1955, pp. 179-95.

Bailey, Hugh C., "The Petersburg Youth of John Williams Walker," in *Georgia Historical Quarterly,* XLIII (June, 1959), 123-37.

Coulter, E. Merton, "A Famous Duel That was Never Fought," *ibid.,* XLIII (December, 1959), 365-77.

Coulter, E. Merton, "Francis Meson, an Early Georgia Merchant and Philanthropist," *ibid.,* XLII (March, 1958), 27-43.

Coulter, E. Merton, "Madison Springs, Georgia Watering Place," *ibid.,* XLVII (December, 1963), 375-407.

Ellis, L. B., "Two Georgia Judges," in *Green Bag: An Entertaining Magazine for Lawyers,* XXI (1909), 20-22.

Few, William, "Autobiography of Col. William Few of Georgia," in *Magazine of American History with Notes and Queries,* VII (November, 1881), 340-58.

Green, Fletcher M., "Georgia's Board of Public Works, 1817-1826," in *Georgia Historical Quarterly*, XXII (June, 1938), 117-37.

Hitz, Alex M., "The Earliest Settlement in Wilkes County," *ibid.*, XL (September, 1956), 260-80.

"King Cotton and his Gin," in *Atlantic Monthly*, XL (August, 1877).

"Letters from Sir James Wright," in *Collections of the Georgia Historical Society*, III (1873), 157-378.

Niles' Weekly Register . . ., XIX (1820-1821); XLI (1831-1832). Baltimore.

Starnes, Hugh N., "The Cotton-Gin; its Invention and Effects," in *Southern Bivouac*, New Series I (December, 1885), 385-95.

Swallon, W. H., "Retreat of the Confederate Government from Richmond to the Gulf," in *Magazine of American History with Notes and Queries*, XV (January-June, 1886).

VIII. Reference Works

Baldwin, Thomas and J. Thomas, *A New and Complete Gazetteer of the United States. . . .* Philadelphia: Lippincott, Grambo & Co., 1854.

Biographical Directory of the American Congress, 1774-1927. Washington: Government Printing Office, 1928.

Fisher, Richard Swainson, *A New and Complete Statistical Gazetteer of the United States of America. . . .* New York: J. H. Colton, 1953.

Georgia and South-Carolina Almanac, for the Year of our Lord, 1808. Augusta: Hobby & Bunce, no date.

Palladium of Knowledge: or, the Carolina and Georgia Almanac, for the Year of our Lord, 1798. . . . Charleston: W. P. Young, 1798.

Sherwood, Adiel, *A Gazetteer of the State of Georgia.* Charleston: W. Riley, 1827. Second Edition. Philadelphia: J. W. Martin and W. K. Boden, 1829. Third Edition. Washington: P. Force, 1937. Fourth Edition. Macon: S. Boykin, 1860.

Index

127, 130, 159, 165; Inferior Court, 73; Grand Jury, 74; jail, 127; Superior Court, 137

Elberton, established, 9; courts, 30; mentioned, 65, 77, 166, 176

"Elegant" merchandise, 134, 192 (n. 53)

Emanuel, LeRoy Pope slave, for sale, 123

Embargo, effect on cotton trade out of Petersburg, 119-20

England, mentioned, 86, 107, 109, 119

Enterprise, steamboat on Savannah River, 54, 183 (n. 15)

"E, O, tables," taxed, 76

Europe, mentioned, 34, 107

Evans, Thomas, free Negro, engages in real estate transactions in Petersburg, 123, 181 (n. 17)

Eve, Joseph, of Bahama Islands, invents cotton gin, 109

Fall Line, 49, 102

Fayetteville, North Carolina, mentioned, 43, 154

Federal Road, 196 (n. 22)

Federalist Party, mentioned, 29, 85, 86, 87, 88

Ferries, 69-70, 96, 159, 160, 166

Few, William, travels to Georgia, 67

Florida, mentioned, 48

"Fine," flour grade, 140

Fishing, as an amusement, 146

Fish traps, in Savannah and Broad rivers, 52, 53, 54, 58-59, 61

Floods, in Petersburg, 30, 72, 79-80

Flour grades, 140

Flour inspection, at Petersburg, 140

Flour mills, on Broad River, 58, 192 (n. 71)

"Forks of Broad-River," meaning of expression used by Asbury, 159

Forsyth, John, mentioned, 127

Forsyth, Robert, Federal marshal in Augusta, murdered, 127; poetry about, 190 (n. 16)

Fort Adams, Mississippi, 168

Fort Charlotte, established by South Carolina, 4, 31; mentioned, 69, 93, 98

Fort James, location, 2; description, 3, 4, 31, 32; mentioned, 31, 47, 69

Fourth of July, celebration in Petersburg, 43, 146, 154

France, 119

Franklin County, established, 8, 35

Franklin Courthouse (Carnesville), on mail route, 65

Frederica, 1826-1827 postal receipts, 166

Freeman, Fleming, of Broad River Valley, marries Martha Bibb, 42, 47

Freeman, Holman, settles in Broad River Valley, 42, 46, 47

Freeman, Holman, II, of Broad River Valley, family, 47; Savannah River Commissioner, 50

Freeman, John, slays Tory, 47; family, 47; mentioned, 119, 129; reports on LeRoy Pope's trip to Mississippi Territory, 167

Freeman, Mary Ann ("Polly"), of Broad River Valley, marries W. W. Bibb, 43, 47; attends school, 156

Freeman, Rebecca, of Broad River Valley, marries Shaler Hillyer, 47; courtship, 147; attends school, 156

Freemans, in Broad River Valley, 10

Front Street, Petersburg, 74

Fulton, Robert, inventor of steamboat, mentioned, 54, 115, 173

Gabriel, slave, 24

Gantt, Benjamin, Petersburg physician, 81; merchant, 124 (most probably this Gantt)

Geese, in Broad River Valley, 14, 23, 46; in Petersburg, 46

George Barnes & Company, Augusta merchant firm, buys tobacco, 107

George Whitfield & Joseph Bunkley, South Carolina firm, deals with Petersburg, 37

Georgia, original settlement boundaries, 1; James Wright's land laws, 3; land laws of 1783 and 1784, p. 7; inspection laws, 32, 33, 103, 106, 116, 118, 140, 141, 142; wealth of rivers, 49-50; improves navigation, 50-71; tax laws, 75-76; enters Union, 85; political parties, 85-88, 97-98; laws for tobacco inspection, 103-105; tavern laws, 148-49

"Georgia," tobacco trademark, 105

Georgia & Carolina Gazette, Petersburg newspaper, 78-79

"Georgia Party," in Alabama government, 170

Gilmer, George, mentioned, 10

Gilmer, George R., attends school in South Carolina, 5, 155; estimate of Broad River Virginians, 9, 10, 11-13;

Hill, Abraham, builds frame residence, 26

Hill, Matthew, Petersburg merchant, 124

Hills, Thomas, Savannah merchant, deals in Petersburg lots, 35

Hillyer, Shaler, Petersburger, marries Rebecca Freeman, 47; an incorporater of Broad River Navigation Company, 61, 131-32; cotton trade in Augusta, 64; trades with New York, 68; plantation home, 73; Petersburg city clerk, 74; Petersburg city tax receiver, 75; mentions Petersburg cyclone, 80; trip to the mountains, 81; Federalist in politics, 87; patriotic fervor, 100-101; deals in cotton, 119-120, 131; slaveowner, 122-23, 129; career, 128-32; moves to Broad River plantation, 128; discouraged in business, 129; mercantile activities, 130-32; laments death of Beggs, 132; trip to New York, 132; opposes stay laws, 138; manufactures flour, 141; distills whiskey, 141-42; trip to North Carolina mountains, 147; summer home at Madison Springs, 147; president of Union Society, 158; mentioned, 167; sends money to father, 191 (n. 33); agent for religious book in Petersburg, 195 (n. 60)

Hillyer & Holt, Petersburg merchant firm, deals in manufactured tobacco, 108; mentioned, 130

Hitt, Daniel, Methodist preacher, visits Petersburg, 161

Hobby, William J., first postmaster of Petersburg, 78; buys Petersburg lot, 125

Holliday, James, Petersburg merchant, 124

Holmes, Hodgen, of Augusta, invents cotton gin, 114, 115

Holt, John Saunders, Petersburg merchant, 130

Horse-racing, 151

Horse-stealing, 151-52

Household and kitchen furnishings, in Broad River Valley, 11-12, 26-27

Howard, Samuel, Georgia steamboat monopoly, 54

Hudson Fork, tributary of Broad River, 60

Hudson River, in New York, mentioned, 54

Huff (Hoff), Richard, sends slaves to Liberia, 24-25; family cemetery, 175

Hugh, James, interests in Petersburg, stockholder in Savannah River Navigation Company, 52

Huguenots, mentioned, 41

Hulls, families, mentioned, 16

Hunter, William, of Savannah, killed in duel with David B. Mitchell, 88

Huntsville, Alabama, mentioned, 35, 38, 168

Illinois, migrations to from Broad River Valley, 13

Indians, cede lands in South Carolina and Georgia, 1, 2, 3, 4; rumors of threats to Broad River Valley settlers, 13; mounds near Petersburg, described, 145-46; hostility after Augusta Treaty Conference of 1773, p. 177 (n. 6)

Indigo, as a Broad River Valley crop, 121

Inferior Courts, regulate taverns, 149-50

Irishmen, in Broad River Valley, 20, 28; in Petersburg, 83

Italy, mentioned, 16, 20

Jack, James, migrates to Broad River Valley, 20-21

Jack, Patrick, career, 21

Jackson, James, statesman, opposes Yazoo Fraud, 86, 88; opposes deception in packing cotton, 118

Jackson, John, Petersburg merchant, 124

Jacksonboro, 1826-1827 postal receipts, 166

James Holliday & Company, Petersburg merchants, 124, 125

Jefferson, Thomas, mentioned, 15, 16; political philosophy appeals to Georgians, 85

Jeffersonian-Republicans, mentioned, 29, 100

J. Holliday & Company, deals in Petersburg lots, 37

John, slave, 24

John & George Tredwell, New York merchant house, 132

John E. Caldwell Company, of New York, money lenders to Petersburgers, 36

Johnson, Dr., Petersburger, 170

Johnson, Nicholas, career, 17-18

Johnsons, in Broad River Valley, 10, 16